YOU ARE MY WITNESSES

You are a letter from Christ, written not with ink but with the Spirit of the living God—not on tablets of stone but on the pages of the human heart...Our sufficiency is from God, who has qualified us to be ministers of a new covenant, not in a written code but in the Spirit which gives life. The Lord is the Spirit, and where the Spirit of the Lord is, there is freedom...Having this ministry, therefore, by the mercy of God, we do not lose heart. It is not ourselves that we preach: we preach Jesus Christ as Lord, for the same God who said, 'Light, shine out of darkness!' has caused light to shine in our hearts, to radiate the light of the knowledge of God's glory, shining in the face of Christ.

2 Corinthians 3-4

Every day before God. Every day hearing with the inner ear. Every day confronted by God's Word. Every day: immersion in Christ's new world to do the work he sets before us...

Pastor Tullio Vinay, Italy

What can a church so few in numbers do before the enormity of violence in our world? We have this promise: we will practice the politics of God, which is love. And it is going to take love alone to transform the mutilations of our times...

Pastor Wilfrido Artus, Uruguay

YOU ARE MY WITNESSES

The Waldensians across 800 years

Giorgio Tourn

with the collaboration of
Giorgio Bouchard
Roger Geymonat
Giorgio Spini

Frank G. Gibson, Jr., Editor

Claudiana - Torino

ISBN 88-7016-089-0

Distributed in North America by
  Friendship Press
  P.O. Box 37844
  Cincinnati, OH 45222
  513-948-8733

Cover by E. Paul Lansdale

Typography:
  Department of Publication Services,
  National Council of Churches of Christ, New York

Printed in Italy

TABLE OF CONTENTS

TABLE OF TEXTS

TABLE OF PRINTS

TABLE OF MAPS

A WORD FROM THE MODERATORS

Nine years ago the first English edition of the story of the Waldensian movement across 800 years was published, in translation from the Italian text written by Giorgio Tourn and published in 1977.

The present work, assembled by the American Waldensian Society, is an entirely new volume, not a reprinting of the earlier edition. The Tourn text has been entirely reworked in light of the revised Italian edition of 1981, and three new contributions have been added to better serve comprehension of the reach and contemporary shape of the Waldensian movement.

One, written by Giorgio Bouchard, brings the reader into the world of Waldensian ministry since WWII. The author, having been directly involved in the national administration (including service in the years 1979-1986 as moderator) of the Waldensian Church in Italy over the past 20 years, is in a capital position to narrate the struggle and controversies of recent decades, as well as the stories of the patience and tenacity which yielded the Waldensian-Methodist federation, achieved in 1979, and of the hope deriving from the 1984 Agreement between the Italian state and the churches represented by the Waldensian National Board.

Roger Geymonat's contribution takes up the story of the branch of the Waldensian Church which has been located in Argentina-Uruguay since the mid-1800s. The struggles of European immigrant artisans, workers, farmers, and intellectuals converge as the Waldensian experience in Latin America takes shape in organizational, ecclesiological and ideological attainments alike. Often history is clothed in the legends of great figures, effectively obscuring the struggles of common folk and minorities. Not so with Geymonat's account, which takes up immigrants' joys, pains and fears, and tells why the little people of this world in their commitment to the gospel have raised up the Waldensian Church in their lands. The chapter does not hold itself out as original; it simply gathers and synthesizes the research, experience and testimony of many. What comes through is the point that the Waldensians are a people with a history shaped in faithfulness to the Lord.

Giorgio Spini's chapter outlines the Methodist experience in Italy, from the mid-nineteenth century initiatives of British (Wesleyan) and U.S. (Episcopal) Methodists, to the creation of the Methodist Church in Italy in 1962, and beyond to the concluding of today's federated arrangement with the Waldensians. A knowledge of the

1

Methodist story in Italy in fact is indispensable for understanding the present federation of Waldensian and Methodist congregations in Italy, a relationship which preserves the historic identities of the Waldensian and Methodist components and permits valued participation in global Reformed and Methodist confessional families.

In this year which commemorates the 300th anniversary of the "Return" of Waldensian exiles to Italy—the historic perilous passage which in a pronounced way has given shape to that which we are today—we publish this volume with thanksgiving for the blessings and for the vocation which God has conferred upon us.

Franco Giampiccoli, Moderator
Waldensian National Board
in Italy

Hugo Malan, Moderator
Waldensian Regional Board
in Argentina-Uruguay

Valdense, Uruguay
Freedom Day
February 17, 1989

FOREWORD

Solidarity in Mission

Across the years, in and out of seasons of crisis, the Waldensians in both Europe and Latin America have raised and continue to raise from within their own very small ranks most of the funds required for the support of local church ministries. A minority church (constituent base in the 1980s: 45,000), Waldensians do accept and, in fact, have compelling need for financial assistance from partners in mission abroad—sister denominations, congregations and support groups—for sustaining the wide-ranging witness of costly specialized ministries (hospitals, homes, schools, centers, etc.) to which they are deeply committed.

On both continents Waldensians also welcome international colleagues for service in Waldensian-Methodist ministries for short-term (one-to-three months), intermediate-term (up to three years) and even longer periods of service.

As circumstances permit, the several Waldensian boards are pleased to respond to invitations from churches abroad for Waldensian-Methodist leaders' sharing in the denominations the story of Waldensian-Methodist witness and ministry discoveries.

Inquiries via the *American Waldensian Society;* The Interchurch Center; 475 Riverside Drive, Room 1850; New York, NY 10115.

The Society, founded in 1906, is a national membership organization (individuals and congregations, across many denominations) dedicated to the raising of funds in support of the Waldensian-Methodist churches and to the development of a program which widens and deepens Christ's love among partners in mission. Mission solidarity places the Society today in the arena of promoting ministry linkages, broadly ecumenical, among the churches in the United States and the Waldensian-Methodist churches.

The Society is governed by a national ecumenical board. Though it consults closely with the Waldensian boards in Italy and Argentina-Uruguay, the Society's board is an independent church agency, not an organic unit of the Waldensian Church. Collaboration across three continents, of course, is a key rule.

Since the Society's office is supported by endowment funds, all current receipts (tax-deductible) are transmitted to the church overseas.

The Society publishes a Newsletter which features reports on the

3

direction of Waldensian-Methodist ministry today, notices of opportunities for dollar support and for voluntary and stipended service overseas, and updates on 'crossings': Waldensian-Methodist people-in-mission in North America, and North American churchpeople in service with Waldensian-Methodist ministries overseas.

Acknowledgments

With the encouragement of the Waldensian boards on two continents this volume has been assembled as a project of the American Waldensian Society on the occasion of the 300th anniversary of the 'Return' of Waldensian exiles to Italy in 1689: daring much for Christ, a devout people returned to preach and to act for everyone's freedom.

The present volume derives from Giorgio Tourn's *I Valdesi*, the first edition of which appeared in 1977. Far and away the best-seller of Claudiana Editrice, the Waldensian publishing house, in recent decades, *I Valdesi* came out subsequently in Dutch, French, German, Spanish and English editions, the latter of which, *The Waldensians*, edited by the American Waldensian Society, was published in 1980. The translator, Prof. Camillo P. Merlino, worked from the 1977 Italian text.

In 1981 Claudiana published the revised edition of *I Valdesi*, which, in translation, constitutes Parts I - IV of the present volume. The revised work in English required full textual review, and for this we are deeply grateful to Christine Spanu, Rome, who translated as well the Spini and Bouchard texts, now appearing as Parts V and VII, respectively. Likewise, our sincere thanks go to Elizabeth Delmonte, Montevideo, who translated the Geymonat text, Part VI.

We acknowledge the insightful editorial counsel of Pastors Giorgio Bouchard, Naples, and Carlos Delmonte, Montevideo, and Dr. Carlo Papini, Turin, Claudiana's director. Special salutes go to Dr. Charles Arbuthnot, my predecessor, who edited the first English edition, a signal moment in the life of the American Waldensian Society; to Sara Gettemy and Laura Porter, whose computer skills yielded the camera-ready copy of the present text; to Drew University, Madison, NJ and the United Methodist Church's Board of Global Ministries, for support of Prof. Spini's research in the U.S.; and to the National Council of Churches of Christ in the USA's Department of Publication Services, for art and composition work. Professionals, with plain-out heart, all.

For the discipleship and discernment of the four collaborating writers, word concerning which is on the back cover, we say— as we say for the ministry of all the aforementioned sisters and brothers—Thanks be to God!

Courage, Church!

Across their 800-year faith journey Waldensian witness has been hewn from the persuasion that preaching—announcement of the grace of God and the call to life with Christ—and the practice of discipleship are indivisible. Had not Jesus commissioned his followers to *teach* and *make disciples* of the nations (Matt. 28)?

Valdesius animated a movement that understood to the core Jesus' promise, You shall be my witnesses, by the power of the Spirit, to the extremities of the earth (Acts 1).

"My witnesses . . . " Obedience, the Waldensians understood, is to God, not to the church. Valdesius and the Poor would teach that the call to discipleship comes from Christ alone, that disciples are the living tissue through which Christ wants to live *his life* for others. Valdesius got into trouble not because of passion for the poor, but because he dared, without the Church's approbation, to interpret scripture in public places. This irrepressible challenge to the teaching authority (the *magisterium)* of the Church—taking Jesus at his word that what witnesses say and do is the *Spirit's* business— centuries later would lead to the Waldensian movement's being hailed *mater reformationis,* the "mother of the Reformation." Living in the way of the apostles, preaching in freedom *(libere praedicare),* not hierarchy, the medieval Waldensians discerned, runs to the heart of the church.

". . . to the ends of the earth . . .": Valdesius and the Poor not only preached of conversion to God's purposes, they practiced as much at the extremities of life, doing freely what Jesus did, opting to live among the wretched and unwashed of this earth — *nudi nudum Christum sequentes* (see text 1, chapter 1). Their inspiration: the gospels' radical discipleship. Waldensians have understood that it is in the gritty trenches of life that the Word becomes flesh. No small wonder that the hallmark of Waldensian spirituality has been the *practice* of the faith, to the point that the current moderator in Italy, Franco Giampiccoli, ventures to assert that in our time the secular equivalent of the word *agape,* Christ's love for others, is the word *solidarietà,* solidarity, which places witnesses in the business of embracing, defending and lifting the mangled, the abused, the weak. It is the testimony of the Waldensian Church that spirituality and solidarity belong together, as do love and justice, grace and discipleship, biblical faith and critical conscience-public responsibility. The new creation in Christ, at once cosmic and intensely personal, transforms both public realities and human hearts. With hearts aflame in the discovery—to which scripture pointed them—that Christ has set humanity free from all fear, the Poor strode right into public places (until driven underground) to call people to new life with Christ. In personal dialog with scripture, and answerable to no church censor, the Waldensians asserted the claims of Christ "where cross the crowded ways of life."

Waldensian theologians in our time distinguish the great sixteenth century Reformation from the first or radical reformation (Valdesius, the Poor, and later, Hus and company) dating from the twelfth century (radical, because it looks to scripture preeminently as pointing to the mind of Christ). Arguably, they say, the Protestant *sola scriptura* motif runs to the first reformation while the *sola fide, sola gratia,* and *solus Christus* master chords, seeded in the earlier reformation, came to full flower in the second Reformation. In both, the centering point is seen as the freedom which Christ has won and confers upon his witnesses. The immediate-past moderator in Italy, Giorgio Bouchard, puts it very simply: "The Protestant phenomenon is based upon the bet that God is manifest more in freedom than in authority."

Grounded in biblical faith (even the lay constituencies learn to mine scripture and to promote *formazione spirituale)*, Waldensian-Methodist people often speak of their church as a *spazio di libertà*— a way for freedom—and a *scuola di responsabilità*—a school for responsibility. Passionately, relentlessly, Waldensian discipleship today seeks to open up "space" for everyone's freedom. Freedom, like love, they realize, cannot be possessed; it must be put to work, that those whom God has made sisters and brothers across this planet can breathe free in their rightful "space."

From the witness of the thirteenth century "bons hommes" to that of today's specialized ministries — traditional and cutting-edge alike — the story is radical, practical love distributed, as the bread and the wine, to the extremities of human need. Between memory and hope, freedom in the service of responsibility!

Whether the ministry is standing with and advancing the reintegration of political prisoners and exiles of the dictatorship era into Argentinian-Uruguayan society, or welcoming, giving sanctuary to and advocating for Third World immigrants and refugees to Italy, or seeking national action to promote the cause of black South

6

Africans and Palestinians, or struggling to secure authentic pluralism in Italy and companion non-confessional teaching of religion in the schools—the centerline throughout is Christ's freedom in the service of responsibility.

Whether a pronounced counterculture (public) amid social configurations which appreciably reflect the Counter-Reformation to this day, or an instrument of evangelization (personal), calling people, as Lazarus, out from the domain of the death forces (militarism, obsession with security, accumulation of possessions, mafia, for example), unbinding and setting free protagonists and artisans of the "new humanity for others," the witness, personal and public, is still *libertad* (Spanish) bound to *responsabilità* (Italian).

Waldensians come in for their fair share of collective infirmities. They are far too contentious among themselves, are possessed of elitist streaks, do not easily accept loving criticism from sister churches. Still, God, whose love never fails, has taken these very sisters and brothers from among the stiff-necked of this earth and crafted a daring people who are not ashamed of witness to Christ. Such is the mystery of God's grace through history. Self-understanding in terms of witness strikes many in this jaded, demented world as truly odd, yet in the midst of idolatrous destruction this robust, down-to-earth minority, just 45,000 believers on two continents, still cries out to the whole church, *Hay que ser valiente!* . . . *Coraggio!* . . . Courage!

Frank G. Gibson, Jr.
Executive Director, American Waldensian Society
New York
Pentecost, 1989

Part One

A DIASPORA OF DISSIDENTS

(1170 - 1532)

The Lord is our light and our salvation: of whom, therefore, shall we ever be afraid? Hope in the Lord: be strong, and let your heart take courage.

— Psalm 27

Jesus said, "Come, Peter, get out of the boat and walk on water..."

—Matthew 14

...Substantive Christianity is biblical, or it is nothing. The church, that is, cannot fabricate whatever Christianity it wishes; the church does not define but bears witness to the biblical message. Nor is the Bible a straightjacket which paralyzes the freedom of the Spirit. To the contrary, across the centuries the Bible has been accredited as the inexhaustible expression of the very creativity and transformation generated by the Spirit.

—"Called to Be Witnesses to the Gospel Today," synod assembly, Italy, 1985

I.

VALDESIUS AND THE "POOR"

1. A man named Valdesius

It is not surprising that a slender band of twelfth century evangelicals, harassed and excommunicated by the Church, should have neglected to make written record of their own beginnings. They were, after all, too much engaged in rediscovering the Bible and circulating it in their native tongue, in preaching and making common cause with the poor to examine their origins. Our story begins, therefore, with a page from the files of the organization charged with their prosecution — the Inquisition. The introduction of an Inquisition functionary's "police report" in the thirteenth century gives us the following revealing picture. It is taken from Church archives in Carcassonne, France.

The Poor of Lyon arose around the year 1170, founded by a certain citizen of Lyon by the name of Valdesius, after whom his followers took their name. The person in question was a rich man who abandoned all his wealth, determining to observe a life of poverty and evangelical perfection, like the apostles. He arranged for the gospels and some other books to be translated into the common tongue, as well as some texts of Saints Augustine, Jerome, Ambrose and Gregory, arranged under titles which he called "sentences," and which he read with great zeal, without, however, understanding very much. Full of his own importance and with little education, he ended up by usurping the prerogatives of the apostles. He dared to preach the gospel in the streets, where he made many disciples, both men and women, and compounded the arrogance by sending them out, in turn, to preach.

These people, ignorant and illiterate, went about through the

11

towns, entering houses and even churches, spreading many errors everywhere. They were summoned by the Archbishop of Lyon, who warned them against such defiance, but they refused to fall in line, cloaking their madness by saying that they must obey God rather than people, since God had commanded the apostles to preach the gospel to every living creature.

And thus, they ended up despising the clergy, accusing them of being rich and of living a life of ease — all the while boldly declaring themselves to be imitators and successors of the apostles! What false profession of poverty and pretended saintly living!

Because of this disobedience and of this arrogant appropriation of a task which did not belong to them at all, they were excommunicated and expelled from their country.

A prosecutor's brief is not without its insights! But let us try to supplement the picture from such fragmentary Waldensian traditions as have come down to us. Surely everything did indeed stem from a certain Valdesius, undoubtedly a man with exceptional vitality, yet seemingly without being overbearing towards his friends. He left no body of written materials, composed no precepts, issued no rules or ordinances. He apparently chose just to live out his faith without demanding that others follow suit. Not a leader, not a self-appointed teacher or model, he was, nonetheless, to become a reference point for many generations of Christians who sought to live as biblical people.

This important fact must be mentioned right at the outset: the Waldensians, unlike the Franciscans, have not embellished the life of their founder with legends and accounts of miracles. They have not turned him into a saint. They have merely highlighted the important features of his life: his call to and practice of the faith.

First of all, what was his name? The primary sources use the Latin form, Valdesius; in the vernacular, he likely was called Valdès.[1] No existing documents, however, speak of the exact year of birth, of his youth, or even of the very last years of his life. Tradition has it that he was married and had two daughters, but the story remains essentially obscure.

He was a man of considerable wealth, in all probability a merchant, a wholesaler. He had diverse financial interests and was probably involved in the political and administrative affairs of his diocese. Perhaps like businesspeople today, he was enmeshed in the area power structure. Wealthy, he was criticized for lending money at outrageous rates of interest.

Then in the 1170s, something happened to this leading member of the Lyonese establishment — something which led to a radical change in his life. We may never know exactly what the story was; various accounts have come down and are worth noting, poetic as they are.

Valdesius, it was said, after mass on a certain day came upon a minstrel who was singing the story of St. Alexis, the rich and spoiled member of a noble family who all of a sudden, on his wedding night, left his bride and family to undertake a pilgrimage to the Holy Land. There, as a result of his saintly life and sufferings, he became so disfigured that, upon return to his city, no one recognized him. Ignored and left to die under an old staircase, he was identified only after his death. This was just the kind of sensational story that people in the streets enjoyed. Valdesius, so the story goes, was deeply touched and invited the minstrel to his home to play the song again. As he listened, Valdesius began to believe that he should follow Alexis' example and renounce completely his previous life.

Another account has it that as a rich merchant in the midst of poverty he was troubled in conscience and sought counsel at the cathedral from a priest. The two were said to have engaged in such prolonged and earnest conversation that at last the priest read to Valdesius the passage from Matthew 19, in which Jesus tells the rich young man to sell all his goods, give the proceeds the poor, and follow him.

There is yet another version. Valdesius was said to have been extremely upset over the sudden death of a friend who was taken in a seizure in the course of a banquet. He is supposed to have asked himself, "If death should overtake me, would my soul be ready for the journey?" After weeks of uncertainty, this tale goes, he decided to give up his former way of life and begin anew.

Beyond these stories' poetic charm this much is clear: Valdesius' dilemma was a spiritual crisis and he saw his conversion as an answer to the call of the gospel. An historian has written, "Valdesius was a medieval man who, in his own town, met the Christ of the gospels."

More than the occasion of his crisis, what interests us are the two remarkable consequences. First, Valdesius decided to have parts of the Bible translated into the vernacular, that is, into the language spoken in and around Lyon. Second, the call to discipleship meant for Valdesius divesting himself of his riches, distributing his goods among those in need, and himself becoming poor. The two decisions were closely related; we do not know whether one had precedence over the other or whether they took place at the same time.

To arrange to have the Bible translated and copied by hand was, of course, an undertaking which could be accomplished only at great expense. We may, therefore, suppose that Valdesius contracted for the translation while still in possession of his wealth. The reading of scripture was no problem for the Church. The great affront to Church authorities was that *laypersons* should read and *interpret* scripture in the vernacular *in public*.

A vow of poverty on the part of the faithful was not unheard of — witness the monks and hermits who were common in medieval times. But Valdesius' case was different. His vow did not lead him to a monastery and to a life of contemplation and obedience. He was an ordinary citizen who chose to *live* among the poor. Further, his renunciation was not an act to earn merit but one to *challenge others*. One of Valdesius' sayings which has come down to us makes the point. It seems that when he was in the act of distributing the last of his goods a crowd of scoffers gathered in front of his house and made fun of him. Valdesius is said to have replied to his detractors, "Citizens and friends, I am not out of my mind, as you seem to think; I am freeing myself of those who were oppressing me in making me a lover of money more than of God. This act I do for myself and for you: for myself, so that if from now on I possess anything you may indeed call me a fool; for you in order that you, too, may be led to put your hope in God and not in riches."

2. The "Poor"

Shortly afterwards, a circle of friends and acquaintances was drawn to Valdesius, attracted by his message and above all by the freshness of his experience. There was thus born a modest community which gave itself a very significant name (from Matthew 5), "the poor in spirit." With this name they wished to show that their aim was to build a community like that of the first disciples of Jesus, men and women who sought to take him at his word and obey him.

The striking thing about this early movement was the freedom by which it lived the Christian faith. It was a freedom full of joy and inventiveness. The thought of challenging the Church or rebelling against its authority was to arise later. The "poor in spirit" wished neither to change nor to revolutionize the Christian faith, only to *live* it in an authentic way. Their movement was one of revival, of which there are many examples from both medieval and modern times, such as the eighteenth century Wesleyan revival in the Church of England.

We should not be misled by their chosen name of the Poor, thinking of them as a band of mendicants roaming the streets. They were men and women drawn from all the social classes, though perhaps the original nucleus was made up of persons who were active in city life, such as merchants and artisans. There were some priests, also, and very soon a number of intellectuals who were attracted by the presence of Durand of Huesca, who was to become the theologian of the group.

The Poor were simply people whose studies of scripture rendered them sensitive to the problem of human suffering and converted them to identify with those who had to endure the misery that surrounded them everywhere.

What is particularly striking in the inquisitor's report is the sense of obligation and determination to live "as the apostles." Christians, indeed, with a profound sense of mission:

> The decision we have taken is this: to maintain, until our death, faith in God and the Church's sacraments; . . . to preach freely, according to the grace given by God to us; this we will not cease to do for any cause.

These are words that Durand of Huesca would write. To "preach freely" did not mean to preach in an uncontrolled manner; it meant that God has the liberty to choose in the church who would be God's own witnesses. The preaching of the Poor was simple, direct, without any pretense of introducing new doctrine; it was centered upon the call for conversion to God's purposes, good works and an authentic Christian life.

Valdesius' followers did not hesitate to include women among their preachers, a fact which profoundly shocked the whole clerical and lay establishment of the time. Their mission and behavior were taken literally from the words of Jesus (Matthew 10) when he sent his disciples forth to preach God's rule — going out two by two, dressed in rough clothing, carrying no money, wearing light sandals. From the latter, in fact, the local folk nicknamed the Poor scornfully, "the sandaled ones."

The problem that the Poor created for the Church did not lie in their practice of the Christian life but in their commitment to preaching and to authentic Christian community. New times were coming and a new kind of society was in the making: what should be the response of Christians to the call of Jesus? Far from being a marginal product of medieval piety, Valdesius and his people struck at the heart of the Christian experience. If they were brushed off as an insignificant minority, it is nonetheless true that often in history it is just such minorities who raise the fundamental questions on which the destiny of a society is based.

Two major elements need to be emphasized in order to understand the special character of the movement and its subsequent history. First of all, the Poor wished to preach while remaining a body of laymen and laywomen. They did not set up a religious order, enter a monastery, or name one of their number as leader who would act as "guarantor" for them before the authorities. Jesus, they said, is our leader. It is he who vouches for us. It was not just by chance that the Waldensians in Lombardy used a commercial term to define their movement — *societas*, a society, a group of partners in a joint enterprise, not an order, but a free association of people who, like merchants setting up a trade organization, have ideas and interests in common.

In the second place, they wished to be part and parcel of the life of the city. They were not hermits seeking the solitude of the desert. Their calling was to be present in the churches, public squares and homes where their message could be heard. They were and wished to remain citizens of Lyon, one of the great cities of western Europe, on the route of the crusades, where St. Bernard had preached, where a great cathedral, St. John's, was under construction. This urban environment was their world; to it belonged the promise of transformation. Here they chose to live out their discipleship.

3. On notice . . .

All this was not so revolutionary. Indeed, the fresh initiative of Valdesius and his Poor could only meet with the approval of the hierarchy, and at first Archbishop Guichard himself accepted it. But a confrontation was not long in coming, and it was over the question of preaching, which both Valdesius and Guichard held to be fundamental. Said Guichard, "We bishops are here to do the preaching; it is a part of the task laid down for us as successors of the apostles." "On the contrary," replied the Poor, "preaching belongs to everyone who chooses to truly live like the apostles of Jesus."

Just as these first points of tension were emerging in 1179, the sessions of the Third Lateran Council were taking place in Rome. It seemed appropriate, therefore, for Valdesius and some of his colleagues to journey to the Eternal City, there to put their case before the Church.

The Third Lateran was the first great Council of the Roman

Catholic Church, the one in which the new papal direction of Gregory VII was sanctioned. The Church was not only freeing itself from imperial power, but was also acquiring a new sense of self-awareness. It was thus a Council of victory — but it was also one in which there lurked a certain fear. The bishops who came from Languedoc and Provence in southern France reported the menacing advance of the Cathari, who threatened to compromise the new equilibrium.

Catharism originated as an evangelical ferment, similar to many initiatives in medieval France which emphasized biblical motifs like purity and faithfulness. However, under the influence of certain dissident elements from eastern Europe, in particular the Bogomils, the Cathari movement underwent a distinct change, becoming involved in extremist philosophical speculation. Holding that the world is where the battle between good and evil takes place, and that the believer must move in it by giving up everything material (evil), the Cathari rejected marriage, refused to eat certain foods, scorned riches, and in general practiced a very austere life. The movement spread little by little, thanks to its strong organization and support of the ruling classes in southern France.

Catharism was by no means a simple matter of eastern philosophical thought, but a real and viable religious community of belief and practice, with its own ministers ("bon hommes" who went about doing good), members (the "perfect") and sympathizers, and with rites, ceremonies, sacred books and deliberative assemblies. Since it strongly opposed the clergy's luxurious lifestyle and the power of the Church, it enlisted the sympathetic support of certain nobles, merchants and others who opposed the policies of Gregorian reform. French society in Provence, one of the most advanced in Europe at the time, was virtually won over to the movement.

It was in this context that the Poor of Lyon, full of confidence, went to Rome and there were welcomed by the church leadership. They brought with them a copy of their version of the Bible to present to the pope, who, upon receiving the delegation, expressed approval for their intentions, but admonished them that the question of their preaching had to be settled by their local bishop. They were also subjected to a severe theological grilling by an English monk, Walter Map, who managed to make them look ridiculous for their lack of theological sophistication. No formal excommunication was pronounced, however.

In their home city, Valdesius' men and women kept up their

preaching — the call to conversion to God's purposes and to living for others — even to the extent of opposing theologically the doctrines of the Cathari. In all this they sought to demonstrate that they were not heretics seeking novelty, but Christians whose life was founded on the good news of Christ.

A certain document (which came to light only in this century) serves to underline Valdesius' awareness of being fully within the body of the Church and his will to struggle for the cause of God's rule. Around 1180, Henri de Marci, a pontifical delegate, was in southern France to organize a campaign against the Cathari, and there encountered Valdesius. The pope's representative proceeded to interrogate Valdesius so as to check his orthodoxy, and then required him to sign a formal declaration of adherence to the Catholic faith. Valdesius' stand was so "Catholic" that he did not hesitate to affix his signature.

It is worth noting that Valdesius inserted in the text a significant expression of his own. For him and his companions, the call to a life of poverty was in consequence of obedience to the command of God; it was not a "counsel of perfection," as with the monks in their obedience to the Church. The fact that he added this particular point was of fundamental importance, even if he was not aware of it at the time. It revealed that for the Poor the vocation of poverty came not from the Church, but from the Lord. The sense of the gospel had spoken to him and to these laypeople directly, without intermediaries of any kind.

When the hierarchy, always wary of any lay activity not fully under its control, issued an order forbidding Valdesius to preach, he and the Poor refused to obey, citing the words of Peter to the Sanhedrin (Acts 4): Is it right in God's sight for us to obey you rather than God? Here Valdesius is Peter, the apostle who defends the word of God against the weight of religious tradition. Expelled from their city of Lyon, the Poor took their mission to the Languedoc region of southern France. Although not yet formally condemned, increasingly they came under strong suspicion.

In their new environment they continued to consider themselves good Catholic Christians. They were zealous missionaries and stirred up questions. They wrote tracts, organized public debates, and preached against Catharism in the market places and the streets. It was not easy for the Cathari leaders, their so-called "good men," to counter the arguments of Valdesius' band. In contrast to the local priests the newcomers, too, were poor. With Bible in hand, they spoke and lived with apostolic conviction and example.

Soon a fundamental experience was to transform their community. The Poor began to encounter other bands of dissidents beyond the Cathari alone. In the disciples of Pierre de Bruys, those of the monk Henri, and others, they heard criticisms of the Roman Church which were far-reaching — charges that Rome was wedded to a love of power and luxury, that Christian doctrine was being corrupted by such things as the veneration of relics and the saints, prayers for the dead, etc. A critical mentality took root, and the piety of the Poor began to be transformed into radical protest. It is not surprising that ecclesiastical authorities took an increasingly stern position toward the Poor, and at length determined to liquidate them as incorrigible dissidents.

The words used against Valdesius' followers by such famous men as Alain de Lille, professor at Montpellier, and by Bernard, the learned monk of Fontcaude, were stinging. Culturally, the Poor were accused of being ignoramuses, self-taught chatterboxes who loved to show off without having studied with the doctors of theology. Socially, they were called drifters, spongers, hysterical females. Morally, they were accused of being frauds who pretended to speak for renewal while actually sowing the seeds of rebellion.

Then came political repression. In 1184 the French bishops prevailed upon the Council of Verona to include the Poor in the list of schismatic movements. In 1190 the Bishop of Narbonne condemned them for heresy. Alfonso of Aragon, whose domain extended to Provence, had them banished from his lands. The Bishop of Toul ordered their arrest and trial before his tribunal.

1. "NAKED, THEY FOLLOW A NAKED CHRIST" (1179)

We have seen these Waldensians at the Council called by Pope Alexander III; they are simple and unlearned people who take their name from their leader, Valdès, a citizen of Lyon on the Rhône. They presented the pope with a book written in Gallic, containing texts and commentaries on the Psalms and other books from the scriptures.

They insisted that they be granted authorization to preach, judging themselves to be experts, while in fact they were merely conceited, like those birds that are unable to see snares and believe they are free . . .

I, who was the least among many thousands of delegates, mocked them because their demands had created an uproar. Called to assist another prelate to whom the Holy Father had entrusted the task of hearing their story, I sharpened my arrows in the presence of many learned men and experts in church law. Two of the Waldensian leaders were brought before me. They had come to dispute the faith, not to search for truth in love, but to close my mouth, to put me into a tight corner as if I had affirmed evil things. I must confess that I felt most uncomfortable, because I feared that on account of my sin, I would be denied the grace of speaking in front of such a large assembly.

The presiding prelate ordered me to proceed in my questioning... To begin, I put to them the most elementary questions ... well-knowing that the donkey which is used to eating only thistles turns down the lettuce:

"Do you believe in God the Father?" They replied, "We do."

"And in the Son?" They replied, "We do."

"And in the Holy Spirit?" They replied, "We do."

Then I added, "And in the Mother of Christ?"

And once more they answered, "We do."[1]

At this last response a roar of derision went up and they withdrew, confused, and rightly so, because they had no one to guide them. And yet these same people expect to lead others ...

These people have no settled dwellings, but go around two by two, barefooted and dressed in wool tunics. They own nothing, sharing everything in common, after the manner of the apostles. Naked, they follow a naked Christ. Their beginnings are humble in the extreme, for they have not yet much of a following, but if we should leave them to their devices they will end up by turning all of us out ...

—Walter Map, *De nugis curialium,* in G. Gonnet, *Enchiridion Fontium Valdensium, I* (Torre Pellice, 1958), pp. 122-3.

2. VALDESIUS' TESTAMENT OF FAITH (1180)

In the name of the Father, Son, and Holy Spirit, and of the blessed and ever-Virgin Mary. Be it noted by all the faithful that I, Valdesius, and all my brothers, standing before the Holy Gospels, do declare that we believe and profess openly with all our hearts, having been grasped by faith, that Father, Son and Holy Spirit are three Persons, one God and that the divine Trinity in full is one essence and substance, eternal and omnipotent, and that the single persons of the Trinity are fully ... one God as affirmed in the creed ... We firmly believe and explicitly declare that the incarnation of the Divinity did not take place in the Father and in the Holy Spirit, but in the Son alone, so that he who was the divine Son of God the Father was also true man ... In him co-existed two natures, God and man in one person,

---

[1]The Waldensians here came up short on two counts. They should have known that the the exact title of Mary, approved by the Council of Ephesus in 431, was Mother of God (*Theotókos*), the only one to guarantee, for the theology of that period, the unity of the person in Jesus Christ, son of God and son of Mary. The title Mother of Christ, on the other hand, had been condemned as Nestorian, not to be used. The second mistake was to extend the formula "believe in" to Mary, whereas official teaching applied the formula only to the three persons of the Trinity.

. . . and he ate, drank, grew weary, and rested after his journeys . . .

We believe in our hearts and confess with our lips one Church, catholic, holy, apostolic and immaculate, apart from which we believe no one can be saved.

We accept the sacraments celebrated in the Church through the invisible and incomprehensible power of the Holy Spirit, even though administered by priests who sin . . .

We firmly believe and affirm that the sacrifice, that is, the bread and wine, after its consecration, is the body and blood of Christ; in this sacrifice the good priest adds nothing more and the wicked priest in no way diminishes the sacrifice.

We believe that those sinners who repent in their hearts, confess with their lips and give satisfaction with their works, according to the scriptures, can receive God's forgiveness . . .

We firmly believe in the judgement to come, and in the fact that everyone will receive reward or punishment according to what has been done in this flesh. We do not doubt that alms, sacrifice, and other good works benefit the dead.

And since, according to the Apostle James, faith without works is dead, we have renounced this world and have distributed to the poor all that we possessed, according to the will of God, and we have decided that we ourselves should be poor in such a way as not to be anxious for tomorrow, and as not to accept from anyone gold, silver, or anything else, with the exception of clothing and daily food. We have set before ourselves the objective of fulfilling the gospel purposes.

We believe also that anyone in this age who gives alms, does other good works with one's own possessions and observes the Lord's commandments will be saved. Brothers, we make this declaration in order that if anyone should come to you affirming to be one of us, you may know for certain that that person is not one of us if that person does not profess the same faith.

— G. Gonnet, *Enchiridion Fontium Valdensium, I*, pp. 32 ff.

II.

THE YEARS OF CRISIS

1. The Lombards

News of Valdesius' movement spread quickly, very soon reaching across the Alps into Lombardy, a most important region in medieval Europe. If Montpellier and Chartres were symbols of thirteenth century culture, Milan and Piacenza were no less examples of renewed economic life. In fact, Lombardy represented an emerging new Europe, where the opposing interests of empire and papacy were to clash.

Criticism of the Church in this bustling region had been common for decades, not only in the aristocratic manner of the Cathari, whose flourishing cells were in all the cities, but in ways even more widespread and popular. A group known as the Patari some years earlier had grown up spontaneously in reaction to an increasingly corrupt clergy. Although by Valdesius' time it had been maneuvered out of existence by a skillful clerical party, there nevertheless remained a certain skillful "patarine" mentality in the cities which was critical of the Church and impatient with its compromises. Present and active, also, were some of the followers of Arnold of Brescia, Abelard's intrepid disciple who had traveled all over Europe making the acquaintance of various dissident groups and who had even started a popular movement in Rome. It was Arnold who first advanced the notion of a complete separation between religious and political powers.

The mission of the Poor in Lombardy was to be quite different from what had been the case in southern France. Here they did not need to present their message as something new. They sought instead to unify and catalyze the ferment of religious unrest already existent in the experience of Lombard religious dissidence. The Poor became a reference point not because they were more numerous or powerful but because they had more lucid ideas.

Thus, in between the sectarian theories of the Cathari and the rigid anticlericalism of the followers of Arnold, Valdesius' people managed to lodge their idea of renewal. Theirs was a broad, straightforward evangelical appeal, not bound to imperial politics and to the struggle against clerical corruption.

We need to note, however, that the witness given by the Poor in Lombardy very soon became quite independent of the Lyonese pattern. The Lombards tended to see the apostolic calling as one rooted in community *(societas)*, and not necessarily implying itinerant preaching. They felt that to travel across the countryside preaching was one way of living "as the apostles," but not the only way. Another was to share commitment unselfishly with one's sisters and brothers in the faith. In other words, the Lombard Poor reflected the emphasis recorded in Acts 1-4 on Christian community, while their counterparts from Lyon honed in on the missionary message of the Jesus they found in Matthew 10.

It was not by accident that the main point of discussion between the two groups was on the way they should regard work. According to the Lyonese, labor was an impediment to witness and a temptation to accumulate wealth. For the Lombards one's daily task was an instrument of service, the opportunity for concrete witness. The Poor of Lyon tended to be pilgrim preachers, bards of conversion not greatly dissimilar from the wandering minstrels of the time. The central figure for the Lombard Poor, on the other hand, was the artisan, the woolcarder in a textile shop, the laborer, the worker.

A deep sense of social solidarity was found among the Lombard Poor. They possessed considerable organizing ability; their life and witness were well structured, and not, as in Lyon, somewhat euphoric and spontaneous.

Although Valdesius continued to serve as the reference point of the movement, the Lombards, the left wing of the Poor, charted a somewhat different path. The more conservative Lyonese current even sought renewed contacts with the Roman Church. Giovanni da Ronco, the Lombard organizer, in the eyes of the aging Valdesius appeared to have betrayed the movement's original ideas and hopes.

Differences among the Poor on both side of the Alps and increasing opposition by the Roman hierarchy led to the crisis of 1205: Valdesius broke with the Lombards and severed them from his community. A few years later, following Valdesius' death, Durand of Huesca and some of his group were reintegrated into the Church of Rome, having been given permission to found a religious order which they called the Poor Catholics.

2. Toward definitive condemnation

All this was taking place around the years 1206-1207, some thirty years after the beginning of the movement of the Poor and at a time historians regard as the most delicate and difficult in the period of medieval Christianity. Already at the time of Valdesius' conversion the Cathari represented a certain menace for the Catholic Church, but by the first decade of the thirteenth century the movement was undermining the Church's very foundations, being welcomed by both nobles and merchants alike. The Waldensians, who might have been a counterforce to the Cathari, had already been repudiated. The Church therefore called upon Cistercian monks to launch a major preaching offensive in France against the heresy. But when the plump friars on horseback arrived in Provence to "evangelize" the people, they were hissed and booed out of the towns.

At this point Dominic of Guzman, a Spanish priest, came forward with another suggestion. Let the Church, he said, accept the nonconformists' way of free dissent and mendacity — all the while presenting the gospel message within the traditional rule of obedience to the pope. This would be the way of an exceptional figure, Francis of Assisi, to whom we will turn presently.

Above all there loomed the figure of Innocent III, the pontiff who was transforming the papacy into an absolute monarchy. In his view the Christian religion was no longer to serve the civil authority but was itself to be the power which orchestrated the civil order. He gave his approval to Dominic's slow and patient methods and also to Francis. One of the results of his strategic maneuvering was to win back to the Catholic fold the Waldensian groups led by Durand of Huesca and Bernard Prim.

In the eyes of intransigent bishops, though, led by Henri de Marcy, the Church was not proceeding vigorously enough against the heretics. In 1208, when this view prevailed, a full-scale crusade was launched against the Cathari (by now also called Albigensians, from their city, Albi). The kind of Holy War which for decades had been proclaimed against the Muslims, now swept through this part of Christendom, destroying in its wake not only the Albigensians

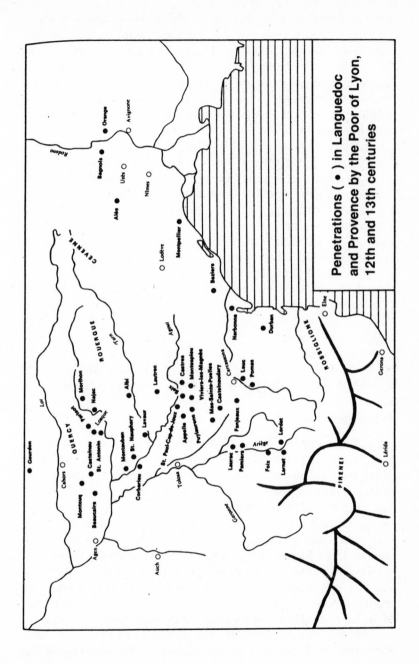

Penetrations (•) in Languedoc and Provence by the Poor of Lyon, 12th and 13th centuries

but many Waldensian nuclei as well.

For 20 long years Languedoc was subjected to a blood bath which not only wiped out the most advanced culture of the time but introduced into the Church, and from there throughout the West, the rule that any ideological deviation must be crushed by force. Henceforth one of the fixed points in European thought was that "the heretic must die!" He or she whose thinking — religious, political, or cultural — was not in line with that of the authorities must be silenced forever.

In 1215, at a solemn assembly during the Fourth Lateran Council, the policy was given official sanction. Heretics, including the Poor, formally condemned by the Council, were to be destroyed by force. Crusades, annual confession and parochial structures all were pronounced instruments of the Church for tightening its control. The centralizing program of Innocent III had its day: the faithful were stripped of their responsibility in the Christian life and made no more than the wards of a watchful clergy.

In 1215 the Waldensian initiative was definitively rejected. The Church had made its choice — one far different from that which the Poor had proposed, one which began a ruthless repression against all forms of evangelical dissent in the West. What was to become of the minute Waldensian community scattered from Languedoc to Lombardy? Oppressed by the great political and religious powers, internally divided and partly reabsorbed into the Catholic fold, it seemed destined to disappear within the course of a few years.

3. Bergamo

All was not lost, however. In the face of repression intended to obliterate them, the Waldensians were discovering a renewed sense of mission and unity. While Rome was bent on decreeing their death, they responded by making plans for the future and by renewing their commitment.

The evidence for this comes down to us in a document of greatest importance, one of the rare Waldensian documents of the era to survive. It is a letter sent to Waldensians in Germany with information on the outcome of a meeting held in Bergamo in 1218. In it we discover that following a long period of preparatory work, with preliminary meetings and exchange of letters, six representatives of the Lombard Poor and six from the Poor of Lyon came together in Bergamo to take stock of their situation, to reexamine their respective positions and to explore anew the possibilities for reaching an agreement. The letter reveals that in the course of discussion there emerged, little by little, a consensus, so that a new sense of solidarity was born. The missionary spirit of the Lyonese was no longer seen as a stumbling block, but as complementary to the more concrete work of the Lombards. The sense of the Lyonese Poor that they were living in the "last days" thus made common cause with Lombard realism. The meeting in Bergamo represented a point of intersection, a mutual recognition of two lines, both valid.

The meeting was also a fresh point of departure. At Bergamo the *societas valdesiana* was born. If Valdesius and his preaching at Lyon 50 years before had led to the birth of the Waldensian movement, it was now the Lombards who supplied the organization, structure and framework in which to carry on. From this time forth the Poor would be more than a fragmented experience; they would be an organic whole.

The Bergamo meeting focused on a new and alternative Christian way of life; it was popular evangelism's reply to the theology of the Fourth Lateran Council. The theological questions of authority and of the sacraments — the overarching issues of the time — were debated at both Rome and Bergamo.

The chosen way of Rome was that of increasing authority and central power. In her view a church faced with renewal movements risked fragmentation, so that it was necessary to reassert unity around the office of the pope and the priesthood. The binding cord would be sacramental dependence; virtue by definition was obedience.

The chosen way of the Poor, on the contrary, was that of *community*. There was nothing at all to be feared from renewal. For the Poor the bond of unity lay not in the sacraments but in their *apostolic mission*. Christian virtue, they held, was in demonstrating love and care for others. Error was to be corrected by admonition, never by force. This was not for lack of theological clarity; it was repudiation of violence. If the Church wished to be freed from imperial power, the Poor argued, it should not itself try to become an instrument of power, but become instead an agent of mission.

One cannot avoid thinking of this contrast in visible, human terms. We can picture a dozen clandestine Christians meeting secretly in a Lombard farmhouse, and we can picture as well a magnificent procession of bishops making their way to the Lateran basilica. Here were two understandings of the Christian faith, two churches — one, that of the "crusaders," the other, that of the "sandaled ones." They no longer faced each other as two hypotheses but as two realities. Which would prevail? The confrontation was about to come very soon. It would not be in the bloodsoaked soil of Languedoc, but in Lombardy.

3. DE HAERETICIS (1215)

As there are people who, according to the apostle "preserve the outward form of religion, but are a standing denial of its reality" (I Tim. 3), and who claim for themselves the authority to preach, although the same apostle affirms "How shall they preach, except they be sent?" (Rom. 10), we decree that all those who dare to take on the ministry of preaching either in private or in public without having been authorized by either the Holy See or the local bishop, are to be excommunicated. And, in the event that they fail, forthwith, to repent, they shall be subject to further punishment according to the law.

— "Acts of the Fourth Lateran Council" in H. Denzinger, ed., *Enchiridion Symbolorum* . . . (Fribourg, 1942), p. 203.

III.

IN THE ITALY OF THE COMMUNES

1. Between Guelfs and Ghibellines

Waldensian protest was born in a city, and for a number of years the cities of Lombardy were the Waldensian strongholds. It was here that the major gatherings were held to distribute offerings, make key decisions, and assign tasks to the members. In the cities were the more or less clandestine centers where people went to receive biblical and spiritual instruction. None of this was by chance.

Lombardy was a region of both economic expansion and religious dissent. Its great city, Milan, had resisted the attacks of Frederick Barbarossa. Proud of its liberties and of its achievements, it was also the capital of protest, a "heretics' Rome." It was not strange, therefore, that Milan should become the center of Waldensian activity.

As the feudal system in Lombardy began to totter, new social forces were beginning to gather strength and to challenge the Church. The latter's response was contained in the declarations of the Fourth Lateran Council, clearly an affirmation of authoritarianism. Communal society in Lombardy, on the other hand, had not yet fully made up its mind: would it opt for the Guelfs or the Ghibellines — a clerical or secular society? This was the question of the time, and the success of the religious movements, the Waldensians included, was closely tied to it. To be Catholic meant supporting the Church totally, accepting its power and control, upholding papal policy at all levels, including the political, and working in every way to increase the Church's might. It was not simply a matter of making one's confession and believing in transubstantiation, but of backing a political current, the Guelfs. In the same way, anyone opposed to clerical power could not fail to be engaged in antipapal and therefore anti-Catholic politics. Such a person could only belong to the opposition stream, the Ghibellines.

For a time the Ghibelline communal magistrates of thirteenth century Lombardy actually welcomed the activities of the dissenters in their struggle against the clergy. They were obviously glad to have any support they could get, and the dissenters were useful allies. There is considerable evidence of this. Genoa and Piacenza, for instance, in the 1220s refused to legislate any laws against heretics; Cremona was a free zone for Cathari fleeing from campaigns against them; both Bergamo and Rimini banished mayors who had sought to round up dissidents, and freed heretics who had been put in jail; Milan took the unprecedented step of permitting Waldensians to construct a meeting place on a piece of municipal property. The latter, to be sure, was outside the city walls, but its construction was carried on in full light of day.

Even among the nobles there were those who assumed the role of protectors for the dissenters, doing so more or less openly and sometimes to the point of risking excommunication.

The golden years of Waldensian preaching in Lombardy, which coincided with this period of inquiry and experimentation, unhappily were not to last long. The Guelfs gained the upper hand. As more of the communal leaders came under the shadow of Rome, their attitude toward the dissenters changed completely; they accused the latter of always criticizing, creating tension, and fostering an atmosphere of constant ferment. The tacit approval given to the dissenters was withdrawn, and they found themselves subject to harsh repression. Milan initiated a series of court actions against the Waldensians.

The Poor, having once been considered good allies, were now seen as too liberal, too independent, too critical. The Ghibelline politicians who had played on the religious unrest in their cities, including the quest for an evangelical style of life, were now succeeded by the Guelf faction, which had no use for dialog with working people who were becoming more and more politically active. This clerical program of the thirteenth century Lombard bourgeoisie was made possible by the new structure which the papacy had created in these same years: the mendicant orders of the Dominicans and Franciscans. Here we meet the most luminous figure in all Italian religious history, Francis of Assisi.

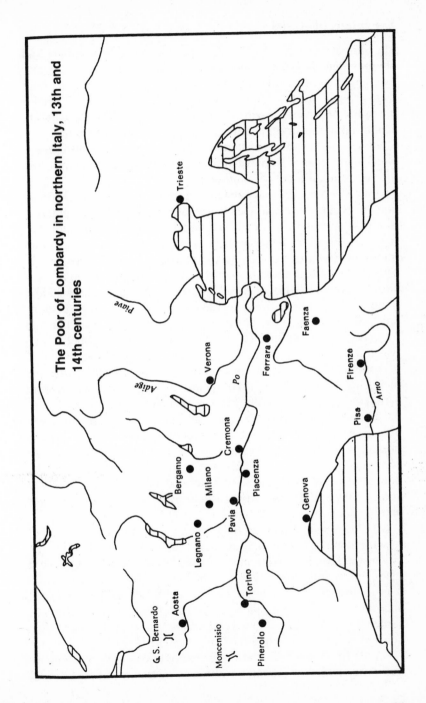

The Poor of Lombardy in northern Italy, 13th and 14th centuries

2. Francis of Assisi

The similarities between Francis and Valdesius are so many and obvious that they hardly need to be underlined. Both were city dwellers, merchants at odds with the society of their times; both were gripped in a radical way by the gospel and were propelled by it to a life of poverty. Each was also on the frontier of the Church, caught up in the struggle between obedience and freedom.

No less evident and substantial, however, were the differences which to the eyes of Rome made of the one a heretic and of the other the very embodiment of sainthood.

Francis was not only an outstanding figure in medieval Christendom; he would be seen as the clearest and most ideal representative of Italian spirituality. Francis succeeded marvelously in interpreting the needs of his generation and of his society, fitting them into traditional Italian religiosity and into the framework of the Church. The need for freedom in the world of the communes found expression in his rediscovery of a faith at once demanding, personal and interior. His criticism of the feudal Church, dominated by bishops and political overlords, became a call to a more fraternal and intimate community life. The need to hear the living gospel, which was felt by so many, was met in his itinerant preaching.

Franciscan piety, with its devotion to the human Christ, its identification with the world of nature, its simplicities which were at times almost countercultural but nevertheless positive and fraternal, elicited sympathy rather than fear. The heritage of humaneness and love of nature present in ancient Roman religion (always present in the Italian soul) was appropriated and transfigured into communion with Christ. This was a piety which reassured the bourgeoisie and the common folk, created inner peace, and allayed conflict. It was the religiosity of a church that draws near to the poor and ministers to them, but does not itself become poor.

All of this was something to be lived not in the monasteries, but in settlements. These new friars built their centers right beside the city walls. They had no intention of spending their time copying old manuscripts or tilling the soil, like the Benedictines. Their vocation was to preach, to teach, to engage in debate and in political activities. Around the Franciscan monasteries grew up clusters of students, congregations, Third Orders, confraternities — new ways constantly invented to live the Catholic faith.

People became convinced that they could be poor, evangelical, and in step with new currents, without going the way of the Cathari,

Patari and Waldensians. One's commitment and struggle for renewal of the Church could be satisfied without falling into heresy. Situating itself in direct opposition to the Waldensian movement, just as the Jesuits would do in the Reformation period, the Franciscan movement succeeded within a few decades in delivering the towns and cities to the political control of the Guelfs.

The Italians did not limit themselves to studying the Waldensian phenomenon; they actively fought it. The first to pen an anti-Waldensian tract was Salvo Burci, a nobleman of Piacenza. Many others followed, such as Rainerio Sacconi, Moneta, Pietro da Verona, Anselmo d'Alessandria, and the militant friars, among whom were ex-Cathari reconverted to Catholicism and thus more Catholic than ever. Their polemics were unremitting in their effort to unmask the Waldensians and to controvert their principles. But the offensive was soon to go even further than words. The Italian friars and Guelf partisans were to become operatives of one of the most tragic institutions in medieval Christendom: the Inquisition.

All of these friars, in effect, doubled as inquisitors, which is to say, they were specialists in tracking down and destroying dissident cells. Clever and ruthless, ready to use espionage, ransom and torture, they arrested and reported anyone whose opinions and beliefs — private as well as public — differed from the official line of the pope.

Here in Lombardy, just as in southern France, the program of winning dissenters back to the Church was accomplished by repression. The disciples of Francis, like those of the violent Dominic, born to humility and the preaching of poverty, became the merciless police agents of the pope. By the middle of the thirteenth century, a promising religious springtime in Italy had come to an end. The Waldensian movement in Lombardy went into decline. But it was to spring up anew, elsewhere.

3. The Waldensian commune

Before leaving Italy, we should take note of some of the features of Waldensian group life in the Italian cities during the period we have just covered. First, we should not, obviously, think of Waldensian congregations in the modern sense, for a good deal of their existence was underground and clandestine. Perhaps the words "commune" or "collective" are most appropriate. The new social order in Lombardy was more communal than feudal. Power and initiative no longer rested with feudal lords, but were in the hands of free people who made their own decisions based on interests which were of their own choosing. Waldensian groups were likewise associations of free people with common interests, except that their interests were religious rather than political or economic. There was this fundamental difference, however: the new bourgeoisie, eager to advance socially and economically, drove the new social order; the Waldensians, on the other hand, were workers on the fringes of society.

Fifty years after the conversion of Valdesius we may think of the Waldensian movement as one with a well-defined structure. No longer united only by natural affinity and religious interests alone, the Waldensians were a people with a pronounced program and with specific projects to be carried out. By this time a distinction was made between those who were totally committed to the movement and those whose adherence was limited. Only the former were called "Waldensian" and addressed each other as "sister" and "brother;" the rest, the sympathizers, were called "friends."

In some cases there emerged a certain hierarchy of deacons, presbyters, and bishops. Tighter organization derived from the Waldensians' need to defend themselves against repression. They borrowed from the prevailing pattern in the Roman Church and from the Cathari, with the latter's distinction between the "perfect" and the "believers."

Waldensian group life revolved around a place of meeting which was quite unique — the *schola*. It was far different from the fine houses where the new, successful businessmen gathered for their meetings or from the great cathedrals and monasteries springing up everywhere and reflecting alike power, prestige, strength and wealth. The Poor had their modest little *scholae* in outlying areas, often clandestine. Such simplicity was dictated not only by prudence but on principle, for the community chose to follow the example of Jesus "who knew not where to lay his head."

4. Toward a theology

In Lombardy, parallel with organizational development, the Waldensian movement began to engage in deep theological reflection. Catholic thought was very clear: outside the Church there was only heresy, a jumble of errors. The Church was the perfect society, the repository of truth, and its bishops were the legitimate successors of the apostles.

Where did this leave the Waldensians? Though rejected by the Roman Church they did not consider themselves to be heretics at all. They accepted the message of the Christian heritage — unlike, for example, the speculative Cathari.

"Just who are you, then, and where are your roots?" the inquisitors would ask, adding "There are only a few hundred of you, tiny groups which have been in existence only for a few decades, while the Roman Church has been present for centuries and counts its faithful among the millions." To answer such questions the Waldensians took a page from church history, from the time of Pope Sylvester, seven centuries earlier.

Ancient tradition declared that in gratitude for a miraculous healing Emperor Constantine in the fourth century gave to Pope Sylvester dominion over the western portion of his empire. This was naturally pure legend, artfully invented in order to prove that the pope had the right to govern the West and that he was not only God's representative but also the heir of imperial power. The legend was backed up by fraudulent documents which at that time were accepted and generally believed without question. How to evaluate this "Donation of Constantine" from a Christian point of view?

Quite naturally the Church's position was that, given her new authority and influence, the Donation had been positive. A good many others, though, saw a negative aspect in the situation, and deplored the fact that the popes had turned their backs on the simple life and had been drawn into an endless circle of riches and vain human pretensions. Of course, the Waldensians agreed with this position; their criticism, however, took them well beyond it. The Donation of Constantine, they declared, not only introduced into the Christian Church an appetite for riches, opening up a life of luxury for the prelates, but it also started the Church down the road of compromise with secular power.

Such a compromise, said the Poor, was a betrayal of the apostolic mission, because it meant giving up the kind of life plainly marked out by Christ. Beginning with the time of the Donation, the Church had actually become the Church of the Evil One. The Poor were Christians who denounced the compromises associated with the Donation of Constantine and who claimed to live the authentic Christian experience.

The question arose: What had happened during the long period from the time of Constantine to Valdesius? Did an apostolic Christian church exist in those centuries? The Waldensians had two

35

responses. The Church, said some, did not fall into error all at once, but only gradually. Valdesius was sent by God to take up the apostolic task only when it was clear that the prelates had forsaken their calling, disdained preaching and obscured the light of the gospel.

Others said that the Waldensian movement had always existed, albeit in a secret and clandestine guise. In this view Valdesius was not the founder, but quite simply the one who restored the community to its authentic, Christian footing. He was one witness in the long line of believers who modelled themselves after the apostles. In the manner of the times, quite naturally, there were some who added bits of medieval fantasy to the account. A certain Leone was said to be the first Waldensian, a man who was a friend of Pope Sylvester's, who foresaw the dire consequences of the Donation and argued against it, and who thereby had to retire in solitude and suffer persecution. Valdesius was sometimes confused with Leone, spoken of as a priest and called a contemporary of Constantine.

Obviously this is pure legend, but it is important to understand the essence of the Waldensian arguments. In the fourth century, the Church betrayed its true nature when it sought an alliance with ruling powers and succumbed to riches. The history of the Church can be divided into two separate and distinct phases, said the Waldensians, the time of the apostles and martyrs (a time of faithful witness), and that after Constantine (centuries of betrayal).

What actually had happened was far more complex than the Waldensians' perception in the thirteenth century. The transformation of Christianity from a banned to a lawful religion did take place under Constantine, but the jump to becoming the religion of the state was later, at the time of Theodosius. The doctrinal elaboration of the church's new status belongs to the Carolingian period (eighth and ninth centuries). It is then that the papacy made its claim for the temporal power. The thirteenth century Waldensians had no knowledge of this and relied completely on tradition, but their theological interpretation was both clear and remarkable.

What happened to the Church after Constantine? The Waldensians claimed that it did not completely lose its way by Constantine's poison. Despite the betrayal, a faithful remnant, the Poor included, would survive. The Church may have betrayed its Christian witness but the light of the gospel was not extinguished outright. This was the essential theological line the Waldensians would pursue for centuries.

Though banished from the cities of Lombardy, the Poor did not disappear. They turned up in different settings, adapting their witness to their new surroundings. In general it can be said that by the middle of the thirteenth century they had been forced to leave their city environment and make their way in rural areas. Expelled from the cultural centers by repression, they tended to find refuge in the peripheral places of medieval civilization — in the plains of Germany, in the Alps, and in southern Italy.

IV.

TOWARD THE BALTIC

1. In the lands of the Empire

The Poor of Lyon had carried their message as far north as Alsace; the major European penetration, however, was the work of the Poor of Lombardy.

Waldensian success in preaching north of the Alps can be attributed to a variety of reasons, one of which was political. In the regions of the Empire where the pope had not yet been able to establish a hold, the Gregorian reforms were hindered by the nobles and sometimes even by the clergy itself, because the reforms were not in keeping with their feudal idea of society. In many areas the people were still semipagan and far from ideas expressed in a movement like that of the Patari of Milan.

Economic factors were equally important, since feudalism was the rule and communal society was still some way off. Nobles to whose lands new immigrants came did not bother to ask many questions; they were interested in people who were willing to work hard and show their loyalty, regardless of their faith. There was a minimum of Church organization and control, which favored the spread of dissenters, including Waldensians.

Because so few of their own documents have survived, it is difficult to trace Waldensian penetration except by inference through the reports of Inquisition agents. From the latter we learn that a major Waldensian thrust was in the valley of the Danube. A 1266 report speaks of no less than 40 Waldensian groups, whose "bishop" resided in the south of Austria, in the vicinity of Ansbach. They had close ties with the Lombard Waldensian movement and were reported to be severely critical of the Roman clergy, seeking exemption from the imposition of the Church tithes and calling for a reduction of properties under the control of the Church. We also learn that in Neuhofen the Waldensians maintained a leprosarium.

One of the first repressive actions against the Waldensians beyond the Alps occurred in the middle of the thirteenth century. Later, at the beginning of the fourteenth century 11 Waldensians were sentenced to death in Vienna, their Bishop Neumeister being likewise sentenced in Hamburg. In 1380 an even greater roundup was begun under the inquisitors Martin of Prague and Peter Zwicker, who were commissioned to bring to trial or to force the conversion of Waldensians through much of Europe. Their systematic effort began in Bavaria, proceeded to the region of Erfurt, and by 1392 took them to the province of Brandenburg. At Szczecin the inquisitors tried 400 Waldensians. Their reports speak of activities in various cities of what are now Germany, Czechoslovakia and Hungary, and of their success in the city of Bern, Switzerland, in getting 130 suspects to abjure heresy and return to the Church's fold. They reported a similar success in Fribourg, with renunciations by some 50 Waldensians. Another Inquisition diary dated 1392 mentions 12 "most wanted" Waldensian leaders in Poland, Bohemia, Hungary, Austria, Bavaria and Switzerland.

The situation in Bohemia will occupy our attention especially, for it was in this "most Catholic" region of the Empire that the collaboration between the Church's inquisitors and the civil powers was most intense. We find the Poor among the German settlers who were seeking more land.

2. Artisans and merchants

Who were these Waldensians, scattered throughout the Empire, whom the inquisitors pursued so doggedly? Once again, unfortunately, documentation is very meager. We do gather in general, however, that they were among the lower middle classes of the time — farmers and artisans in Bohemia, Brandenburg and the German cities; perhaps small-scale merchants in Switzerland.

A series of crop failures in fourteenth century Bohemia led to not a few Waldensians losing their holdings and becoming indentured to more prosperous farmers. As a general rule, however, they were neither rich nor poverty-stricken, but a hardworking, modest sector of the local population. The 12 leaders mentioned above, for example, were engaged in the crafts as tailors, shoemakers, smiths, and weavers and all belonged to the same class.

A fourteenth century inquisitor has left us a lively account of a Waldensian preacher who went about disguised as an itinerant merchant. Upon his arrival at a local manor all the townspeople, including masters and servants, would gather around while he artfully displayed his various wares — fabrics, jewelry and trinkets. But even as he sold he would make allusions to more precious goods in his possession, to jewels of inestimable value he was in a position to offer. When the curiosity of his audience was kindled, the Waldensian preacher would then speak of the pearl of great price, the gospel of Jesus, and gradually proceed to contrast the way of the gospel with the way of the Church, in its love of power, riches, and luxury.

The story of the itinerant peddler of simple wares ever ready to surprise his audience with the announcement of the gospel, was repeated with great success in the edifying literature of the Waldensians, inspiring poetry and sketches right up to the last century. There is no reason to doubt that the stories are based upon fact, since ties always existed between the world of the Waldensians and that of the merchants, beginning with Valdesius himself. When Waldensians were tried in court they sometimes referred to their initial experiences at the hands of the merchant-teachers.

Waldensians evidently considered this kind of activity as a useful cover which permitted them to travel without creating suspicion. In order to escape the Inquisition the itinerant preachers had to be ready to move around constantly and in great secrecy, thus lending to their lives an air of mystery. Unknown by name, they would arrive in a place, stay a few days, then disappear into the night.

These "apostles," as they were called in the German lands, were regarded as true teachers of life and piety, highly respected by the faithful. A Polish document affirms they were "men who tell the truth," that one could make confession to them in full confidence and that their absolution was valid.

Many were the legends narrated about them of an evening by the fireside. Once a year, it was said, they went to heaven to contemplate the blessed, and one or two had even descended to the gates of hell to ponder the punishment of the damned. In the words of an old Austrian woman, "Our teachers are good; they are saints because they fast and live a life of abstinence . . . Their authority derives from God and from the apostles."

3. A familial piety

All of this creates the impression of strong in-group attachments, closely tied to the teachers. Catholics were regarded as outsiders. It was a clandestine world throughout, one that made the most of night meetings in stables and back rooms of little shops. Each generation was careful to transmit the faith to the succeeding one, the young sitting at the feet of elders, who in turn had received instruction from their parents.

The terror of the Inquisition made public preaching, such as the earliest Waldensians had engaged in, impossible: now the Poor were constrained to keep the faith alive within the walls of their homes — indeed, within the recesses of their own hearts. Yet if the streets were closed to them, they still had their gatherings in the kitchen, at their washing places by the streams and in their shops. The Lombard *schola* thus lived again in the Waldensian home, a secure place where teaching and mutual strengthening in the faith could be carried on.

The community was not entirely devoid of means of reaching out beyond the family circle, for the desire to communicate, to teach, and to evangelize was always present. One inquisitor's remark may be typical: "Not one of them, old or young, man or woman, by day or by night ever stops learning and teaching others." He also quotes, in the same vein, one of the Poor who had been brought before him: "In our home, women teach as well as men, and one who has been a student for a week teaches another."

Each evening meal was a special occasion for worship. Before the head of the household took his place at the table, he or she would say the grace: "May the God who blessed the five loaves and two fishes for his disciples in the desert, bless this table and its provisions." Then would follow the Kyrie and the Lord's Prayer, with the sign of the cross. After the meal, all would stand, join hands and lift their eyes as the leader repeated the verse from Revelation 7: "Blessing, and glory, and wisdom, and thanksgiving, and honor, and might be unto our God forever and ever." Then, "May God bless all who do good, bless us with material and spiritual food, and abide with us."

There was also a regular time for worship in the community, centered around a reading and a meditation from a Bible passage. The leader would read a portion of scripture (although it might be necessary to recite it from memory, since a Bible found in one's possession could compromise one before the authorities) and make comment. The latter, likely to be more moral than theological, served to clarify fundamental convictions. The service would end with everyone kneeling and repeating the Lord's Prayer in unison a number of times. This was the only prayer, used deliberately in place of the Ave Maria.

We have a memorable glimpse of what was apparently the deepest point of Waldensian piety — the gathering on the Thursday before Easter to commemorate the institution of the Lord's Supper. It is a picture in stone, the work of an anonymous sculptor whose great work of art in the from of a *bas relief* at the Cathedral of Naumburg reflects Waldensian influence. There, just six persons are grouped around Jesus at the table, all local people. They are rustic, simple folk. Christ is distributing the bread among them, some are drinking from a cup, others are eating fish. (It is well-known that Waldensians from Provence partook of fish during communion.)

It is not suprising that in these northern lands Waldensian piety emphasized intimate communion with the Lord, personal meditation and prayer. All of this accorded very well with German piety and devotion which they must have absorbed, but with their own noteworthy feature: the focus was not on the Church, on the sacred as such, or on the Virgin Mary, but on Jesus. Waldensian piety was familial rather than sacramental, communitarian rather than individualistic.

By the end of the fourteenth century Zwicker had extended his crusade against the Waldensians all over German lands, and the fourteenth century ended by the light of burning fires — with the Waldensians at the stake. One of the first victims was an old Waldensian woman in Austria, El Feur; condemned to wear the cross of the penitents, on a feast day she was trampled on by the faithful as she lay pinned down at the steps of the church, after which she was burned at the stake. This was the image of the German Waldensian community, seemingly headed for death.

4. Waldensians and witches

A part of Europe which has figured little in our story so far is northern France and Flanders.

Even before they were exiled from Lyon, there is evidence of Waldensians in the regions near Toul and Metz (Lorraine). In the following decades, their numbers increased, even in the face of persecution. As in Lombardy, towns flourished where artisans were employed in the textile industry and it was there that Waldensians were to be found with their message of poverty.

In the following centuries Waldensians declined and virtually disappeared, but they still were confused with a veritable hotbed of heresies. Here "Waldensian" lost its character and became synonymous with "heretical," so much so that Joan of Arc was condemned for Waldensian heresy, even though she was by no means a Waldensian.

Dissidents around Arras acquired a certain notoriety at the end of the fifteeth century when they were accused of the "crime of Vauderie" (the Waldensian way). The group, both men and women, was questioned, tortured and sent to the stake by the inquisitors as in many other parts of Europe. The striking aspect of this persecution, which affected nobles and middle classes alike and provoked the intervention of the ruler, was the charge of "Vauderie" levelled against them. "Vauderie" was synonymous with witchcraft; to go to the "Vauderie" meant taking part in a witches' gathering.

One most interesting contemporary treatise, *Traité de Vauderie*, describes the Waldensian phenomenon as one of the many forms of witchcraft. The Waldensians are accused not only of heresy, but of monstrous connivance with diabolic forces. The idea became so ingrained in the culture that some time later, Theodore di Beza, in Geneva, referring to Reformed people in Piedmont, felt constrained to defend those believers "who unjustly have been defamed with the name of 'Waldensian.'"

4. AN INQUISITOR'S REPORT ON WALDENSIAN OBSERVANCE OF THE LORD'S SUPPER ON HOLY THURSDAY (1320)

Question addressed to a Waldensian: If, according to their custom, he could not consecrate the bread and wine, could he bless the bread and wine, if not in the sense of accomplishing a sacrifice or offering, in the sense of a remembrance of the blessing of the bread and wine which Jesus gave when he transformed the bread and wine into his body and blood. He answered that he could not do it.

He said that after nine o'clock when the supper has been prepared, it is the leader who washes the feet of his companions and dries them with a towel which he wears as an apron. Having done this, the leader sits at the table with the others. Then taking the bread, fish and wine, he blesses them, not as an offering or sacrifice, but as a remembrance of the first supper. In so doing he pronounces the following prayer:

O Lord, the God of Abraham, Isaac and Jacob, and God of our fathers, and the Father of our Lord Jesus Christ, who has commanded that, in many places and by the hands of the bishops and priests, your servants, offerings and sacrifices should be made unto you: May Jesus Christ, who blessed the five barley loaves and two fishes in the desert and who turned water into wine, bless, in the name of the Father, Son, and Holy Spirit, this bread, this fish, and this wine, not as a scarifice and offering but as a simple commemoration of the most holy supper which Jesus Christ our Lord instituted with his disciples. Lord, I am not worthy to offer with impure hands such a precious gift, nor are my impure lips worthy to receive the most holy body of our Lord Jesus Christ. Merciful Father, we ask you, nonetheless, to bless the substance of this bread and this wine, in the name of the Father, Son and Holy Spirit. Amen.

So direct my soul, body, and all my senses and dispositions by your grace, that in my every gesture I may be worthy to offer to you this holy body which is revered by the angels in heaven, O God, who lives and reigns forever and ever. Amen.

Having offered this prayer of blessing, the leader eats and drinks such bread, fish, and wine, then gives to all his companions, who in turn eat and drink. And nothing is given to others nor do they wish that the latter know anything of the meal . . .

— "Testimony of Raymond de la Côte at his trial in 1320," in J. Duvernoy, *Le Régistre d'Inquisition de Jacques Fournier, I* (Toulouse, 1965), pp 40 ff.

V.

THE BASTION OF THE ALPS

1. To the mountains!

In southern Europe, the Waldensians found particularly favorable conditions in the valleys on the slopes of the Cottian Alps along what is now the Italian-French border.[2] This region, destined to become one of the major medieval Waldensian centers — and later the sole point of refuge for the Waldensian Church — was at first only one of many areas visited by the itinerant Waldensian teachers.

For a long time it was held that the Waldensians of the Alps were the Poor of Lyon who had taken refuge in these mountains. There, it was said, they found hospitality among a population which for centuries had remained faithful to the gospel while the Roman Church had triumphed throughout the West. It was an attempt to show that the Waldensians were directly linked to and successors to the apostolic community — a thesis driven by faith but supported by neither history nor scholarship.

The factors which really led the Waldensians to settle in Alpine villages were more social and political than religious. In the Middle Ages the region was divided into roughly two parts: on the western slopes was the French Dauphiné (so-called because its nobility's coat-of-arms bore a dolphin) and on the eastern side were the lands of the abbey of Pinerolo and the counts of Luserna. The Dauphiné, originally an imperial fief, came under French domain, while the Piedmont side came under the influence of the House of Savoy. The political frontiers, however, did not coincide with present-day national boundaries. Parts of the Val Susa, the Val Varaita and the Val Chisone belonged to the French Dauphiné.

From the point of view of church administration, the two lands were under the jurisdictions, respectively, of the bishoprics of Embrun and Turin, but the ecclesiastical boundaries did not coincide precisely with the political ones. This created a mosaic in which the interests and power struggles of the kings of France, the dukes of Savoy, the local lords, archbishops, priors and inquisitors intermingled and sometimes even cancelled each other out. The Cottian Alps region in the thirteenth century thus was politically very complex while culturally homogeneous in language, custom, and trade. The area was not entirely peripheral, for the Susa-Briançon route was one of those well-known avenues of trans-Alpine communication at the time.

The region was in economic crisis because it had experienced the full ravages of the Saracen invasions and needed to be repopulated. Thus the authorities were eager to encourage new settlements.

The first evidences of a Waldensian presence in the area date from the beginning of the thirteenth century. The early settlers must have multiplied very rapidly, for the Inquisition was directed against them by the end of the century on both sides of the Alps.

The inquisitorial practices apparently led more to legalized plunder than to full-scale religious repression. Under the threat of trial in courts, the population was kept in constant fear and forced to pay abusive heavy taxes. It was a time of psychological warfare.

The first known person in the region to be burned at the stake was a woman, condemned in Pinerolo in 1312 for adherence to the Waldensian way. The transference of the papal court to Avignon early in the fourteenth century was apparently the signal for a brutal repression against Waldensians in the Dauphiné, for the pope was evidently not disposed to tolerate any expression of dissent so near to his see.

Another incident indicative of the times was the arrest of Martin Pastre, a *barba*[3] and key organizer among early Alpine Waldensians. News that Waldensians in this remote corner were holding services in the Val Angrogna reached all the way to Pope John XXII, who ordered an inquisitor from Marseilles to go and carry out the necessary punitive measures.

Or again, in 1335 Pope Benedict XII issued an order against Waldensians in the Dauphiné which resulted in yet another toll of lives. Nor did the situation change when, in 1349, the region was given over to French control.

A period of relative calm apparently followed, but in the latter part of the century the Inquisition was resumed in full intensity

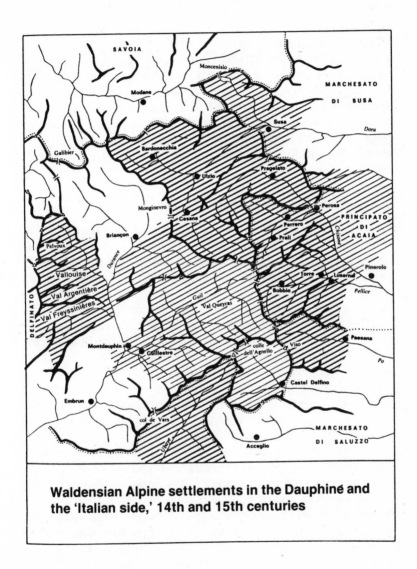

Waldensian Alpine settlements in the Dauphiné and the 'Italian side,' 14th and 15th centuries

under the direction of a Franciscan, Francesco Borelli. So obsessed was this monk with the pursuit of heretics that it was said that every prison from Embrun to Avignon was filled to overflowing. As a result, Pope Gregory IX himself had to appeal for alms for the hapless prisoners.

The century closed in shame for all of Christendom, with popes in Rome and Avignon recriminating and mutually excommunicating each other, and the faithful not knowing whom to obey. Nor did their respective campaigns against the Waldensians relax in the slightest — with one exception. In that time of abuse and violence, of imprisonments and burnings at the stake, a certain Dominican monk, Vincent Ferreri, sent to the valleys to preach against the heretics, mercifully stopped his preaching and limited his mission to dialog with the people.

2. Rebels with a cause

If we should try to picture the typical Alpine Waldensian or the movement sympathizer who welcomed the visit of a Waldensian teacher, of whom should we think? Certainly not the pilgrim of Valdesius' own generation, nor the sturdy weaver settled in a city of the Lombard plain. We should have to imagine, rather, a highlander, enclosed in his or her rustic, mountainous little world. Whether a farmer, isolated from the world in the high valleys of Vallouise or Freyssinières, a hired hand in the the fields of the counts of Luserna, or a shepherd in Pragelato, one thing was sure: he or she would be a person of the soil.

The little towns like Embrun, Pinerolo, and Perosa, nestled in the lower valleys near a castle or cathedral, remained firmly under the control of feudal and church power. Their inhabitants had to make do with a limited degree of tolerance.

Some centuries later, Frederick Engels' definition of the Waldensians in this setting would become well-known. Engels considered the movement to be patriarchal, a heresy which expressed "reactionary tendencies contrary to the movement of history," insofar as it was in opposition to feudal power. In his opinion the Waldensians were nothing more than country bumpkins in their mountain retreats who wanted nothing to do with modern society.

The definition of Alpine Waldensians as essentially reactionary needs to be corrected. There is no doubt that theirs was a patriarchal society; they did oppose feudalism — in the interest of survival, not because they were reactionaries. Even if they do not qualify as revolutionaries (it was not their intention to overturn any social order) they nonetheless can be considered rebels toward the established order, for they claimed to be beyond the jurisdiction of the *magisterium* of the Church.

Engels' notion of the Waldensians as shepherd folk scattered across the high mountains has no basis in fact. Fourteenth century heresy trials against them took place not only in the high valleys, but much more in the towns on the plain, from Pinerolo to Chieri. These latter folk were not rough mountaineers but artisans, merchants and innkeepers — forward-looking people alert to new ideas. And there were indeed many new religious ideas making the rounds in Piedmont at the time, fed by Cathari refugees who had escaped the crusade of Innocent III.

It is clear that the Waldensian movement was not limited to the higher mountain regions but reached to villages and towns and their new social classes.

It is further plain that in these Alpine areas the Waldensians were no marginal group but a proactive element, stirring up opposition to the status quo. Indeed, at times they seem to have strayed from the essential pacifism they had inherited and appear to have been drawn into quasi-revolutionary activity. One revealing incident in the middle of the fourteenth century, for example, concerned a local uprising which followed the arrest of the *barba* Martin Pastre, mentioned above. The people of Angrogna suspected that it was the local priest of San Lorenzo who had informed against their leader, and in their rage they seized the priest and killed him. An inquisitor was sent in to restore order, but the embattled farmers were too much for him, so that he had to beat a hasty retreat.

Certainly it is not unusual to find evidence of direct resistance to the Inquisition in the Middle Ages. The inquisitors Peter of Verona and Conrad of Marburg were assassinated; not a few priests in Bohemia who were caught up in the repression there came to the same end.

3. Theology of the two ways

The importance of the role played by Alpine communities is evidenced by the fact that with the exception of a few texts in Latin, practically all of the Waldensian documents which have come down to us were written in a dialect — some would go so far as to call it a language — derived from Provençal and spoken throughout the whole Waldensian diaspora. It is noteworthy that these records were carefully preserved locally right up to the mid-seventeenth century, when they were transferred for safekeeping to university libraries at Geneva, Cambridge and Dublin, where they remain to this day.

When one looks at these precious little notebooks, the mind does not run to the great libraries of medieval monasteries. Written in a miniscule hand and no larger than a pad to be carried around in one's pocket for economy of space and concealment, it is obvious that these little volumes were not designed for the spacious shelves of a library but for the homes of the hunted — dark kitchens and the back rooms of shops. Written in a plain style for the edification of unpretentious folk, the little volumes were not the literature of the firmly established, but of a counterculture commmitted to daily struggle for sheer survival.

The most important documents were translations of scripture. Valdesius himself had begun his own pilgrimage of faith upon having parts of the Bible translated, so that it was quite natural that succeeding generations should be true to his example. Actually, this attachment to the Bible derived from a very precise faith and outlook. In the Waldensians' view the Bible was not a "sacred" book in Latin for use among the learned, but one to be studied and meditated upon day in and day out by all in their own languages. One cannot claim that the Waldensians "gave" the Bible to the medieval church, but they undoubtedly contributed to its wider circulation. It is thought, for example, that the earliest translation of the Bible into the Tuscan vernacular, the so-called Dugentista Bible of the thirteenth century, was derived from the Latin Vulgate version current in Provence, itself likely based upon earlier versions of the Waldensians or their sympathizers.

In addition to scripture, the little notebooks included miscellaneous writings which were read and passed along from hand to hand: sermons, poems, edifying treatises on the Christian life and on the renouncement of possessions.

The Waldensians did not go about making a spectacle of their conversion, despising the created world after the manner of the Cathari. Nor were they obsessed, as were so many Catholics, by the desire to accumulate merit and to do good works to escape purgatory. They acted upon the insight that this earthly pilgrimage means *responsibility* ventured in light of the judgement of God.

Waldensian piety was eschatological rather than dualist or ascetic. An example may be found in the long fifteenth century devotional poem, the "Noble Lesson," which begins as follows:

Sisters and brothers, give ear to a noble lesson:
We ought always to watch and pray,
for the world is nearing the end;
we ought to strive to do good works,
for the world is nearing the end.

From surviving Waldensian literature what may be called the "theology of the two ways" can be discerned. Life's pilgrimage, the Waldensians taught, will be marked as good or evil, ruled by sin or grace. All are *responsible for choices* made in life, and the church cannot redeem the choices made. Thus, the Roman Church's doctrines of purgatory, intercessions of the saints and madonnas and the countless masses said for the deceased, all such practices the Waldensians denounced as religious frauds. The Waldensians were conscious of being an autonomous Christian community, distinct from Rome in both doctrine and organization — an altogether different kind of church. The hierarchical structure of the Church with its sacerdotal power had been overcome.

Waldensian theology refused to countenance lying or taking an oath. To do either was to commit mortal sin. This conviction stemmed from strict adherence to Jesus' admonition in Matthew 6. In medieval society, furthermore, to take an oath was not a mere matter of standing on one's word; it was, rather, the very basis of all social relationships. To swear by solemn declaration loyalty to a superior was an act which carried with it a promise of obedience and assistance at every turn. It followed logically that the pope was the summit in the hierarchy of obedience and that he had the right of excommunication or interdiction upon anyone refusing an oath.

The Waldensians' refusal to be bound to any superior by swearing an oath thus led to their living outside the law. Theirs was a *radical criticism* of the social norms which bound people to one another in a *chain of dependencies*. The religious and temporal powers immediately realized the implications of this protest and were not slow to repress it.

In general, the Alpine Waldensian way was not very different from that in Germany. Both were founded on closely knit family life in an agricultural setting; both handed down the faith from generation to generation. One Alpine quality, however, which deserves special mention, was its unusual ability to impact the social fabric as a whole. In the valleys there was a lively spirit of critical ferment which awakened conscience and love of freedom even to the point of popular uprising.

4. To the south beyond the Alps

There were two other southern regions where Waldensians maintained a presence — in Provence and Languedoc of southern France, and in southern Italy. Of the first we have already noted that the crusade of 1208 against the Cathari was followed by decades of repression, inquisition and court trials which virtually destroyed the non-Catholic religious movements. This was not entirely so in the case of the Waldensians, however. At the beginning of the fourteenth century there were enough survivors for the inquisitor Jacques Fournier, who later became Pope Benedict XII, to undertake court trials against them. This was also the region which gave the Waldensians their liturgy of communion on Holy Thursday, thought to be the most important event of their liturgical year.

Documentary evidence is still harder to come by regarding the Waldensian experience in southern Italy. Waldensians were there during the rule of the House of Anjou, when the French kings who opposed the Saracens promoted colonization by settlers from their old fiefs in France. Other Waldensians in the region of Cosenza gave names to their villages (one was called Guardia Lombarda, later to be called Piemontese) which indicates that they came from Piedmont.

For a time these little groups of religious dissenters must have enjoyed a certain protection from the central government of the region at Naples. They figured prominently in the great struggle between the papacy and the Fraticelli, the most radical wing of the Franciscans.

5. WATCHING AND PRAYING (FIFTEENTH CENTURY)

Sisters and brothers, give ear to a noble lesson:
We ought always to watch and pray,
for the world is nearing the end;
we ought to strive to do good works,
for the world is nearing the end.
A thousand and one hundred years are fully accomplished
since the coming of the last days was set.[1]
We must desire little, for we are at the very end.
We see the signs of the end every day —
the increase of evil and the decrease of good.
These are the perils of which scripture speaks,

---

[1]Reference to Constantine's "Donation" to Pope Sylvester I in the fourth century, which in Waldensian theology was the crucial point, ushering in the "last days."

the gospels and Saint Paul.
No one can know when the end shall be;
therefore we ought the more to be vigilant, not knowing
if death shall seize us today or tomorrow.
But when Jesus shall come at the day of judgement,
all shall receive full payment,
those who shall have done ill, or done well.
But scripture affirms, and we ought so to believe,
that all of the world shall pass two ways —
the good shall go to glory, the wicked to torment.
And any that shall not believe this
should search the scriptures from the beginning.
Since Adam was formed, until the present time,
the reader shall find, if he or she has understanding,
that few are saved.
But every person who would do good
will honor God the Father above all else,
and invoke the help of his glorious Son, the son of St. Mary,
and of the Holy Spirit who leads us in the way.
These three, the holy Trinity,
one God are to be invoked,
full of power, of wisdom, and of goodness.
To this God we must pray without ceasing,
that God give us strength against our enemies,
to overcome them before our end —
they are the world, the devil, and the flesh.
God give us wisdom, accompanied with goodness,
that we may know the way of truth,
keeping pure that spirit which God has given us,
the spirit and body in the way of love . . .
Now after the apostles there were certain teachers
who taught the way of Christ our Saviour,
and who are found even to this day,
known to very few,
who would show the way of Jesus Christ.
They are so persecuted that they are able to do but little.
Many are the false Christians blinded with error . . .
who persecute and hate those who are good,
and let those live quietly who are false deceivers.
But by this we may know that they are not good pastors,
for they love not the sheep, but only the wool.
Scripture says, and we know it to be true,
that if anyone is good, loving Jesus Christ,
that person will neither curse, nor swear, nor lie,
will neither commit adultery, nor kill, nor steal,

nor be avenged over the enemy.
Now such a person is a Waldensian, and worthy to be punished,
and they find occasion by lies and deceit,
to take from him that which he has gotten by his just labor.
One that is thus persecuted for the sake of the Lord,
takes courage is this,
that the kingdom of heaven shall be inherited at death . . .
This I dare say, and it is very true,
that all the popes from Sylvester on,
the cardinals, bishops, abbots, and the like,
have no power to absolve or pardon
any creature so much as one mortal sin.
It is God alone who pardons, and no other.
This is what pastors ought to do:
preach to the people, and pray with them,
and feed them with teaching from on high . . .
May the Lord who made the earth
number us to dwell in his house forever.

—"La Nobla Leyczon," in J. Léger, *Histoire générale des Eglises Evangéliques des Vallées du Piémont* . . . (Leyden, 1669), pp. 26ff.

6. TESTIMONY OF A *BARBA'S* ASSISTANT (1451)

Having been interrogated on the charges which had been read to him, he answered that it was true that he had once at his home made his confession to a *barba*, a teacher of the sect called the Waldensians, who had been introduced in his home by Stefano Rigotti, of the parish of Usseglio. Asked what was the name of that *barba*, he answered that he was called "Big Michael" from Freyssinières; asked if he had seen other *barba*, he said that he had: one from Meana, near Susa . . . Asked if during his life he had seen other *barba*, he replied yes: one who was from Manfredonia in Puglia . .

Asked as to how he knew they were *barba* of the so-called Waldensian sect, he said that every year they came to the valleys, and that the people of the valleys and nearby (Roman) parishes made their confession to them, and that when they were leaving the valleys the *barba* named him as their delegate, along with Francesco Aydetti of Val Perosa. In their name he and Francesco carried out the task of representing them in the valley . . . receiving confessions from men and women of the so-called Waldensian sect . . . He said that they had collected money from these Waldensians and given it to the teacher in Puglia.

Asked concerning when — month and day — and where he had gone in Puglia and how much money he had taken, he answered that it was in March of 1448 and 1449, and that the sum was 300 ducats. Asked how they had gone to Puglia and managed not to be recognized, he answered that they disguised themselves as merchants, that the two went through the towns offering their merchandise for sale . . .

Asked about the teaching he was imparting to the above-mentioned people when he was receiving their confessions and when he was preaching to them, he answered that in their confessions he taught that they should not celebrate any feast day of any saint nor that of the Virgin Mary, that such feasts days of the saints and of Mary were not valid, and that it was not a sin to work on those days. He said that one should not believe in the eucharist, the host, and in the sacrifice at the altar, that at the time of the elevation the host does not become the body of Christ, that it is only bread, and that one should not believe that Jesus was born of Mary as virgin.

Further, that he taught that there are only two ways open to all and which determine whether one will be saved or will be condemned, that one who does good will go to paradise, and one who does evil will go to hell and damnation; purgatory does not exist. Indeed, whoever believes in purgatory is condemned already. Further, charities for the benefit of the deceased should not be done for they make no difference as far as the deceased's salvation is concerned . . . Further, Mary, the Son, and the saints have no power to perform miracles or signs or to bestow grace, but only God; that all things performed in churches have no value and no bearing — it would be much better that they should be performed in stables rather than in churches.

Asked about what the *barba* said when he came to give the sermon, he answered that now and then they met in a home, 50 or 60 of them. Then the *barba* would come and would deliver his sermon explaining that they should not do to others what they did not wish done to themselves, that they should recite the Lord's Prayer often every day but not the Ave Maria, and that if they wished to give offerings they should do so in this world, for offerings to benefit the dead have no efficacy whatsoever.

—G. Weitzecker, "Processo di un Valdese nell'anno 1451," in *Rivista Cristiana, IX* (1881), pp. 363-67.

VI.

THE WALDENSIAN-HUSSITE "INTERNATIONAL"

1. The Bohemian revolution

By the early 1400s, after more than two centuries of witness and martyrdom, the Waldensian movement appeared to be in decline. Relentless extermination had reduced Waldensians to a clandestine few, and it seemed that the movement would be snuffed out. Following the lead of Innocent III, the Roman Church dominated Europe, although the great body of medieval Christendom was really without life. A tragic question was making itself felt in the conscience of the people: Is this really the church of Jesus Christ, this curia which administers vast wealth, dispenses indulgences and exercises such encompassing power? This was the very question which had been raised by Waldensians all along, their only reply being torture and the stake. Now the question of reform arose not only from known dissidents but also from within the ranks of the Church's theologians, bishops and religious orders.

The work of two figures in widely separated countries now stood out in the struggle for reform—John Wycliff in England and Jan Hus in Bohemia. Wycliff, with good reason, was called "Doctor Evangelicus;" his determination to be faithful to scripture led him to translate and circulate the Bible among the people. Wycliff's work spread to the continent, precipitating the greatest spiritual upheaval of the century — the reform movement of Jan Hus.

Like Wycliff, Hus was a scholar and university professor, keen to put his gifts and his culture to the service of "the least." Week after week at the Bethlehem chapel in Prague he expounded the scriptures, having exceptional gifts as a preacher.

Hus' life ended tragically. Ordered to appear before the Council of Constance to defend the actions and given a promise of safe conduct, he was nevertheless taken into custody, condemned for heresy and burned at the stake. A year later the same fate befell his disciple, Jerome of Prague. Hus' death at the stake ignited a real revolution which in the end was to envelop all Bohemia. The Hussite demands were for freedom in preaching, and for an end to the oppressive taxes and to rule by Church courts. Faith was seen as the exercise of personal responsibility, not subjection to the Church. The communion chalice on Hussite banners symbolized insistence on an intensely personal faith.

The Hussite revolution passed through several phases, the first of which was a national and popular uprising which included the nobility. For a time the crusading army called out by Rome was held at bay by the Hussites. A moderate wing, however, made its peace within the Church, having been satisfied by Rome's promise, among others, that laypeople should receive the cup at communion. When the moderates gained the upper hand, a more intransigent group reorganized itself in southern Bohemia near the city of Tabor and there vowed to continue the struggle. The Taborite movement became the Church of the Unity of the Bohemian Brethren (Unitas Fratrum), a church which was to play an important role in the spiritual maturing of central Europe.

Even though it suffered military defeat, the Hussite revolution was an event of major importance in the history of the Christian church. For the first time, a dissenting movement had raised a popular army to defend itself against the constituted authorities. In doing so it resisted the inroads of the crusades, liberating a part of Christendom from papal oppression and from the Inquisition. On the spiritual and theological level, Hus and his disciples demolished Rome's claim to universal jurisdiction in Europe, having founded an alternative Christian church, one based not on obedience to an institution but on the gospel and human solidarity.

2. The "International"

In the wake of these events in central Europe, the timid Waldensian groups which had survived persecution began once again to take heart. For their part, the Taborite theologians recognized the importance of the Waldensians' protest and alternative practice of the faith. In one remarkable incident at the Council of Basel the military hero of the Taborite campaign, Procopius the Great, came to the defense of the Waldensians and justified their faith before the Council. Such are the strange paradoxes of history: here a military general defended, before Catholic bishops, Waldensians who were both "heretical" and pacifist!

The Hussites did not accept all of the beliefs and practices of the Waldensians, nor did the latter give up their own tenets in the light of the Taborite revolution. However, the two groups did remain extremely close to one another. The bonds between them were such, for example, that on one occasion the Waldensians in the French Dauphiné raised money for the Bohemian war effort. And at Paesana, a town in the Po valley, a group of Waldensians in the early sixteenth century expected to be liberated by a Bohemian intervention.

The Hussites strengthened the hand of the Waldensians in the field of theology, so critical for future generations. The Prague theologians, in retracing the ground worked over by the Waldensians, brought it within the world of the university. Hussite scholarship and the Taborite Confession of Faith were translated, summarized and circulated in the Waldensian communities.

A fresh missionary thrust by Bohemian Hussites spread throughout Waldensian communities on the continent, strengthening the ties between the two groups. German Waldensian ministers visited the communities in Bohemia. Together they envisaged an evangelical movement which, beginning in Bohemia, would radiate across the whole of Europe along the axes of the Waldensian diaspora. A. Molnár, the Czech church historian whose research has added so much to our knowledge of the pre-Reformation Waldensian experience, has appropriately called this fifteenth century missionary vision the "Waldensian-Hussite International."

The role of the leaders in the Waldensian communities, meanwhile, was undergoing real change. For the Waldensians the traditional name *barba*, which freely translated means "uncle," obviously had a controversial ring to it. The *barba* were ministers who had authority but no power; they were elders, not priests, "uncles" not "fathers" as in the Roman Church. By the fifteenth century, the *barba* were no longer, as in previous centuries, travelling artisans who fortified contacts between the Waldensian groups scattered throughout the diaspora; they were now truly teachers of faith, and even of culture. To them fell the duty of circulating Waldensian literature, collecting sermon material and writing poems.

This is not to say that the *barba* were to be compared with the humanists of the time. Their collection of books was quite small, suited to those constantly on the move, but such books as they had were well used. The *barba* were capable of reading theological works in Latin, of studying mathematics, and of knowing enough botany and rudimentary medicine to enable them to deal with simple diseases.

Their ministerial work was now better organized, less casual than before. Young Waldensians who had gifts and desired to work hard for the community would be apprenticed to an experienced *barba* for some years. They first became familiar with the various places to visit, mastered languages, and studied the Bible thoroughly, much of the time in clandestine schools. A major school, tradition has it, was located at Pra del Torno, deep in the Angrogna Valley. Organization and communication across the *barba* network must have been very effective, for it was only in rare instances that the Inquisition succeeded in trapping one of these leaders.

Two *barba* who were indeed caught and martyred deserve special mention —Frederich Reiser, burned at the stake in 1458, and Martino, who suffered the same fate some 40 years later.

Reiser, as his father, was a Waldensian merchant whose work centered around the largest German cities of the time, as Nuremberg, and at Fribourg in Switzerland, where he was continually in contact with Waldensian cells. When Reiser was 25 or so years of age, a friend of his father, convinced that Reiser should give himself entirely to the task of preaching, put him in touch with the Bohemian communities. Ordained as a Taborite minister, Reiser was drawn into the Hussite revolutionary movement.

After the Hussite revolution, in 1435, Reiser began visiting and reorganizing the Waldensian diaspora. From a base in the city of Zapek and with the support of the friendly Bohemian communities, he and his Taborite colleagues managed to cover the entire area from Cracow in Poland to Basel. In the end he was arrested at Strasbourg, condemned and burned at the stake. Two months later that same fate befell a disciple, Matthew Hagen, at Brandenburg, and a few years later Reiser's chosen successor, Stephen of Basel, was likewise put to the torch.

The *barba* who went by the name of Martino and whose real name was Francesco di Girundino, came from the Italian region of the Marche. His arrest, along with that of a fellow *barba*, took place in the Chisone Valley in 1492. At his trial he told the story of his life and his journeys as a *barba*. The son of a *barba*, he had accompa-

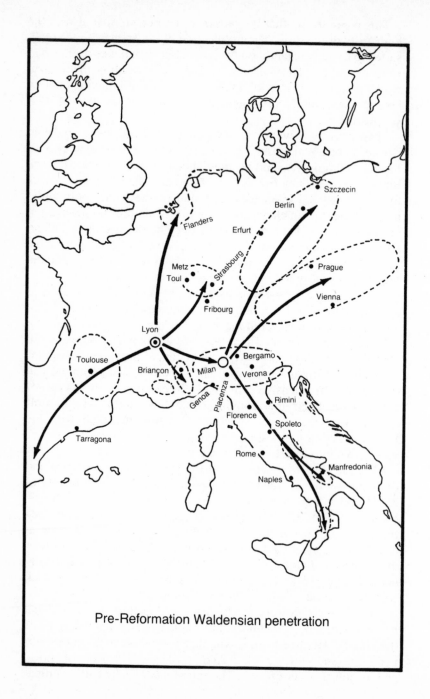

Pre-Reformation Waldensian penetration

nied his father at first, then other *barba*, to communities all across Italy.

Through surviving accounts of the itineraries of the *barba*, the quite astonishing and far-reaching spread of the medieval Waldensian way can be pieced together.

3. Relentless Inquisition

Due to the work of Reiser and the encounter with the Taborites, the most dynamic part of the Waldensian movement in the fifteenth century was in the diaspora in the German lands. It was from there that new ideas began to filter toward the south through Switzerland. There were also important communities in the Kingdom of Naples and in the region east of Florence along the Adriatic, which raised up a good many *barba*. When, for example, the well-known Hussite theologian, Luke of Prague, sought to get in touch with key persons in the Waldensian world, it was to central and southern Italy that he turned, rather than to Germany or even to Piedmont. Waldensians in the latter area, although less prominent at this time, were a compact group. They were to become increasingly more important and were to suffer the next wave of repression.

After only a few decades of relative tranquility under Amedeo VIII, the inquisitors were sent to deal with the Alpine dissidents. In 1450 the whole Val Luserna was placed under interdiction on the charge of having resisted the authorities. Another inquisitorial sweep took place in 1475. Ducal authorities were ordered by Duchess Yolanda, regent for her son, Charles I, to come to the support of the inquisitors in their actions (threats and fines) against the counts of Luserna themselves, charged with being too lenient toward the Waldensians.

More and more the Waldensians were being persecuted not so much for their religious beliefs as for the economic exploitation which could be gained from them through punitive taxation. In corrupt times Charles I at last called for full-scale military action against the dissidents. On the French side, meanwhile, the papal legate Albert Cattaneo led a crusade against the Waldensians in 1487-89.

The occasion which provoked action by Charles I very likely centered around a local uprising against the counts of Luserna. The fighting took place mainly in Val Angrogna between two disorganized and ill-equipped bands. On one side was the rag-tag feudal militia, and on the other, the poorly-equipped Waldensians who were armed, however, with a steel will. The clashes must have brought biblical images to mind: a Savoyard captain of fortune struck down by a Waldensian rustic's well-aimed sling shot stone; hand-to-hand combat which lasted far into the night, and so forth.

In the end, Charles I agreed to negotiate. When the Waldensians arrived the palace was amazed to discover that they were not the hairy devils or one-eyed monsters of anti-Waldensian propaganda, but sturdy mountain folk. The outcome preserved the status quo, although a gesture of ducal clemency did result in tacit acknowledgement of some rights for the dissenters.

On the French side the story was sheer devastation. There, Philip of Savoy, with the full consent of Charles VIII of France, undertook a merciless and far-reaching crusade against the hapless population. As in other places and times in the Middle Ages, the sweep was under the patronage of the pope and organized by his legate. Like the papal campaigns against the Cathari and the Muslims, the Alpine offensives became organized piracy, full of greedy noblemen, local fanatics bent on their vendettas, adventurers and plunderers everywhere.

Cattaneo prepared his campaign meticulously, choosing his troops carefully and making sure of his backing by local authorities. The Waldensians, meanwhile, tried their usual tactics of temporizing, seeking to defend themselves through appeal to tribunals.

It was in this context that the Waldensians of Pragelato wrote the Declaration of Faith which is included at the end of this chapter — one of the Waldensians' most significant statements. The work of a community purified in suffering, it expresses the faith of a mature, responsible Christian people.

Pragelato, right in the path of the crusaders, was invaded and sacked in March 1488. Some of the inhabitants managed to escape further up the mountains, while others were hidden by friends in nearby valleys. Still others gave themselves up in exchange for immunity. At Prali, a pitched battle between the local inhabitants and the crusaders ended when Count Hugo La Palud pulled back his troops.

A fate similar to that of Pragelato was in store for the Waldensians in the valleys of Argentières and Vallouise. These folk had been consistently pacifist by tradition, so they did not resist when the invaders came. The geography of the closed-in valleys allowed no opportunity for escape. The crusaders proceeded to level their villages. A few tried to escape massacre by hiding in caves, but they were tracked down and slaughtered. A symbol of this violent and merciless attack was the "barme Chapelue" cave, where scores of women and children were burned alive. Those who managed to flee the area eventually made it to Waldensian enclaves in Piedmont or in the deep south of Italy.

Thus ended an inglorious chapter of papal dominance, an epoch of Hussite revolution on the one hand and of councils of the Church on the other. The age which produced the Cattaneos was also the age of Savonarola, preaching his fiery sermons in Florence. Machiavelli and Erasmus were just young men.

Relentless Inquisition, crusades and pillage had done their efficient work, so that by the end of the fifteenth century a veil of silence hung over much of the Waldensian world. Any evidence of activity during the first years of the sixteenth century came mainly from the sector in southern Europe — from Provence and the Dauphiné in France, and from Calabria and the Luserna Valley in Italy.

Later historians would offer the views that at the time of the Lutheran Reformation the Waldensians were all but extinct and that their revival at the beginning of the sixteenth century was a virtual resurrection. This was not the case. While it was certainly a time of rethinking rather than expansion, the Waldensians were by no means inactive and far from being enfeebled.

Proof of this thesis is that the Archbishop of Turin, Claudio di Seyssel, while on a pastoral visit to the Alpine valleys in 1517, the very year of Luther's protest, recorded the presence of numerous Waldensians practicing their faith. Waldensians at this time were active enough in their missionary endeavors to print and publish tracts in the Italian language (as distinct from their own tongue), daring to circulate them in Piedmont and Liguria. It was against these tracts that the eminent friar De Cassine published his polemics. We can only conclude that a community which had access to that marvelous new instrument called the printing press — invented only a few decades earlier — and which had the ability to raise the necessary funds for a considerable propaganda effort, could hardly be considered at the point of extinction.

7. DECLARATION OF FAITH (1488)

We true believers of the Val Chisone ask that you, Reverends and Illustrious Lordships, not let yourselves be deceived by the talk of our enemies, and that you should not proceed to our condemnation without having taken cognizance of the truth. We are indeed authentic believers and obedient and faithful subjects of the king. Those who are teachers of our religion, noted for their holiness of life and doctrine, can show you in any synod or general council, on the basis of the authority of the Old and New Testaments, that our way of understanding the faith is authentically Christian, so that we deserve praise rather than persecution.

We do refuse to follow those who betray the rule of the gospel and who forsake the tradition of the apostles, and we are not willing to obey their evil institutions. Instead, we take pleasure in the poverty and innocence which have been the source and strength of true faith. We disdain riches, luxury, and the thirst for power by which our persecutors are possessed.

You state that you have decided to destroy our people and our manner of life. But beware in doing this, lest you offend God and provoke God's anger, and lest, in thinking to do well, you commit a serious crime, the like of which, according to scripture, St. Paul was once guilty.

We put our hope in God and we strive to please God rather than humankind. We do not fear those who kill the body but cannot kill the spirit. Know, all the same, that all your efforts will be in vain if God does not will them.

— Declaration of Giovanni Campi and Giovanni Desideri, delegates from the Chisone Valley, to the papal legate, Albert Cattaneo, in Emilio Comba, *Histoire des Vaudois* (1901), p. 406.

VII.

THE REFORMATION

1. Luther and the Waldensians

In the century after Hus it was Martin Luther who opened up the whole question of reform in the church. His intention was not to break the unity of the Church, but to bring about a return to the gospel.

Although Luther was well aware of the work of the Hussites and Waldensians, he first considered them to be rebellious and dangerous schismatics, once exclaiming, "I shall be taken for a Wycliffite or a Waldensian!" — as if this were an absurd eventuality.

What a change followed upon his examination of the dissenters' literature! Seeing so many parallels between the earlier protests and his own protests over papal abuses, the doctrine of purgatory, and the Church's misuse of its authority, he cried out, "We were all Hussites without knowing it!" Partly to make amends for his previous harsh judgment against the pioneers, he wrote his famous preface to the Taborite Confession of Faith and caused it to be circulated widely; in that same preface he referred to the Hussites as "Waldensians."

Luther's theology really went far beyond that of the medieval evangelical movements — not because he was more radical than his predecessors, but because he grasped the fundamental issue of the time: justification by faith.

Luther's struggle was naturally welcomed in the Waldensian world. Before long, scholarly works from Germany were in the hands of a good many *barba*, where they were read, translated, discussed and circulated to every region. In 1526 an assembly of Waldensians held at Laus, in the Chisone Valley, was so eager to make personal contact with the new movement that it decided to send a discovery team across the Alps. The two chosen for the journey were an older *barba*, Giorgio, from the group in Calabria and a young man from Angrogna, Martin Gonin, who had been won over by the new ideas and who were ready to undertake the risky task of bookseller.

That journey turned out to be of capital importance for the whole course of Waldensian history. At Aigle, in what is now a part of Switzerland, they encountered the man who was to play a decisive role in the formation of the Waldensian Church, William Farel. From the Dauphiné, Farel had been a militant and progressive Catholic, but now was active in spreading the new Lutheran ideas. He had become a fiery and fearless critic of the papacy and superstition. It was he who later insisted before a hesitant Calvin that the scholarly theologian should stay in Geneva to guide the destiny of that newly Protestant city instead of quietly continuing his studies. The young Gonin, after meeting Farel, became convinced that the Waldensian groups should adopt the new way of reform.

Another assembly of *barba*, held four years later in Mérindol, in Provence, less than fully enthusiastic, decided all the same that it needed more precise information about the new stirrings. So it decided to send another two *barba*, Morel of Freyssinières and Masson of Borgogna, on an exploratory mission. Morel in particular, a good theologian, was already known for his openness to Reformation ideas.

Their plan was not to go all the way to Germany,[4] but to consult reformers in Bern, Basel and Strasbourg. Here the Reformation movement was not led by the nobles but by the middle classes who were becoming increasingly influential in the cities. The leaders were found in the town councils and humanistic circles. The organization of the first Reformation parishes was entrusted to outstanding figures such as Bucer and Oecolampadius.

The Swiss reformers found much to appreciate as they listened to the two *barba*, finding in them a very biblical spirituality. Still, they expressed some reservation, sensing that the Waldensians seemed to have certain Anabaptist and perfectionist tendencies. They had good reason for this judgment, for in Waldensian thinking one cardinal point had stood out from the beginning: an insistence on a clear separation between civil power and the practice of religion. The Waldensian pair were counselled to rethink their medieval ways of clandestinity, to abandon their dependence on itinerant *barba*, to leave behind their little *scholae* and their biblical literalism. In short, the reformers wished the Waldensians to rework their theology and to declare themselves openly a part of the mainstream of the Reformation.

Returning to Provence, and to another assembly at Mérindol, the two emissaries found their communities eager to debate but unable to come to any conclusions. Three possible directions were on the table. The first would keep the Waldensians on a conservative path, maintaining the line of the past. The second, found in the young Gonin, supported joining the Reformation movement. The third, the position of Morel, was that of dialog with the reformers. The onrush of events, however, gave the Waldensians little time to work through the several directions in a deliberate manner.

By 1530 the Reformation was no longer a question to be discussed primarily among the theologians. Suddenly it burst out as a popular force, sweeping aside venerable institutions like a flood. Just five years previously Prussia had become Lutheran; Sweden followed two years later, Basel in 1529. By 1531 military lines were drawn right across Switzerland; the leader of the Reformation in Zürich, Ulrich Zwingli, met his death in pitched battle.

This was also a time when political and military turmoil spared no one. In 1527 Rome itself was sacked by imperial troops; in 1529 the Turks besieged Vienna. Confronted with immense problems in his realm, the young emperor Charles V signed a treaty with the Protestant princes which recognized — provisionally, but as a fact — the Reformation. The Confession of Faith written by Melanchthon, outlining the theological standards of the new movement, thus received sovereign sanction.

How did Piedmont fit into this picture? Although it was just a small corner of Europe which seemed to count for little, its geographical position gave the duchy a key place in the political chess game of the time. Like Flanders in the north, Savoy was situated between the great powers of France and the German empire. The sovereign, Duke Charles III, was a typical prince in the Italian style — skeptical, calculating, and defenseless as his large duchy, which extended all the way from Nice to Lake Geneva. Politically, he was pure Savoyard — agile, never stepping too far in any one direction, always ready to change course at a moment's notice. As he balanced himself between the pope's warnings and the new wave from the north, he might even have wished to follow the lead of the Duke of Saxony — but he didn't dare.

Charles' manner of dealing with his subjects on religious questions was also in character. One day he might decide to send his nobleman, Bersatore di Miradolo, into Provence for a general roundup of all Waldensians. A day later he would issue another order forbidding any harassment of the same people. He was perfectly capable in one moment of vowing to root out every trace of heresy within his domain and in the next of providing for the liberation of the Genevan preacher, Saulnier, arrested in Savoy.

His political undoing, however, came about in 1529. Like all the Italian princes, he was forced in that year to take a stand which put an end to any balancing act. Spain by now had assumed the leadership of the anti-Reformation forces and Savoy had to go along, which meant adopting a repressive policy in religious matters. The assault against the Alpine population triggered the reaction of Bern. The ensuing conflict was to bring an end to the old Duchy of Savoy.

As the largest of the Swiss cantons, Bern had gone over to the Reformation in 1527, soon extending its influence across the southern and western regions of the country — to the Valias, Vaud and the southernmost gateway at Geneva. In a decisive clash with the duke's forces, in 1529, the Bernese armies prevailed so that, by the treaty of St. Julien, Charles forfeited his rights over the Swiss lands and paid a heavy indemnity.

Thus the powerful claws of the bear (Bern's cantonal flag depicted a fierce bear, ready to spring) had not only rent the old duchy, but had opened a way for the Reformation to impact regions to the south.

For the "lords of Bern," the burghers who had come to power, the Reformation was not merely a religious question — it was a political, economic and social reality, as well.

Zwingli's dream of making Switzerland the center of a revolutionary force which would envelop the lands to the south seemed about to become a reality. The Bernese troops had succeeded in inserting a wedge between Savoy on the east and France on the west, a wedge pointed straight at Provence. To the one side stood the Dauphiné, and to the other, the valleys of Luserna and Saluzzo, regions long since prepared by the Waldensians for a new day. The 20 cannons and 2,000 armed men in Geneva's command some years later were to be more than a wound in the pride of Savoy; they were to be a harbinger of conquest.

This was the international backdrop for the eventful assembly of Waldensians in Val Angrogna in September of 1532, which would thereafter be known as the historic Synod of Chanforan.

2. Chanforan

We learn from the historian Scipione Lentolo that *barba* came to Angrogna from all over the Waldensian diaspora with the express intent of "reforming their church." This was not, then, an ordinary meeting of the *barba*. Today it would be called an "extraordinary" or "constituent" assembly, open to the public so that the Waldensian people could fully participate. No clandestine meeting, its setting was that of an open field, one in which discussions could be held in the full light of day. Only five years separated Chanforan from the assembly at Mérindol, but the two events were worlds apart.

Who could have taken the initiative to convene an assembly of this sort? We do not know for sure, but it could well have been the school of young Gonin activists who would have been capable of transforming a meeting of leaders into a popular decision-making assembly. Gonin and colleagues must have been the ones who invited Saulnier and Farel to interrupt their labors in Geneva to come to Chanforan.

Thanks to the records which were kept, there is no doubt about the theological consensus which was achieved in the course of the debates. The Bible's preeminent place in faith and practice was once more underlined. Sacraments were limited to two — Baptism and the Lord's Supper. It was also decided that the *barba* should no longer itinerate but be assigned to communities. A good deal of attention was given to problems of a practical nature. Could a Christian rightly seek public office? Was it right to lend money at interest? The answers to such questions generally followed the lines of Morel. In other matters Farel's more radically anti-Catholic influence stood out, as with the call to put an end to confessions, fasts and "meritorious Sundays." In short, wherever Waldensian medieval theology and spirituality showed any remaining traces of Catholic piety, they were to be brought into line with theological foundations more biblical in character.

The synod's readiness to embark on a quite new course was also revealed in a decision to raise money to provide for the translation and publication of the Bible in the French language. The Waldensians were eager to seek a wider audience for their witness than was possible with their old Bible in Provençal, and were anxious to take advantage of the most recent textual studies. The translation task was entrusted to Pierre Robert, called Olivétan, a relative of Calvin's, who withdrew to an Alpine village to do his work. The remarkable translation he produced (for which Calvin himself wrote the preface) has come to be known as the Olivétan Bible, the first of the French Reformation. Printed in Neuchâtel, it was delivered to the Waldensians in 1535.

Behind questions of a theological or practical nature, there was at Chanforan the question of the Waldensians' relationship to the Reformation itself. Waldensians were of one mind in recognizing that the great new movement abroad could not be ignored. But how was it to be done? There were those who wished to be true to the past and to maintain their special traditions, while working in collaboration with the new Reformed currents. For his part, Morel advocated a middle course, one which foresaw a gradual Waldensian assimilation of the reformers' theology. The most radical elements, on the other hand, insisted that the whole thrust and organization of the old Waldensian movement should be fully integrated into the Reformation effort now taking place in the Swiss and French areas. The latter persuasion finally carried the day, doubtless due to the strong personalities of Farel and his companions, who succeeded in convincing the assembly that the new wave of religious ferment sweeping across Europe was just the fulfillment of the long struggle against an unfaithful Church, the very struggle in which the Waldensians had been engaged for centuries.

The decision was not unanimous. The traditionalists, believing that Chanforan could be a dangerous turning point, called for reconsideration. To seek further counsel, the assembly decided to turn to the Bohemian brethren, who had given such useful guidance to the Waldensian diaspora throughout the fifteenth century.

It was thus agreed to send two *barba* to Mladá Boleslav, where the Unitas Fratrum had its headquarters, to seek advice. The counsel the Waldensian emissaries received was closer to the position of Morel than that of Farel. They were told not to be hasty in giving up so precious a heritage as they had received from their forebearers, to reflect at length before taking any action, to guard against extremism and novelty. To consider the report of the emissaries, a second assembly was held at Prali in 1533; the outcome was reaffirmation of the basic direction taken at Chanforan — integration into the Reformation.

At Chanforan, as at Bergamo in 1218, the Waldensians closed one chapter of an illustrious history and opened another. Now, as three centuries earlier, they knew what they had left behind, while what lay before them was anything but clear. They knew only that they would press on in the quest for a church which was authentically Christian.

What was at stake was adherence not to a church, but to a reform movement. Protestant "churches" as such did not yet exist in the year 1530. There were, to be sure, vast areas which had affirmed the Lutheran movement and discovered the gospel, but these same people still awaited a great council, one which would formulate the main tenets of the Reformation. For Waldensians, then, it was not a question of becoming Protestant in the sense of streaming into a church with a confession, a firmly defined theology and a distinct organization — it was a question of taking part in a religious revolution, seeking theological clarity and leaving questions of structure open.

The Waldensians' turning point at Chanforan has been given quite opposing interpretations. According to some, adherence to the Reformation at Chanforan was a decisive step forward on the path of evangelical witness — a deeper commitment to struggle with theology than the medieval Waldensian diaspora had ever achieved. The contemporaries of Chanforan generally read events in this way, not sensing any major break with their past. Nor have most later Waldensian historians treated adherence to the Reformation as a real rupture with the past, since they have seen a spiritual continuity across the whole of the Waldensian experience.

Some Catholic authors, on the other hand, have written a quite negative account of these same years. They profess to find that sixteenth century Waldensians became more rigid in their outlook, forsaking many elements of Catholic faith and piety which had been present in earlier times. Even among some Waldensians today, there is a certain tendency to view Chanforan with a more critical eye, lamenting in particular the decline of criticism of "Constantinianism" in the Waldensian Church. It is said that there was also at Chanforan a turning away from that kind of Christian discipleship which had been nourished by a literal reading of the Bible.

But these judgments are beside the point. In light of the actual conditions before them, the Waldensians had to choose to become a part of the Reformation or to disappear. The decision taken at Chanforan to give up aspirations for maintaining an independent course and to find renewal within the framework of a wider Protestant movement was a difficult but very clear choice. It was a choice made not "above" history, but *in* history, as has been the case across the entire Waldensian experience. It was a choice grounded in the realization that faithfulness to the gospel means readiness to yield to transformation's way *in* history.

8. THE CHANFORAN DECISIONS (1532)

The following proposals were discussed in the presence of the ministers and people assembled in Angrogna on September 12 in the year of our Lord 1532.

1. A Christian may swear by the name of God without contravention to what is written in Matthew 5, provided that one who so swears does not take the name of God in vain. . . One may swear before magistrates, because anyone who exercises the office of a magistrate, whether a believer or non-believer, derives that power from God . . .

2. No work is called good, but that which God has commanded, and no work is bad but that which God has forbidden . . .

5. Auricular confession is not commanded by God, and it has been determined according to holy scriptures, that the true confession of a Christian is to confess to God alone, to whom belongs honor and glory . .

6. God does not forbid a Christian to stop work on Sunday. . .

7. Speaking is not always necessary during services.

8. Kneeling, established hours, the uncovering of one's head and other external things are not necessary nor required for services. Worship can be performed only in spirit and in truth, as we find written in John 4 . . .

9. The laying on of hands is not necessary . . .

10. It is not lawful for a Christian to take revenge upon one's enemy in any manner whatsoever . . .

11. A Christian may exercise the office of magistrate over Christians who have done wrong . . .

12. There is no certain determination of time for fasting . . .

13. Marriage is not forbidden to anyone . . .

15. Enforced lifetime virginity is a diabolical doctrine . . .

17. Not all usury is forbidden by God. This is clearly so because God only prohibits usury which damages one's neighbor; as the law says, 'Do not do to others that which you do not wish to be done to you.' . . .

19. All those that have been and shall be saved have been elected of God before the foundation of the world.

22. The minister of the word of God ought not to itinerate from place to place, except it be for some great good of the church.

23. It is not a thing repugnant to the apostolic communion, that ministers have some possessions for the welfare of their families.

Concerning the matter of the sacraments, it has been determined by the holy scriptures that we have but two sacramental signs left us by Jesus Christ: the one is baptism, the other is the eucharist, which we receive to show that our perseverance in the faith is such as we promised when we were baptized being as children, and moreover, to recall that great benefit given to us by Jesus Christ, when he died for our redemption, and washed us with his precious blood . . .

— Manuscript 259 of Trinity College, Dublin, in V. Vinay, *Le confessioni di fede dei Valdesi riformati* (Torino, 1974), pp. 139 ff.

Part Two

THE PROTESTANT OUTPOST

(1532–1689)

Let imprisonment and afflictions befall me. Bound in the Spirit, I aim to accomplish the ministry which I received from the Lord Jesus, to testify to the gospel of the grace of God.

— Acts 20

The "Return" (1689) came along at a really crucial time in European history, the time of passage from the Catholic absolutist regimes (Louis XIV) to nascent Protestant (Anglo-Dutch) constitutional forms of government. In this same stream the "Return" of the Waldensians to Italy in the late 1600s prefigured the difference that the Reformation would hold out in that land, notwithstanding a pervasive Counter-Reformation environment.

It was in the late seventeenth century, with its values of freedom, tolerance, personal conscience and democracy, that modern Europe began to stir. To this day Italy's hold on these values remains infirm: mafia, regressive religion-in-the-schools practices, cynical avoidance of morality in public life—all this and more point to our society's need to make democratic values its own at last. No small wonder, then, that the "Return" raises afresh the issue of the very shape of our "modern" land...

—Tercentennial Committee statement, "Three Hundred Years Later," Italy, 1988

I.

REVOLUTION'S HOUR

1. A Protestant Piedmont?

As the *barba* returned from Chanforan and the high country around Angrogna, the autumn sun cast the Piedmont plain below in quite a new light. The hamlets and towns which for centuries had been under the tight control of inquisitorial friars, were no longer forbidden ground. The plain was a land now full of promise, a new world to be won over to the reality of the gospel.

For them and for the Waldensian rustics of Angrogna it was not alone a matter of affirming the Reformed movement, but also of enlisting actively in the great campaign that was dividing Europe, including Italy. The Italian states had also begun to feel the effects of this excitement at various places — at the ducal court in Ferrara, where Calvin was to visit the Duchess Renata; among the merchants in Lucca; at the salons of the nobility in Naples; and among the monks in their cells in Veneto. Already some prominent Catholic intellectuals of the most cultured circles were numbered among those who accepted Luther's thought and who spread his teaching.

The assembly at Chanforan is not a page from Waldensian history alone; it is one from the spiritual and religious history of Italy. Chanforan had made a clear decision to accept Farel's call to extend the Reformation to the south and to give it all possible support.

There were some daring fellows — Gonin and his companions, for instance — who were ready to run any risk in trying to take the land before them by force. The more prudent *barba*, on the other hand, accustomed to their clandestine activity, preferred to keep to their old itinerant ministry. Everyone, it seemed, looked out on the plain, waiting for the right time.

That occasion was not long in coming. French troops in 1536 invaded the Duchy of Savoy, routing the army of the duke. In their wake the Reformed movement in Piedmont exploded like a fire, enveloping not only the villages in the Luserna Valley, but also larger places on the plain like Chieri, Carmagnola, Fossano and even Turin itself. Soldiers of Reformed persuasion in the French army circulated books and manifestos. Chaplains in the army who had come under Lutheran influence preached against the abuses of the Church. In spite of prohibitions and arrests, artisans, merchants, and nobility drawn to the new ideas organized groups and held meetings.

To counter the turmoil the Parliament in Turin, which was responsible for law and order and for the maintenance of official religion, introduced court proceedings and issued decrees which sent many Reformed sympathizers (the Miolos, Paschales, Salvaggios) into exile, including Pinerolio, who was to become Calvin's publisher in Geneva. These measures did little to stabilize the situation. French policies themselves were ambiguous regarding religious matters, alternating liberty with periods of repression. France was an occupying power and, for her, military priorities were uppermost. Among French troops were soldiers from Germany and Switzerland who had sacked Rome and who called themselves "Lutherans." It might well happen that someone of the Reformed persuasion would be condemned by Parliament only to be liberated by a sympathetic military governor, or that a "Lutheran" soldier in the occupying force would help a prisoner to escape. Or again, it was quite possible for Savoyard courts to lock up booksellers of Reformed literature, but the authorities were helpless under the circumstances to silence Reformed chaplains in the occupying army if they elected to preach in Turin.

The sudden eruption of the Reformation in Piedmont was not confined to the religious sphere alone. The determined folk from the countryside and the middle class in the cities who threw in their lot with the Reformation cause were challenging a whole culture, its social structure included. It was perfectly logical, for instance, that Reformed leaders in the Waldensian Valleys should seek to do away with the whole system of inherited feudal privileges so long maintained in the area. In 1549 soldiers and farmers went so far as to assault the castles at Bobbio and Bricherasio. As these formidable structures tumbled, the Valleys folk believed that at last they could see an end to feudal servitude — that old regime of lords, monasteries, and oppressive taxes.

The French occupation itself represented a fundamental change in the Valleys; it meant that the religious and social victories could be consolidated and popular self-awareness strengthened. We have noted that among the French troops were a number of soldiers who called themselves Lutheran. This was also true of some of the officers, one of whom was Gauchier Farel, no less determined than his brother, William. The same could be said for the Prince of Fuerstemberg who governed the region.

Protected at home and backed by allies abroad, the Waldensians could turn their Valleys into a liberated and secure base for the Reformation, one from which operations could be directed elsewhere in Piedmont. If a preacher who ventured out onto the plain below suddenly found himself in danger of arrest, he could still find a secure refuge back home.

The upshot of all this was that Waldensians were now enlisted in the grand strategies of European Protestantism. When Francis II of France declared his intention to destroy every evidence of Protestantism in his domain, Theodore Beza, Calvin's strong colleague at Geneva and rector of the Academy, was ready to intervene and to set in motion the considerable diplomatic pressure of Geneva, managing to obtain the intervention of the German princes. So the Waldensians, beyond their intention, became one of the pieces in the whole European political game of chess. Gone were the days when they were merely a tiny corner of religious dissent; now they had become the Protestant outpost looking down on Catholic territory. They were to remain in this strategic and exposed position for the next century and a half.

2. "Rise up and build the church anew!"

The course of the Reformation in Piedmont, as in France, was by no means planned, but took advantage of fortuitous circumstances as they arose. It had in Geneva a center and constant point of reference. It was in Geneva that Farel implemented the proposals he had put forward years earlier at Chanforan, and on a much larger scale. Here was a whole city, strategically located, which had gone over to the Reformation. In John Calvin Geneva possessed a man with an extraordinary ability to guide and direct public affairs. City of refuge for many in Italy, France, and Spain who had had to flee from the Inquisition, Geneva was also a veritable school of the

Reformation. Presiding over its Academy was Calvin himself. Young people from all over Europe came for schooling in biblical and theological studies, returning afterwards to their home countries to continue the work of the Reformation.

The nerve center of the Protestant International, Geneva was where theology, policy, and programs were charted. An early contingent of Waldensian students who completed their training and received approbation from the Venerable Company of Pastors included G. L. Paschale of Cuneo, who was sent to Calabria, and Giaffredo Varaglia of Busca and Scipione Lentolo of Naples, both sent to Piedmont.

It is worth emphasizing again that these young pastors were not called to organize Protestant congregations as we know them, with their parish registers, schedule of worship services and meetings, etc. Their first task was to arouse interest in the Reformed way of thinking. The center and focus of their work was preaching, above all; liturgy and the sacraments were subordinate.

The preaching, so different from our time when it means a few minutes of reflection on a biblical theme before a weekly gathering of the faithful, was discussion, debate, biblical and doctrinal teaching, and even journalism, all at work together. Preaching took place every day and lasted for hours on end. Many stirring drawings have come down to us which evoke the sixteenth century scene — children sitting on the floor; women perched on their backless stools with their men behind them; standing by, perhaps some of the local gentry, hands on their swords. Preaching took place everywhere — at a clearing in the woods, in the middle of a public square, or inside a "liberated" church.

The Reformation centered in Geneva took off in earnest in the mid-1550s. Dozens of young ministers set out for France, there to organize the first Reformed churches. In 1555 two events of capital importance took place in the Alpine region: the Pragelato Valley was won over to the Reformation and the Waldensians in Val Luserna constructed their first church buildings.

At Easter of that year, Jean Vernou and Jean Lauvergeat reached Fenestrelle from Geneva. There they preached and celebrated holy communion in public; from that moment the Reformation spread throughout the upper Chisone Valley.

The first churches, fruit of the new missionary thrust, were built at S. Lorenzo-Angrogna, Coppieri-Torre, Roccapiatta, Villasecca and Prali. Constructing church buildings designed for preaching, and replacing mass by the communal act of breaking the bread, were revolutionary events. It was plain for everyone to see that the new Reformed communities were a visible alternative to the Roman Catholic Church. If it was not possible to reform the Church which spurned renewal, there was no other way than to rise up and build the church anew! (*Dresser l'Eglise!*)

The parliaments at Grenoble and Turin tried to suppress the Reformed upsurge in their areas, but to no avail. In the late 1550s, resident pastors, some from abroad, were installed in key Alpine communities. The hope and thrust of the Piedmont Reformation found its symbol in the little Ciabàs church at the head of Val Angrogna, a modest structure set in the middle of fields and vineyards — and the object of derision by local Catholics. Covered by a straw roof, it had no bell tower, altar, candles, or sculpted pulpit. All the same it had a chair for the minister, a place where people could sit and break bread, and some copies of the Psalter set to music. Lacking the visible characteristics of a Catholic church, it was a church in a different style, meant for people who had discerned a radical new way of life with Christ.

This community was not merely assemblies which gathered around its preachers; it was organized bodies of believers. The popular assembly which 20 or so years before had met at Chanforan and had decided to stream into the Reformation was not an isolated event, but one which became a common experience. The assemblies with their preachers were the heart of the struggle for transformation of political and social life in the Valleys, and for securing for everyone land and rights from the clutches of the feudal lords. Waldensian local church organization as we know it today can be traced to the early Reformation-era popular assemblies dedicated to addressing human need and the administration of finances.

3. Martyrdom

The period from 1530 to 1560, although one of revolution and of great hope, was likewise a time of great suffering and martyrdom. Before everyone was the grim possibility of imprisonment, torture and death. It is not surprising that in the Reformed literature of the time we find so many letters from prison and letters written to prisoners who were condemned to death. Two letters from a Calabrian prisoner, G.L. Paschale, may be found at the end of the next chapter. How impressive is the serene and unshakable faith expressed here!

Piedmont, too, had its share of martyrs — among the better

educated people, in the main — people at the fore in circulating Reformed literature. The authorities evidently sought to stamp out the movement by striking down its intellectuals.

In 1536 Gonin was arrested in Grenoble while traveling from Geneva to the Valleys with a load of books and tracts for popular use. After a summary trial he was condemned and put to death by drowning. The life of this courageous bookdealer and courier who chose his profession with open eyes underscores what the movement owed to those who dealt in and circulated the printed word. A major source of Reformation strength, printer's ink flowed freely in those days. The author or distributor of books, pamphlets, and tracts was as much in the thick of the battle as any of the reformers.

On that same road to Grenoble from Geneva a few years later, five young preachers, making their way to the Valleys, were caught at Chambéry, tried and burned at the stake. A colporteur, Bartolomeo Héctor, trapped when he was in one of the high villages, died at the stake. Niccolò Sartoris met a similar fate at Aosta. He was the son of Leonardo Sartoris, a well-respected notary, who, imprisoned on the charge of being of the Reformed faith, died of hunger and cold in the Chieri prison. The young Niccolò, who managed to escape and become a citizen of Bern, did not hesitate to return to a town as dangerous as Aosta to witness to his faith.

Another who embodied in his person the hopes and travail of the Reformed churches in Piedmont was Giaffredo Varaglia, for a time minister at Angrogna and in charge of missionary work on the Piedmont plain. The son of nobility and promising member of the Franciscans, he was delegated by his order to study and refute Reformed doctrine. His reading, however, resulted in his becoming convinced that the reformers were right. He fled to Geneva, where he studied under Calvin and was ordained a minister. Returning to Piedmont, he was based at San Giovanni and the Ciabàs church and he proved to be a very eloquent and persuasive preacher, engaging in debates up and down the land. At length he was arrested, tried and condemned to the stake. After months of incarceration, in 1558 he was brought to a large public square in Turin to be burned. Just before the torch was applied he was granted a last wish — to preach a sermon before the multitude. It was said that as he preached, the mob, primed to jeer, fell into a deep and respectful silence.

Just one year later, in 1559, the Reformation was to face its most critical hour. Charles V's fiercely Catholic Spain overcame Francis I's Renaissance France. It was total victory — political, cultural, and religious — one which allowed Philip II of Spain, Ignatius

Loyola and Pope Pius IV to prepare for the Counter-Reformation. The dreams of a gentle Erasmus to reform the Church from within were just that — dreams. In their place was the reality of two worlds, two churches, two civilizations, which were to face each other in an inevitable clash. The protracted wars of religion were at hand. The treaty of Cateau-Cambrésis foresaw considerably more than a change in boundaries and a division of territory; it expressed the determination to reconquer Europe for the Roman faith.

The young bemedaled Duke of Savoy, Emanuele Filiberto, returned to his land from his battles to find Piedmont in ruins and mired in debts. He had no alternative but to align himself with victorious Spain and to set out to reclaim his land for Catholicism.

9. THE MARTYRDOM OF G. VARAGLIA AT TURIN (1558)

Concerning the death of Varaglia, one of the believers wrote the following to the churches.

The grace and peace of God our Father, his son Jesus Christ and the communion of the Holy Spirit abound with you.

Dear brothers, . . . I feel it is my duty to send you news of what it pleased God to happen among us these days for the advancement of his word, that is, the calling home of our good brother and minister, M. Giaffredo Varaglia through the cross of martyrdom.

When an emissary of the court announced his sentence to death, Varaglia replied that he had nothing to fear, and though it went against human nature . . . he spoke with an admirable steadfastness without becoming agitated.

Later, as he was leaving the prison to go to the place of his martyrdom, a priest approached him and begged him to be converted. Varaglia smilingly replied, "Be converted yourself, because, through the grace of God, I am already converted." He was led bound to that other good old man you know who suffered greatly himself for the same reason, as he had been condemned to be present at the execution and to be whipped, branded with the king's mark and banished. M. Giaffredo went on ahead, consoling the old man and reciting aloud the Psalm which says, "In you, Oh Lord, I put my trust." When they reached the stake, he turned to his friend, smiling, and said, "Do not forget to greet all the churches you visit; you will remain here, but I go to the glory of my Father!" Finally, with a rope around his neck, he climbed onto the pyre and began to speak to the crowd:

Dearest brothers, first of all I very willingly forgive all those who are the cause of my death, because truly they do not know what they do; I pray to God to give light to them. What is the cause for which I have been condemned to death? It is to hold and to make a confession of faith, that same confession which St. Peter and St. Paul and all the other apostles and martyrs made to defend the gospel of our Lord, Jesus

Christ. It is that good news which was given for the remission of our sin, through Jesus Christ, whom God raised as Advocate, Mediator, and Intercessor between God and us poor sinners.

When I served the devil, I died every day for my great sin, blaspheming God's holy name. If I had died at that time, I would have died damned. But now I die to live eternally with God, not that I believe that this death is the reason for my salvation, which is only by the blood of Jesus Christ.

If there are any among you who know the gospel and all the other sacred texts, I exhort you to study them, and let yourselves be ruled by them, because only they point us toward the right way. Cast off all those sins like idolatry, fornication, slander, theft, and similar crimes. This is the example I have always followed since God cast light upon my way, and I ratify it with my death, awaiting the reward from the One who has given me so much grace and honor: having been a herald of God's word, I have now been made one of God's knights and martyrs.

I want you to know that I believe in the Holy Catholic Church; I have received mediation from no person, but lean solely on God's word. I beg you not to trust in human mediation . . .

Having spoken on these and other matters for a quarter of an hour, he begged the crowd to pray to God with him, and kneeling down, he recited the Lord's prayer and the articles of faith in Italian, loudly and clearly without showing that he was in any way frightened. His color did not change and his face was joyful, so much so that many in the crowd marvelled, saying that he looked as though he were going to a wedding. When he recited the articles of faith, a murmur rose from the crowd and some questioned "How come? They told us that he did not believe in God and that he slandered the Virgin Mary. But we see that it is not true!"

He bid the executioner to get on with what he had to do. The latter begged forgiveness, to which he replied, "My friend, I have already pardoned you, and again I pardon you with all my heart." Thus, his spirit having been commended to God, he was strangled to death and burned. So was the passage of M. Giaffredo Varaglia, the Lord's faithful servant and martyr, to the promised new life on 29 March 1558, in Turin.

— Scipione Lentolo, "Historia delle grandi e crudeli persecutioni . . . " in T. Gay, ed., *Manoscritto della Biblioteca di Berna*, codicil 716 (Torre Pellice, 1903), pp. 111-113.

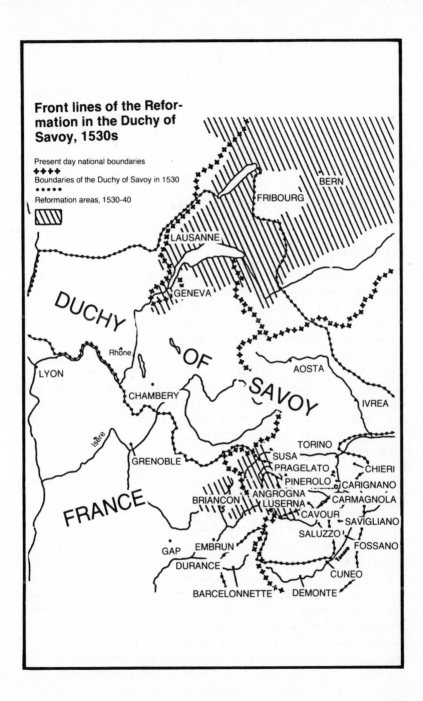

Front lines of the Reformation in the Duchy of Savoy, 1530s

Present day national boundaries
++++
Boundaries of the Duchy of Savoy in 1530
•••••
Reformation areas, 1530-40

BERN

FRIBOURG

LAUSANNE

GENEVA

DUCHY

Rhône

OF

LYON

AOSTA

SAVOY

CHAMBERY

IVREA

Isère

TORINO

GRENOBLE

SUSA

PRAGELATO

CHIERI

PINEROLO

CARIGNANO

BRIANCON

ANGROGNA

CARMAGNOLA

LUSERNA

FRANCE

CAVOUR

SAVIGLIANO

SALUZZO

GAP

EMBRUN

FOSSANO

DURANCE

CUNEO

BARCELONNETTE

DEMONTE

II.

SCORCHED EARTH AND MASSACRE

1. In Provence

Two years before Chanforan, in 1530, the Waldensian assembly was held in Mérindol. That site had been chosen with good reason, for at this time Provence — especially the Lubéron hill country — was one of the strongholds of the Waldensian diaspora, from the point of view of both numbers and the quality of life.

There were both social and religious reasons for these settlements. Many families had migrated from the Alps in search of land to cultivate and had settled in a region which was Waldensian or which at least viewed Waldensians in a favorable light. In this well-developed area, according to a Catholic report of the time, there lived some 10,000 families of "heretics."

The religious reasons were equally important. In the first half of the sixteenth century there was a vast movement of evangelical renewal; it could not yet be called Protestantism, but it was not medieval Catholicism, either.

Lefèvre d'Etaples was publishing his translation of the New Testament, Calvin at Bourges had teachers with Lutheran sympathies, and at the court of Marguerite of Navarre the gospel was being openly preached.

The Lubéron Waldensians became in effect a central nucleus for the entire movement, so much so that when the subject of the Waldensians came up, Provence above all came to mind. For several years before the 1530 assembly the Inquisition in France had been taking a harsher turn, led by one of the most degenerate and despicable of its leaders, Giovanni da Roma. Greedy and cruel, his excesses stirred protest from Erasmus. Farel wrote about it to

Calvin, who penned a letter to the King of France, defending the rights of the Reformed believers.

The threat hanging over the area abated for a few years, but shortly the "religious question" was put into the hands of the local parliament at Aix-en-Provence. In 1540 a ghastly thing happened: 19 Waldensians were accused of sedition, condemned, and burned at the stake; further, an order was issued to destroy the town of Mérindol. In the wake of this series of terrible acts, Farel prevailed upon Melancthon to draw up a protest in the name of the German princes which was duly sent up to the king's court. Francis I, in turn, rebuked the Aix parliament and ordered an investigation which resulted in the Waldensians' being cleared of any wrongdoing.

In 1545, however, Francis I, ever a wavering monarch, changed his mind and commanded the president of Aix's parliament, Jean Meynier, to lead personally the papal army from Avignon to clear the area entirely of the Waldensian presence. The Lubéron folk were suddenly caught in a vice.

The sweep did not stop until it had devastated the whole region and obliterated every trace of the Waldensian villages. A few survivors did manage to escape to Switzerland, but for the rest, it was either death or its grim equal: a life sentence as galley slaves on French ships.

The massacre gave to France a bitter and frightening foretaste of what was in store for her in the coming wars of religion.

2. In Calabria

A similar fate awaited the little Waldensian communities in the extreme south of Italy. They had heard the reverberations of the religious revolution going on in the north. In particular, upon learning that Valleys folk were daring to build churches, they believed that a new day had arrived. The Calabrian Waldensians had been living very discretely, separated from Waldensians to the north, but not completely isolated, thanks to the regular visits by the *barba* to all the various points in the Waldensian diaspora. Their settlements were quiet little enclaves. The feudal powers were compliant and even the Church authorities were relatively silent about them, so that they lived without too much strain in a land rich in cultural autonomy and spiritual ferment.

The Calabrian Waldensians, increasingly aware of their responsibility in the Reformation movement, decided that the moment had arrived to send a delegation to Piedmont with a request to Geneva for ministers and means to build up Reformed communities. The effort ended in tragedy. Giacomo Bonello, after a time of preaching in Calabria and in Puglia, dared to undertake an exploratory mission into Sicily, where he was arrested in 1560 at Palermo, condemned, and put to death as a martyr at the stake.

G. L. Paschale in many ways personified the remarkable Waldensian spirit in the middle of the sixteenth century. A native of Cuneo in Piedmont, he turned from a military career (again the influence of Lutheran fellow soldiers) to study theology with Calvin in Geneva, where he became an author, publisher, and bookseller for the Waldensians. Among a series of biblical works he issued was his own translation in 1555 of the New Testament in Italian, a first.

Already well-known in Piedmont, he volunteered to go to Calabria. His fearlessness there, however, led him into a trap which resulted in his arrest and confinement in Naples, Cosenza, and Rome prisons, where he wrote his moving letters which have a permanent place in Italian religious literature. He was hanged at Castel S. Angelo in Rome in 1560.

As with Varaglia at Turin and the five young ministers caught at Chambéry, it was thought that by hanging the Reformation leader Paschale, the movement would come apart. However, the Waldensians managed to reorganize and in the end Philip II of Spain resorted to harsh and violent repression.

Late in 1560 Cardinal Alessandrino, who was to become Pope Pius V, sent two inquisitors, Alfonso Urbino and Valerio Malvicino to Calabria. Once at Cosenza, aided by the efficient arm of the governor of the region, they spread terror with their torture, secret accusations and arbitrary fines. The Waldensians had no alternative but to abandon their villages and flee to the woods and mountains, where a most unexpected turn of events occurred: well hidden, and in a moment of desperation, the Waldensians fell upon their pursuers and killed a number of them, including the governor of the province himself.

Authorities from Naples reacted with a vengeance. Punitive action was carried out by the Spanish military who had shown their prowess during their campaigns in America. The jails were also emptied of convicts, dregs of the realm, with the promise that they could purge their crimes with the blood of the "heretics."

What followed belongs to the chronicle of unspeakable violence. There were sporadic attempts at resistance by a few. Their old tradition of non-violence, however, with its simplicity of heart and innate respect for constituted authority, led the Waldensians to give themselves up. On June 5, 1561, the town of San Sisto, with its 6,000 inhabitants, was burned to the ground. Guardia Piemontese, its neighbor, was likewise destroyed. Prisoners were burned like torches, sold as slaves to the Arabs or condemned to die of starvation in the dungeons of Cosenza, where the ropes which bound them were so tight that their flesh rotted. The massacre reached its height at Montalto Uffugo on June 11, when, on the steps of the parish church, 88 Waldensians were cut down one by one, like animals brought to the slaughterhouse.

If the military operation lasted only a few weeks, the work of Catholic indoctrination, Jesuit style, continued for years. The Jesuits were determined to obliterate every trace of Waldensian presence in Calabria. They succeeded, except in one small respect: there is to this day a trace of Alpine dialect in the speech of the inhabitants.

The martyrdom of the Waldensian communities in Provence had the effect of arousing indignation all over Europe. To men and women steeped in the spirit of the late Renaissance, it had all the marks of an inexcusable crime. The equally savage Calabrian massacres, however, had no profound repercussions. Hushed up in the stagnant and gloomy climate of the Spanish Counter-Reformation, they had nonetheless foretold something of the mindless and ghastly carnage of the next century.

10. LETTERS FROM A CALABRIAN PRISON (1560)

To the beloved and honored people in San Sisto:

Greetings in Jesus Christ. The first lesson that our heavenly Master teaches us is this: "If any one will come after me, let that person deny himself or herself, take up the cross,and follow me." . . . I now have no doubt at all that to be denied country and possessions, and to expose oneself to a thousand dangers, is not an impossible burden for the flesh; I know equally well that to forsake Jesus Christ is much greater loss for both the body and the spirit . . . How foolish are those who would fill their bellies but are content to be deprived of spiritual food . . .

I can testify that with a little bread and water the body can be satisfied, whereas the soul will never have satisfaction until it finds food which nourishes the hope of eternal life. And what is that if it is not the preaching of the holy gospel? . . . If, therefore, you desire to be fulfilled, go to the place where your soul is fed, and thus you will fortify your conscience, you will find rest, you will confess Jesus Christ, you will edify the church, and you will confound your enemies.

> Your brother in Jesus Christ,
> G. L. Paschale

To Camilla Guarino, my beloved and honorable wife:

I confess to such a great benevolence of the Lord our God toward me that I am almost beside myself in thinking of it, so many are the blessings that God grants me — among which is this present opportunity to be able to greet you with this letter and to have you share in my consolations . . . I know well that the patience and constancy of Christians by no means are gross stupidity, nor insensibility to the afflictions of the body . . . May God, who has honored you greatly in your life of service, comfort you in the spirit in such a way that you may be able to overcome any trial in your life . . .

Bid farewell to my dear colleagues. Tell them to sharpen their scythes well, for the harvest is great but the laborers are few.

> Your husband and brother in Jesus Christ,
> G. L. Paschale

—A. Muston, ed., *Lettere di un carcerato* (Torre Pellice, 1926), pp. 87 ff.

III.

WAR OF RELIGION

1. The enigmatic Emanuele Filiberto

When the duke returned to his ruined land from the wars and was put under Spanish pressure, he issued repressive anti-Reformation decrees. Already his courts had begun a search for heretics. Turin became unsafe for Waldensians and the number of refugees who left from there and elsewhere for Geneva increased considerably.

Emanuele Filiberto was no Spanish *hidalgo*, visionary and fanatical, but a calculating Savoyard. He knew very well that in carrying through his "restoration" the Catholic religion suited his plans much better than any Protestant ferment. But he also knew that it was better to put out little fires than to massacre a whole population.

In dealing with the scattered Waldensians on the plain, he showed no mercy, but in the Luserna Valley, where they were far more numerous, he offered to negotiate. The first phase was organized by a group of Jesuits led by Antonio Possevino.

There was a rash of discourse and debate in public places. Some of the most notable of these encounters took place at the Ciabàs church between Possevino and Scipione Lentolo, the Waldensian pastor who succeeded Varaglia. Before the people, local clerics and the nobility of Luserna two determined young men got up and argued vociferously, citing scripture to support their positions. Lentolo, standing for the Reformation, argued for a new society while the Jesuit spoke up for the Counter-Reformation and the preservation of the status quo. It became clear that the answer of the Angrogna folk to the Jesuit conception of the Church and even of society was a resounding No. Emanuele Filiberto now realized that he had to swing into action.

The debating at the Ciabàs was but an earlier and smaller version of the "great debates" which would take place a few months later between Reformed and Catholic theologians assembled at Poissy before Catherine of France; the open, if uncertain climate was not yet that of the Spain of Philip II. Racconigi, a royal prince, was among Lentolo's audience as the preacher delivered one of his fiery sermons. As he listened, the prince did not seem uneasy at all. Hoping for the best, the Waldensians presented their royal visitor with documents, including their confession of faith, to support their point of view. Was Racconigi a curious intellectual, an interested party, or just another politician? Who could say? It was clear that he belonged to the nobility and that the Duchess Marguerite at the court was likewise of the nobility and a Protestant. In her role as a duchess in a Catholic country Marguerite had to move with a great deal of tact and clear-headedness as she sought to protect the rights of her Protestant people.

Discourse seemed to go nowhere, so the duke decided to try a military solution. In September 1560 he entrusted to Giorgio Costa the command of an armed unit whose goal was to reestablish order in the Luserna Valley. His chaplain for the exercise was to be none other than Possevino. What the duke assumed would be a minor police action became a full-scale military campaign. For the Waldensians the moment of truth appeared to be at hand.

The campaign was to develop in several well-defined stages. First came a period of uncertainty as to just what would happen. By the end of October, the hill folk, bringing in their last harvests and seeing winter approaching, were already fearful that their fate might be like that of their brothers and sisters in Calabria. Meanwhile, they continued to hope that the threats they heard everywhere would remain just so many words and that the ducal authorities could be appeased by declarations of loyalty and obedience. November, however, saw the first of the skirmishes; more troops arrived, forts and castles were rebuilt and bands of mercenaries began to plunder the lower valleys.

This was a turning point. The populace refused to have any more to do with negotiations. Now, they said, was the time to defend themselves in the name of all that their heritage stood for. Scipione Lentolo wrote:

> Some ministers maintained that people in such dire necessity have every right to repel violence inflicted on them by their enemies, …that what they were doing was in defense of a just and holy issue, which was the maintenance of true religion and the preservation of

their lives, that this war was instigated by the pope and his men, not directly by the duke, who was forced into it by these evil spirits.

The Waldensians now set about raising an army for their defense. With this action they were not only overriding their own policy of non-violence, but also the Reformation way of obedience to the sovereign. In doing so, the Waldensians disassociated themselves from the stated line of Geneva, where their position was not fully appreciated. In embarking on a new course they risked isolation. They pointed out that at issue was not freedom so much as truth. Thousands of Reformed Piemontese had chosen another course — that of exile — in order to serve God according to their consciences. In doing so they, too, had broken with their past. This time it would be to fight rather than to flee.

The arguments put forward to Geneva were both juridical and theological. Concerning the former, the Waldensians maintained that their decision to resist did not constitute rebellion but legitimate defense. They would simply seek to protect what was rightfully theirs from the plunders of evil men.

The theological argument was more telling. The struggle now going on, they said, was not between subjects and the sovereign, but between Christians of Reformed conviction and the pope. The duke was no problem; he was acknowledged as the rightful ruler. The hard fact was the menace of tyranny at the hands of the pope. Centuries before, the Waldensians had freed themselves from the pope's authority, but now they saw that same tyranny reappearing in the duke's troops drawn up before them. What was at stake, therefore, was something more than a question of obedience; it was still Valdesius' issue: honoring God through preaching and teaching set free from episcopal controls. It was, in the Reformation expression, a "battle," a challenge of faith for the cause of *witness*.

Just at this point something unforseen occurred in France to strengthen the direction the Waldensians were taking. Francis II died, and Catherine de Medici showed her willingness to continue the discussions. The Valleys of Pragelato and Chisone (regions still occupied by France) formed a coalition with the Val Luserna. At a popular assembly in the hamlet of Puy, near Bobbio, a document promising mutual support was signed, which has come to be known as the Covenant of Puy. The date was January 21, 1561.

The covenant deserves a special place in Waldensian history, for it defined the entire Alpine Reformed area as an autonomous and responsible unit. It gave notice, in effect, that Waldensians would no longer be a simple pawn on the Reformed chessboard, a southern outpost for Geneva or a peripheral part of French Protestantism. For the first time a community of country people, led by a dozen or so intellectuals, their ministers, decided to resist the absolute power of their sovereign. In medieval times there had been many revolts of the poor and spontaneous uprisings, but this was a concerted action joined to military resistance, for the cause of the people's right to reform the church.

Within weeks Waldensians began to put their covenant to the test, attacking the fortifications built by the duke's men. They assaulted the garrisons, set fires at different strong points and sacked the Catholic church at Bobbio. The reaction in Turin against such effrontery was immediate — this was war.

Military operations began on February 14 and lasted until the end of April. The duke's force consisted of noblemen on horseback, followed by archers, and behind them a band of "volunteers," mostly intent on picking up booty. It was very much an expedition of medieval character, in which the local gentry recruited and equipped the farm folk on their estates — usually with picks and swords.

The commander of the duke's force was right in identifying Pra del Torno — deep in the Val Angrogna — as the Waldensian command post, but he made mistakes in judgement which would be fatal to his campaign. He thought their camp was a classic military fortification and failed to take into account the protection that the mountainous terrain offered. His repeated attempts to overcome the little hamlet nestled at the bottom of the snow-covered mountains were a complete failure, and his men were dispersed on the slopes and steep gorges below. As the weeks passed the invaders' situation got worse and worse. For their part, the Waldensians demonstrated courage and daring in combat that — as has been retold down through the generations — must have been of epic dimension. The stories tell of Waldensian sharpshooters with slings who scattered the invaders, of ducal officers losing their way and drowning in icy torrents, of how one fellow, a certain Carlo Trucchietti from Perrero, was caught in the snow in his ridiculously heavy armor and ignominiously brought down by a mountain rustic.

If all this has come down to us with biblical overtones, it is not inappropriate. It was indeed David against Goliath, Gideon routing the Midianites. One of the notable characteristics of Reformed spirituality of the time was identification of its own struggles with those of the Old Testament Israelites: prophets up against a corrupt priesthood's idols, faithful kings versus apostate kings, a Josiah against a Jeroboam. The familiar Old Testament stories suggested to the Waldensians that in pitched battle the people who relied upon God's help would finally prevail against their enemies.

Literature and legend portrayed the Valley of Angrogna as a "land of Canaan," the theater in which the redeeming hand of God was revealed. Waldensians up against the "papists" was Israel up against the Philistines. The rout of the enemy or a fog which descended at the right time to permit escape were signs of God's intervention on the side of truth. Each battle was preceded by prayer and accompanied by the prayers of the people. Combatants knew that they were forbidden to use reprisals, to plunder or use unnecessary violence. Strange as it may seem, because Waldensian fighting had pronounced theological overtones, it became better reasoned, more disciplined and more effective.

The last assault against the defenders on the heights in the late spring ended in failure like the others. With the attacking force disorganized and weary, the duchess and Racconigi, who had been following events very closely, decided to intervene and a truce was reached.

True, Emanuele Filiberto could have mustered sufficient force to extinguish once and for all this little hotbed of resistance. In so doing, doubtless he would have been acclaimed a hero of the Counter-Reformation, but at what price? The enigmatic Emanuele Filiberto was a man who had read his Machiavelli, and he knew that reason should rule over passion. The Luserna corridor in which these troublesome folk would have to be hunted down, he was aware, was partly in the hands of the French, and military complications outweighed any promise of glory. Reason counselled that it was much better to surround the area and snuff out resistance little by little. If hostilities could be ended, a solution might be found which would save the honor of the ruler, insure the stability of the state, and, above all, provide the international credit needed for the reconstruction of Piedmont. The obvious course for a clever ruler was to offer negotiations with the adversary without granting recognition.

2. A watershed parchment without a name

The new state of affairs was officially ratified June 5, 1561 at the meeting held at Cavour between the Waldensians and the authorities. It was the same day that the Waldensian colony in Calabria was destroyed. The Waldensian delegation arrived not as suspects being brought to trial but as free people, properly respectful, as befitted subjects being received in a sixteenth century princely court. One part of their history included Mérindol and Guardia Piemontese, but Cavour was different. Of the three Waldensian areas which, after Chanforan, seemed to have possibilities for growth, two had now been annihilated. Only the third, Piedmont, had been able successfully to resist.

The document which was drawn up offered the duke's pardon, absolved the defenders from all acts committed during the war, and forgave damages to ducal property. It acknowledged certain Waldensian rights and authorized Waldensian worship in places such as Angrogna, Villasecca and Coppieri.

Drawn up in Italian, the document was unique. It was not a treaty. The duke could not deal on an equal footing with rebellious subjects who scorned his laws and opposed his army in pitched battle. The two parties simply were not on the same plane diplomatically. Nor was it an act of clemency. The Waldensian delegates (two pastors and two others) had a clear conscience about what they had done and they would not have affixed their names to a document seen as the duke's generous pardon. In their eyes it was an agreement.

The formal aspect of what happened in Cavour may not have been so important, but the substance was without precedent and of revolutionary significance.

This strange parchment spelled out for the first time in European religious history the fact that subjects who practiced a religion different than that of the ruling power possessed officially recognized rights. Up to this time the rule had always been that the religion of the prince determined the religion of his subjects: *cuius regio eius religio.*

Yet here was the case of a Catholic prince who tolerated the presence of dissident subjects in his land — even ones who were spiritually rebellious. Not only did he tolerate them; he came to terms with them, recognizing their existence and extending guarantees for their worship. Even more important was the fact that a Catholic prince tolerated "heresy" and renounced the destruction of it.

How different this was from the melodramatic gesture of Philip II, who swore that he would give up his empire, his wealth, and even his life to root out and destroy the hated "Lutherans." Yet here, for all the world to see, was a little duchy astride the Alps becoming an outcast in the eyes of Catholic Europe.

Certainly the duke himself did not sit down at the negotiating table. How could he without losing his honor? He did not give up any territory; he just saved face by recognizing reality. The signature of Prince Racconigi was a firm pledge, and it provided a new premise for Savoyard politics, namely, that the Waldensian question now belonged to the political order of things.

The bold, legible signatures of the Waldensians bound their communities to an irrevocable, if unforseen, responsibility. The designated localities for open churches, certain rights won, and the clear recognition of Waldensian "territory" all became new frontiers in the life of a singular community which could be surrendered at the price of death alone.

As the Waldensian delegates returned to the mountains from Cavour, they must have taken a long look back toward the plain. It was the same Piedmont as 30 years before, but no longer, as at Chanforan, a land of promise, where, it was hoped, the spirit of the Reformation would give rise to great events. Now the plain was emptied of Waldensian families, for thousands had fled the land where the Inquisition was snuffing out the last stirrings of the Reformation spirit. Yet these delegates must have said to themselves that it was precisely in this wilderness that preaching of the gospel, somehow, must continue at all costs, even if prospects of success appeared dim.

In a certain sense, Cavour closed a chapter opened in hope at Chanforan. Instead of fanning out in this new land and seeing it transformed by the preaching of the gospel, the Waldensians now found themselves confined to the mountains. True, they were protected within certain limits, but all the same, they were prisoners.

Cavour, likewise, was a time for taking stock, for reflection on the battles, debates and decisions of the past decades. Had the march of the Reformation perhaps been checked? If so, the real resistance was just beginning.

From now on, the Waldensians would no longer be just a fragment of the Protestant diaspora or an outpost of Geneva. Now they were a distinct reality in their own right. In the face of the papacy and of life in a country now dominated by Spain, they saw themselves as a bridgehead of Protestant Europe south of the Alps, in the very front lines up against the Counter-Reformation. The Reformation offensive in Piedmont was perhaps over, but the Waldensian Church had been born.

11. THE COVENANT OF PUY (1561)

To find a suitable solution to their problem, Reformed believers sent two of their pastors along with other leaders to the sisters and brothers in Val Chisone, which meant crossing mountain passes despite heavy snowfalls. When they had described their sad plight, it was decided to renew their old covenant of union, which from father to son had been handed down among the Waldensians of the Dauphiné and of Piedmont. They solemnly promised to come to each other's aid whenever they suffered persecution on account of their religion, so that they might keep their faith intact and pure, according to the sacred scriptures and the tradition of the authentic apostolic church, without prejudice to the obedience due to their rulers. A delegation of pastors and leaders from Val Chisone then accompanied the group from Val Luserna back to their valley to renew there the covenant they had made togther.

They crossed the Giuliano Pass on January 21 and that same evening made it down to Puy of Bobbio where they spent the night. They offered fervent prayers to God, asking for guidance and assistance; then they all agreed that as they had no wish to attend mass, they had to decide whether to face great suffering and take flight — a near-impossible venture because of the severity of the winter and because they had nowhere to take such a large number of people — or to defend themselves courageously until death.

This last proposal was accepted unanimously and the covenant was renewed with great feeling. All present raised their hands and swore never to submit to the papacy and to remain rooted in their inherited and true faith, grounded in the word of God, for defense of which all declared readiness to commit their lives and possessions, to defend persecuted sisters and brothers, and forsaking individual interest, to await not upon people but upon God.

Then they decided that the next day they would go to hear the word of God instead of attending mass as they had been commanded . . . The following morning people came from all the surrounding hamlets to the church at Bobbio; the men were all armed, and once they had cast out all images from the church they gathered to hear the word of God preached.

— P. Gilles, *Histoire ecclésiastique des Eglises Vaudioses . . ., I*, P. Lanteret, ed. (Pignerol, 1881), pp. 226-228.

12. THE POPE AND THE DUKE (1561)

The Duke of Savoy convened a meeting with the Waldensians from the Valley of Moncenisio. For more than a year he had tried to bring them into line, inflicting various forms of punishment, but after they had organized their own defense, he sent an army against them (which the pope helped to finance). At first, owing to the mountainous terrain, there were skirmishes rather than pitched battles; finally a battle was arrayed. The duke's army of 7,000 soldiers was routed while the Waldensians lost only 14 men.

The duke, seeing that the action had had the effect of hardening the rebels while weakening the country and costing large amounts of money, decided to pardon them. He convened them on June 5. At this meeting they were absolved from all acts committed during the war; freedom of conscience was recognized; they were assigned certain places where they were allowed to hold services, but in all others they were forbidden to preach, only to aid the sick and carry out other offices pertaining to their religion. The agreement enabled exiles to return and those who had been banished to reacquire their property; the duke, however, would be able to send away any pastor he pleased, but they could be replaced with another. In every place provision would be made for Catholic worship; no one, however, would be forced to attend.

The pope was greatly disgusted that an Italian prince, whom he had aided and who could not manage without his help, should let heretics live freely in his state. Above all, the pope was highly concerned about the example this would set to other princes who might wish to allow other religions in their states. Extremely angry, he distinguished the duke from the Catholic King of Naples (who, in those days, had captured a group of over 3,000 Lutherans who had left Cosenza for the mountains in order to live according to their doctrine; many were hanged, others were burned at the stake or sent to the galleys) and exhorted all the cardinals to find a remedy . . . He sent for the duke to justify his act, but once the pope had heard his arguments, he fell silent, not being able to respond.

—P. Sarpi, *Istoria del Concilio Tridentino, V* (Biblioteca Sansoni), p. 563.

IV.

COUNTER-REFORMATION EUROPE

1. Lésdiguières' Huguenots

John Calvin, the last of the generation of the great reformers, died in 1564. Just one year before his death the Roman Catholic Council of Trent had adopted the lines of the Counter-Reformation: stricter doctrine, rejection of the Reformed tenets, and a return to a medieval spirit of obedience. Such a program required rigid and fanatical popes, Jesuits with their authoritarian politics and a revitalized Inquisition.

It was a time, also, of attempting to revive the spirit of the crusades, resulting in such actions as the battles against the Turks at Lepanto and against England in the North Sea, and the massacre of Protestants throughout France which took place on the feast of St. Bartholomew, that night of infamous memory.

If the Waldensian redoubt was able to resist the enormous pressure of the Counter-Reformation, it was in large part thanks to a fortunate combination of geographical and political factors — a mountainous terrain, sparsely populated, difficult to police, and always under the threat of invasion by France. Wedged in, as they were, between the Marquisate of Saluzzo and the Pragelato Valley, both under French dominion and Reformed influence, and with the Dauphiné at their flank, the Waldensians passed these years in relative quiet.

The wars of religion which tore France apart did not similarly ravage this border country, and by 1570, when the Duke of Lésdiguières was named governor of the Dauphiné, conditions were fairly stable. The remarkable Huguenot (French Protestant) general was able to make the whole area from Susa to the Rhône river into a Reformed bastion, and this had its impact in the nearby Savoyard lands, politically, culturally and religiously. Indeed, in 1592, Lésdiguières actually invaded Pinerolo, Cavour and the Waldensian Valleys, controlling them for several years and encouraging a movement which would have made them a part of France.

The House of Savoy rose to the challenge and deployed the necessary forces to keep control over its traditional lands; in the last decade of the century it actually regained the area of the Marquisate of Saluzzo. The Reformed folk there who had enjoyed French protection were immediately subjected to harassment, so that many of them sought refuge in more hospitable areas; some settled in the Luserna Valley, others went to Dauphiné, while still others joined the considerable Piemontese refugee colony in Geneva. In this period more than a third of the pharmacists in Geneva were Piemontese, and among Geneva's typesetters, textile workers and mechanical craftspeople, a large number were from Piedmont.

The Marquisate was not conquered for the Catholic cause without considerable resistance. In 1590, for example, the communal council of Dronero asked that its citizens have the right to attend Reformed services in the Valleys of Pragelato and Luserna. Protestants had definitely taken over Val Pragelato, where Catholic services were suppressed.

The Waldensians also showed their strength in winning over the last remaining Catholic valley, that of Pramollo. As the story goes, the pastor of San Germano one Sunday went up to the high Alpine village to confront the local priest publicly on his own ground. Challenging the priest, he asked the latter to explain the meaning of the rites of his Church. When it was evident that the priest was not able to defend his Church, the pastor launched into his own discourse before the people, advancing the Reformed way, grounded in the gospel, as distinct from the Catholic practices which the priest himself did not understand. The Catholic people sized up their situation anew, including the fact that they were surrounded by those of firm Reformed conviction. They accepted the preacher's call to become Reformed and ended all Catholic services in their village.

2. Friars and debates in the squares

One of the most notable aspects of the Counter-Reformation was the new surge it brought about in the activities of the religious orders. The friars were indeed much more eager to do battle for the Catholic faith than were the bishops and the priests. Jesuits, naturally, were in the front lines, though the Capuchins were not far behind. Together the orders reopened closed churches, preached, founded schools and seminaries, and wrote catechisms and polemical books to hold in check the Reformed message.

It is not surprising that the Counter-Reformation's attack on the Waldensian Valleys should have been put into the hands of the friars. We have already seen something of the work of the Jesuit Possevino around 1560. Firmly established by 1583 in Luserna, the Jesuits followed their classic strategy of first gaining a foothold in local power centers and from there going about their conquests. In Luserna, however, the counts responded rather lukewarmly to this effort to restore Catholicism. They were not even enthusiastic when a prominent son of one of their families, Marco Aurelio Rorengo, was named to a leading position in local ecclesiatical life.

It was this same Prior Rorengo who was responsible for inviting the Capuchins, and for housing them in his own palace at Torre. The Capuchins were supposed to be warmer, more popular and better preachers than the Jesuits. They set about to open centers in various Waldensian localities, such as Bobbio, Villar, Rorà and Angrogna, It was in vain. In spite of intense efforts, the friars for years celebrated mass alone, unable in the slightest to breach the wall of Waldensian resistance. Finally, they withdrew. As legend has it, the local population wanted to be rid of them at any price but didn't dare drive them out by force, lest they contravene the law. Waldensian women, therefore, are said to have hoisted them onto their own backs and carried them out of town.

In 1572 the two religious orders of Sts. Maurice and Lazarus merged to more effectively combat the Turks and the Waldensians, considered to be the Turks of the Piedmont. Their missionary activity was intense and was aimed not so much at reconverting the population as at opening Catholic services, however small and poorly attended, in order to establish a base for a more favorable time.

They naturally clashed with the Reformed preachers; market places and squares became areas where the local folk could listen to debates and animated discussions between friars and pastors. It was clear that true dialog was not their purpose, however. Like men in combat, they were earnestly trying to exploit an adversary's point of weakness.

3. Geneva and Huguenot France

The test of strength with Emanuele Filiberto had galvanized the Valleys churches, but it had also raised some difficult problems. The first of these was economic. The brief but violent war had quite disrupted the economy of the region. Political problems arising within Waldensian ranks were equally serious. The Reformed hard-liners were eager to go beyond the Cavour concessions and to consider all of Piedmont as the field for an intense missionary and propaganda activity which could lead to a general uprising, planting the Reformation in Turin itself. "A dangerous illusion," replied moderates who were closer to Geneva, feeling that the Valleys should take their cue from the international situation, which in their eyes did not appear propitious at the moment. War of religion, as in France, they said, was not the solution. It was much better to fortify present positions and to organize church life for heavy times surely to come.

The divergent points of view found leading pastors as their protagonists — Scipione Lentolo and Stefano Noël. Lentolo, volatile and an impassioned preacher, was of Neapolitan origin and pastor of the Ciabàs church. Noël was French, with a thorough grounding in the ways of the city of Calvin. Each of the parties associated with these men tended to draw inspiration from a Reformed neighbor, from France or from Geneva. We look at the latter first.

With the triumph of Calvin's party and the foundation of the Academy, Geneva in the late 1550s went through a radical transformation. The Ordinances, which gave the Geneva church its structure, actually date back to 1541. These provided for elders to oversee individual conduct, deacons to assist those in need, ministers to preside at worship and to preach, and bodies called consistories to unify all of the church functions. It was another body, however, the Venerable Company of Pastors, which gradually assumed more authority than the consistories, for it had the last word in doctrinal matters. In effect, therefore, it was really the pastors who determined the lines of conduct for the entire city.

Such an arrangement was possible, of course, in an independent republic possessing a solid mercantile class. The Waldensians, by contrast, had to struggle for emancipation from a rule which was monarchical and semi-feudal. What Italy lacked most at the time was a middle class capable of taking control of the situation.

The other possible model for the Waldensians was that of

Huguenot France. The French Reformed Church assembly was called the synod, a body which brought together pastors and lay representatives on a regional basis. The synod also made provision for the inclusion of certain leading Protestant figures of national importance. In the French Reformed situation there were very close ties between the grassroots of the church and the political and cultural leadership. Unlike the Waldensians, the Huguenots at this time were a considerable political force; they possessed their own party organization and were capable of putting an army into the field. The wars of religion in France were to reflect this.

Which of the two patterns open to them would the Waldensians in Piedmont follow? The people living in the mountain area around Pragelato were drawn to the example of France. Those in the other Valleys in general sought a more independent course. They looked to Geneva for a certain lead theologically and used the city's Ordinances as a fundamental guide for their own church's organization. But they did not hesitate to modify the latter in the light of their own situation, especially after what they experienced in the fighting of 1560-1561.

In setting up an organization, the Waldensian churches had to keep two considerations in mind: maintenance of Reformed doctrinal integrity and expansion on a local level. Following the direction set out by the synod of 1558, which laid down the foundations of their Discipline, Waldensian churches in the early 1560s organized themselves in a completely original way. Like Geneva they provided for ministers to preach the word, elders to run the churches and deacons to care for the poor, but organized in the framework of a rural rather than a middle-class mercantile community. As in France, they held synods, but in the Valleys the synods were deliberative assemblies of the whole community of believers rather than of party people. The main concern was to provide a structure and a way of life to advance Christian community, rather than to formulate social policy as in the French experience.

The rallying point throughout this period remained the Covenant of Puy, a free affirmation of faith which had unified the Reformed people of Piedmont at a critical hour of need. The covenant was to be a living inspiration across the years, since for the Waldensians faith had meant and would mean holding fast to the gospel which is discovered and lived in the context of solidarity and in the concreteness of history. Their church would not be rigorously centralized, as in Geneva, nor still would it be a political-confessional movement, as with the Huguenots. The Waldensian Church would be a *free union of congregations and believers, bound together by a common commitment to solidarity*. No wonder that from 1571 on the covenant was to be reaffirmed over and again.

V.

A TIME OF VISITATIONS

1. Violence and war abounding

Giordano Bruno was burned at the stake in the year 1600 — a sinister portent of what was in store for Europe in the seventeenth century. The Catholic Church, having survived the first shock of the Reformation, was ready to go on the march again, militant and self-assured. Its aim was to reconquer the continent.

The Thirty Years War broke out in 1618; in its wake the Church could mark impressive successes: Austria, Hungary, Bohemia, and Poland became "re-Catholicized," and the armies of Lutheran Germany were saved only by the timely intervention of Gustavus Adolphus of Sweden. In 1622 Rome founded the "Congregation for the Propagation of the Faith" to disseminate the Catholic faith throughout the world and to "extirpate the heretics" from European soil.

What was to be the fate of the Waldensians in the face of this ideological offensive? They lived in their remote mountain areas, and perhaps many were even unaware of the tremendous battles being fought to the north over the Reformation. The armies most to be feared, those of Spain and France, had soon neutralized each other, but this does not mean that the situation was calm. Even in Piedmont the war of religion continued to take its toll, although it was not quite as tragic and fierce as in the rest of Europe.

In 1601 the Marchesate of Saluzzo passed to Savoy in exchange for land on the other side of the Alps. Edicts issued after the armistice forced the Reformed inhabitants to choose between conversion to Catholicism or exile. The death of the Reformed churches in the Saluzzo area was slow and marked by the adventurous politics of Carlo Emanuele I, who alternated concessions with repression. His dream of military conquest burst like a soap bubble, when his troops, upon assaulting Geneva, were forced to withdraw ignominiously by the women of the city who hurled pots and pans at them. The campaigns for the conquest of Monferrato resulted in the combatants' being infested with the plague.

To conduct the war, the duke had to employ in his army mercenary Huguenot troops from France and even some Waldensian soldiers, which meant that he had to adopt a more prudent policy towards the Reformed churches, enabling them to enjoy a few years of truce.

In 1619 the truce was broken when two leaders of the Reformed movement, Pietro Marchisio and Maurizio Mongia, were arrested and executed. The French synods protested but to no avail. All they could do was to provide financial means to help the Reformed believers of Saluzzo on their way to exile. The sad story of those years is told in an anonymous work published in Geneva in 1620 *(Bref Discours des persécutions . . .)*, with which the author tried to arouse public opinion to the threat of the Counter-Reformation.

Two churches in the area of Paesana in the Upper Po Valley, which were of Waldensian origin and which had always kept in close contact with the churches of the Valleys, managed to survive as an underground movement until around 1630 when they, too, were destroyed.

2. Onerous laws, paper wars, scholarly works

Piedmont stumbled through the Counter-Reformation. It was a land of red tape and busy little notaries, a tangle of laws that defied every attempt to unravel them. A classic description of the period may be found in Manzoni's *Promessi Sposi*.

Legislation concerning religious matters, in particular, was a thicket so dense and confusing that it was practically impossible to find one's way. Abstinence from meat on Fridays, observance of every feast day, doffing one's cap to the priest carrying the sacrament on the street, were only the beginning. Work was forbidden on feast days. No more than six Waldensians could accompany the dead to their burial place. And such penalties! — confiscation of possessions, heavy fines, even death. It was a terror of words, of maddening gestures, like the statues of the time, all arms and contorted limbs.

The law was only rarely enforced. Power was arbitrary and

arrogant. For 20 years Waldensians had to suffer the swaggering governor, Sebastiano Grazioli, called Castrocaro, installed in the Torre palace with his henchmen. It was he who listened in on the synods, conducted searches everywhere, fixed onerous taxes and levied heavy fines to line his own pockets. It was he who engineered the exile of Scipione Lentolo as a way of getting rid of one of the community's most articulate leaders.

Life did not undergo marked changes, except in efforts to organize for proper defense. As in the past, the synod governed the life of the Waldensian community, although the ministers still played a leading role. New Valleys-born leaders came forward to take the place of such vitalities as Noël and Lentolo. One of those who emerged was Antonio Léger, a man of such unusual personal and intellectual gifts that the Geneva authorities prevailed upon him to accept the key diplomatic post of chaplain to the Dutch embassy in Constantinople. There Léger had important conversations with the Ecumenical Patriarch, Cyril Lucaris, encouraging the latter's interest in Reformed theology and in certain reforms in the Orthodox Church. The relationship was cut short in 1638 when the patriarch was assassinated by the sultan's men in a plot instigated by the Jesuits. Léger had come to the Valleys the year before and was able to give leadership to his people for seven years. At the end of that time, however, he was threatened with arrest and had to flee to Geneva.

Counter-Reformation assaults in the seventeenth century also had the effect of hardening theological positions in the Reformed churches, including those in the Valleys. Holland, in mortal combat with Spain, was the source of an especially rigorous Calvinistic orthodoxy which separated itself from the Arminianism prevalent in the Dutch parishes. At issue was the doctrine of predestination. In the 1618-1619 Synod of Dordrecht, conservatives won the day, which had a considerable influence not only on the Waldensians but on all Protestants in the Latin countries. According to the Dutch at Dordrecht, to yield on a single point was to risk being crushed by the Counter-Reformation. In fact, a Waldensian minister at Pragelato, finding the acts of Dordrecht too rigid, ended up embracing Catholicism.

The arena for polemics was shifting from public square to literature, where the focus was now more historical than doctrinal. The most prominent apologist on the Waldensian side was Pierre Gilles, the moderator. His Catholic counterpart was the Prior Marco Aurelio Rorengo. Their confrontation began in 1632 with

Waldensian emblem (P. Paschetto). Many variants have arisen over the centuries and are found across the Waldensian Church today. Commonly included are a candle, the John 1 citation (...into the darkness, Light...), and the seven stars representing the churches in Revelation 1-3.

the Prior's *Breve narratione dell' introduttione de gl' heretici nelle valli del Piemonte* — to which Pastor Gilles replied. The exchange was taken up by others like Belvedere and Grosso, who turned out hundreds and hundreds of pages to fill the book shelves.

These works, which have only an historical value for us today, were, nevertheless, the instruments of serious battle for that generation, for they sought to justify and legitimize the Reformation itself. The problem was not confined to the local Waldensians, but concerned the defense of a whole Reformed culture. Everywhere the Catholics leveled the charge that the Reformed were schismatics with hardly a century behind them, whereas the Catholic Church had existed for centuries.

In 1616 there appeared in Holland an unusual book by Baldassare Lydius with the arresting title, *Waldensia*, in which he argued that it was not true that the Reformed had only a century of life. They had existed for centuries, he said, and the proof was that the Waldensians and all those like them had for centuries been persecuted by the Roman Church. Once again the Poor came to the fore.

The same line was followed in a book by Perrin, a pastor in the French Dauphiné, entitled *Histoire des Vaudois et des Albigeois*, commissioned by the French Reformed Church. In 1643 Pietro Gilles updated the work of Perrin, producing the first real classic on Waldensian history, *Histoire Ecclésiastique des Eglises Réformées autrefois appelées vaudoises*. For Gilles, the Valleys had become so much a part of the Reformed world that the name Waldensian belonged only to the past. He found the traditional name interesting only because it demonstrated the antiquity of the Reformation itself.

In passing, let us note that in 1643 there appeared for the first time (in pastor Valerio Grosso's *Lucerna Sacra*) the Waldensian emblem (which, in one form or another, has been used by the church ever since), a candlestand and the words *In Tenebris Lux* surrounded by the six (later seven) stars.

3. The plague

Any history of the Waldensians must include a section on the ravages of the plague of 1630, one of Europe's last and most disastrous epidemics. In Manzoni's novel, *Promessi Sposi*, the plague stood for a grand purification in which the wicked were punished, the penitent redeemed, and the poor found their peace. The reality for the Waldensian Valleys, however, was that of wartime devastation, for it involved the whole region in terrible suffering.

The pestilence broke out in May of 1630 in the town of San Germano. By July it had reached the Pellice Valley, where it spread with exceptional virulence throughout the summer. Documents of the time tell of the dead in the streets, of homes abandoned and pillaged while the thieves themselves fell victim to their booty, and of doctors and pharmacists enriched by the peddling of useless potions. Acts of extraordinary devotion and personal sacrifice occurred side by side with those of cruelty, neglect and superstition.

One of the most alarming consequences of the plague for the Waldensians was the sudden decrease in their population. Gilles wrote of some 9,000 deaths; many families were completely wiped out. All the hamlets in the high pastures had to be abandoned. Nor were the Valleys alone in their sufferings. Throughout Piedmont everyone was so preoccupied with the dead and dying that no thought could be given to a move against the Waldensians.

Of the 13 Valleys pastors, only two survived, Gilles at Torre and Grosso in Val San Martino. It was urgently necessary to turn to Geneva for help, an appeal which was met generously but which was to bring startling changes in Valleys life.

In due course, a new body of ministers, all educated at Geneva's Academy and similar in outlook, was installed. This was no time for gradualism: the newcomers set out to do things in the Genevan way. Soon the moderator's office assumed more importance than before, and the patriarchal, family-centered pattern in the churches tended to disappear. The term *barba* no longer seemed appropriate for these young pastors, who were called "Monsieur."

Of greater moment was the fact that Italian was discontinued in services. Although the villagers were fluent in both Italian and French, they had made a point in using Italian in their churches because this was the language of the people in Piedmont they wished to reach. With the arrival of the new pastors from Geneva it became necessary to use French as the official language of the churches — a practice that was to extend well into the nineteenth century.

Using French as their religious and cultural medium, of course, tied the little Waldensian world more and more closely to that of European Protestantism generally. At the same time it spelled isolation with regard to Piedmont. The Waldensians now had their faces more to the west and north — to Geneva and Leyden — than to the east and south. The hostile world around them now spoke a language which the mountain folk themselves would soon no longer use.

Gilles, who had already completed his history in Italian, had to rewrite it in French, and, although in 1644 he published in Italian his "150 Sacred Psalms," he would be the last pastor for the next two centuries to write in Italian.

13. SNAPSHOTS OF THE SEVENTEENTH CENTURY WALDENSIAN EXPERIENCE

1. Waldensian soldiers

... The troops from the Valleys were housed in the city of Vercelli, where they enjoyed their liberty . . . During the time our soldiers traveled in Monferrato and neighboring provinces, they came across many people who on account of our faith, showed them special interest and attention. They wanted our Waldensian soldiers to be billeted in their homes to learn of our faith; they regretted their sad plight and showed a real desire to free themselves to live in the true church. There were others, however, especially those who lived in isolated villages far from the towns, who had been indoctrinated with strange ideas about our religion. They had been given to believe that our soldiers came from certain valleys in Piedmont where only a few Christians lived among monstrous people who slandered God, the Virgin Mary and the saints. They believed that some had just one eye in the middle of their foreheads, that they had four rows of long dark teeth used to devour children who had been roasted on a spit. They had been warned that the soldiers who wore yellow cloaks belonged to these people, so the brave ran to see these monsters, while those from distant villages fled, petrified at their arrival. . . .

2. Kidnapped children

... This Friar Bonaventura, a man who was expert at flattering and other "monkish" arts, having unsuccessfully tried to convert more wary, older people, started to stir up the children from the lower valleys where Reformed and Catholics live side by side. Before anyone could guess what was happening, some children between 10-12 years of age from good families disappeared. In vain their families searched for them and presented petitions, but no sign was to be found of either the children or their kidnappers. Just one inhabitant of Luserna heard that his son was to be found in a monastery at Pinerolo. With the help of some influential friends, the man was given permission to go and see his son on the condition that he would do nothing to convince him to return home. Petitions and reports to the authorities were all in vain; the reply they received was that they had no authority over the friars and that the children were no longer in the country. There were, however, no more kidnappings and the parents were careful not to let their children be around friars.

This affair was just over when something else equally disturbing happened. On June 9, 1627, several men of the faith were arrested at Luserna, Bibiana, Campiglione and Fenile and immediately transferred to Cavour, where Senator Barberi was waiting for them with a large detachment of guards, and from there they were taken to Villafranca where they were detained for several days.

The churches of the Valley of Luserna immediately sent a delegation to the nobles of the Valley . . . to make it known that these arrests had violated the agreements . . .

— P. Gilles, *Histoire ecclésiastiques des Eglises Vaudoises . . .*, II, Lanteret, ed. (Pignerol, 1881), pp. 206-207, 309-310.

14. DECLARATION OF THE REFORMED BELIEVERS OF SALUZZO (1603)

Since time immemorial from generation to generation our ancestors have been instructed and nurtured in the doctrine and faith which we have openly professed since our infancy and in which we have instructed our families. When France occupied the Marchesate of Saluzzo, it was possible to profess our faith without being molested, a situation similar to that which our sisters and brothers in the Valleys of Luserna and Perosa and others enjoy today. On the basis of an explicit treaty signed by our prince and sovereign, they enjoy the free exercise of the Reformed religion. As the ruler, on the advice of wicked counsellors and troublemakers, rather than on his own will, has decided to take measures against us through publishing an edict, we intend to point out that we do not deserve to be oppressed or robbed of our goods and houses, because we have in no way committed any crime against the person of our prince, nor have we rebelled against his edicts, nor committed crimes or theft.

We are utterly convinced that the faith which is taught and professed by the Reformed churches in France, Switzerland, Germany, Geneva, England, Scotland, Denmark, Poland and in other regions and lands, the religion in which we have made an explicit profession of faith, in obedience to our sovereigns, is the one and only true Christian faith, established and approved by God, the only one that can please God and lead us to salvation.

We are resolved to keep our faith even if it means putting our life, goods and honor at risk, and to follow it for the rest of our days. If anyone thinks we are mistaken, we would ask that person to prove it . . . [for] we promise to follow the religion which is proved to be best, desiring above all else to follow with a clear conscience the true and legitimate worship which we poor creatures owe to our Creator, in order to reach true everlasting happiness. If, on the other hand, force is used to make us give up the true path of salvation and to make us embrace errors, superstition and false doctrine invented by people, we prefer to give up our houses, goods and our very lives.

We humbly beg our ruler, whom we recognize as our legitimate prince and lord, not to permit that we be in any way unjustly molested, but to see to it that we may continue for the rest of our days, ourselves, our children and our descendants after us, to be loyal and faithful subjects, as we have been up to now; we do not ask other than the opportunity to faithfully render to our ruler what is expected of us and what we are bound to do by divine commandment — to render to God the honor and worship which God demands of us in the holy word.

In our isolated and precarious situation, we ask the Reformed churches to recognize us as their own; we are ready to seal with our blood, if God so desires, their confession of faith, which we recognize to be in conformity with the doctrine taught by the holy apostles. We promise to live and die in the faith. If on account of our profession [of faith] we are persecuted and afflicted, we render thanks to God for having allowed us to suffer in God's name. We put our fate in the hands of the divine providence, who will free us when God judges the time to be right.

We beseech God, who has power over the hearts of kings and princes, to touch the heart of our ruler so that he may take pity on those who have never offended him or even had in mind to do so, so that he may recognize that they are more loyal and faithful than those who instigate him to persecute us.

We pray that the Lord will sustain us in these trials, giving us patience and perseverance to hold to the truth until the end of our days.

— J.P. Perrin, *Histoire des Vaudois* . . . (Genève, 1619), pp. 185 ff.

114

VI.

A SPRINGTIME OF BLOOD

1. The circle closes

By the middle of the seventeenth century, after a hundred years of struggle and endurance, the Reformed enclave in Piedmont still showed vitality and courage, although it was notably smaller in numbers than in the century before. Catholic attacks had forced it to be on the defensive. We now come to the most dramatic moment in the Waldensian story — the 35 years from 1655 to 1690.

On the international level the stage had been set by a great confrontation between two civilizations, Catholic France and Protestant England. In the former, Louis XIV pursued his policy of centralization in a climate of bigotry and servility. Dissident forces among the nobles or within Parliament were repressed; the king centered all power around himself.

In England, Charles I sought to embark upon the same course of authoritarianism and hoped he would be able to lead his country back to the Church of Rome. But Charles' efforts had just the opposite effect, for in his realm it was the dissidents who emerged victorious. An antimonarchical and anti-Catholic movement led by a combination of minor nobility, Scottish Presbyterians, and dissidents of various types, was able to launch a great revolutionary cause against the king. Unlike Charles I's mercenaries, the dissident Puritans did not fight for money but for a cause, in the conviction that they were not only safeguarding their own rights, but were defending the truth of their faith. These "round heads" (as they were scornfully labelled by the nobles in wigs) prevailed in battle and Charles I was condemned to death. The ensuing Puritan revolution went through various phases under the guidance of Oliver Cromwell, who took the country's destiny in hand, taking in 1653 the title of Lord Protector, and ruled with a firm religious and social realism.

In Piedmont, the regent was Christine, widow of Carlo Emanuele I. A sister of Louis XIII of France and understandably sympathetic toward the new French policy, Christine was also sister-in-law of Charles I of England, and, like all Catholic monarchs, was keenly aware of the danger that Reformed communities, with their lively spirit of independence, posed for authoritarian rule. There were Reformed communities very nearby, she knew, hardly 35 miles from Turin.

Repression became the policy. A Catholic sovereign could "rule" over a mass of subjects who were silent and obedient; the Reformed folk, who opted to think for themselves, had to be wiped out.

The first to be struck were the churches in the Pragelato Valley. As long as the governor of the Dauphiné had been under Lésdiguières, the Reformed people had enjoyed the relative security which stemmed from the Edict of Nantes (1598). In the late 1620s, however, the authorities once again imposed Catholic worship in the Valley. After long and painstaking efforts, the Prior of Mentoulles and the Jesuits recovered the Catholic churches and other properties and restored payment of tithes. Following the classic Counter-Reformation maneuver, they set about to win over local authorities, landholders and civil servants in the Valley.

The justification for this offensive was a certain clause in the Edict of Nantes which forbade Reformed worship in "lands which lie beyond the mountains." Politically, the Valley belonged to the Dauphiné and was therefore French; geographically, it was indeed on an eastern slope of the Alps. What interpretation should prevail? The law, in the hands of a repressive power, became an instrument of repression, and a wily political authority succeeded in slowly suffocating the Reformed faith in the Valley.

In the Waldensian Valleys further south, relations with the authorities were regulated by the Cavour agreements, but the problem was the same. Waldensians there were trying to secure some breathing space for themselves, hoping at last to break out of the straightjacket that had long imprisoned them. Waldensians in Val Pellice, hard-hit economically by the restrictions, had acquired lands on the plain a dozen miles beyond their own boundaries. This "colonization" again raised the old charge of Waldensian "conquest" of the open country and sounded the alarm at the court of

Turin. In the 1640s an increasing number of incidents occurred in the Valley. Determined to hold worship services, the Waldensians dared to build a chapel in open violation of the Cavour document. The ducal authorities ordered the little church to be demolished, only to find that the Waldensians would rebuild it. In 1641 the governor gave orders to confiscate the goods of about 100 families who had settled outside the boundaries. In 1653 the monastery at Villar Pellice was set afire by a band of extremists. The facts of the latter incident were not clear, but Pastor Manget was accused of having had a part in it. Two years later Pastor Léger was falsely accused of the murder of the priest of Fenile.

Accustomed as they were to the exhausting war of edicts and provocations, the Waldensians regarded all this as part of their continuing struggle. They did not take into account the real change which had come about in the political climate, and so failed to realize that the fanatical elements in the Catholic Church and French imperialism had decided to liquidate for good the Reformed presence in the Alps. By the time the first contingent of troops had been amassed at the Waldensian borders it was already too late for a political solution. A bloodbath was at hand.

2. . . . And still more massacre

Lined up on one side were 4,000 ducal soldiers, plus the rabble from local militias, all under the command of the Marquis of Pianezza, a perfect son of the Italo-Spanish Counter-Reformation. Of the nobility, religious and calculating, Pianezza was totally convinced that the end justifies the means. On the other side stood the Valleys folk, clustered around their young moderator, Léger, nephew of Antonio Léger, known to be a man of courage and vitality, but unprepared for a confrontation of this sort. Léger was more at home in legal struggles than in leading his people in battle.

At first glance everything seemed to recall the scenario of a century earlier, in 1560: the presence of a fanatical Catholic army, see-saw Savoyard rule, and a lack of preparation on the part of the Waldensian population. In reality, however, the scene had changed profoundly. This time Waldensian behavior betrayed a certain fatalism and resignation — more of a willingness to submit to events than to resist, struggling in faith. Those hurried gatherings of the first war of religion, with their urgent preaching and fasts, were but a memory, as was the dramatic tension between loyalty to sovereign and obedience to the gospel which had dominated the earlier years. What the Waldensians were now facing seemed like a natural calamity, like a plague or a famine. The defenders just hoped that the duke would somehow call an end to the punishment.

The climate in which Pianezza's men carried out their 1655 sweep through the Valleys was that of a medieval crusade or pogrom. To the fanaticism of the Piemontese militia was added the anti-Protestant passion of the refugees from Ireland who had suffered Cromwell's iron rule in their homeland. Everything took place in an air of total disorder, seemingly without plan; the mob proceeded to loot at will while one Waldensian delegation after another, with words of submission and genuflections, made its rounds in the Piemontese camps. Actually, the Marquis' general staff had carefully planned the actions of its militia and soldiers in order to test Waldensian resistance and to strengthen its hand.

Pianezza then ordered the Valleys citizens to quarter his troops in their homes as a sign of their loyalty to the sovereign. It was the end of April. The fateful consequences of the maneuver could easily be foreseen, yet to refuse his command would constitute an act of insubordination. After a good deal of inconclusive debate the Waldensians submitted to the order, whereupon the occupation degenerated rapidly into a sheer massacre. It was a day of infamy which has gone down in Waldensian history as the "Piedmont Easter."

More travail was to come. On April 24, Pra del Torno — the Waldensians' high ground refuge and bastion of resistance over the decades — was taken by assault, reduced to rubble and plundered. Within a few days the same fate befell Villar and Bobbio. Similar ghastly scenes were multiplied throughout the Valleys — unarmed people were tortured sadistically and massacred; the terror-stricken fled for their lives while the soldiers came down from the mountains laden with booty.

On May 3, Pianezza ordered a great celebration to take place in the villages which had been conquered and returned to Catholicism. In the presence of his victorious soldiers and the surviving population, he planted a cross as a "countersign of the faith and the coat of arms of the sovereign."

3. Janavel, Puritan rustic

It was just in these devastating times that the Waldensians discovered a resolute leader in the person of a farmer from Rorà, Giosuè Janavel. In the face of the massacre to which his people seemed willing to submit, he stirred up a resistance force of a handful of men. Although poorly armed, Janavel's skilled and daring guerrillas managed for a time to repulse the onslaught of the ducal troops. For a few days Rorà survived, the last free territory in the Val Pellice.

In these days of desperate resistance a drama was being played out in the Waldensian communities which was noteworthy both historically and spiritually. Just when Janavel and his men, helpless onlookers to the destruction of their culture, were being overrun by the enemy, a prophetic sense of vocation came to them. Like the Scottish Puritans, they now saw that the Counter-Reformation was not merely a restatement of certain religious doctrine, but an ideology based on violence and death — in Turin as in London. The Court of Savoy now disclosed itself as a regime with which taut co-existence was no longer possible. It had become an outright instrument of death.

The Waldensians, Janavel perceived, were no longer the "Reformed" subjects of a Catholic duke, but people who were to be told what they should believe. Freed at last from any obligation to the ruler, Janavel's band determined to be answerable only to God for their conduct, to fight and die as free people.

Pianezza's military action continued relentlessly. After the fall of Rorà it shifted to the Chisone Valley, where the Waldensians sought in vain the mediation of the French governor at Pinerolo. The sole avenues of escape were across the frontier into France or into the Pragelato Valley. By May 8 the whole Val Germanasca submitted to avert outright devastation.

After the massacre came the edicts. Anyone connected in any way with the resistance — including Janavel and Léger — was banned. Heavy indemnities were levied. Then followed the "big show" characteristic of the day. Forty Waldensians, with two of their pastors, were brought to the cathedral at Turin, to take part in a ceremony in which they were made to renounce "the detestable sect of Calvin." The reconquest of Reformed lands was now thought to be complete and the way thus opened for a new drive by Catholic missionaries. What the crowds in Turin did not know, however, was that a storm of protest was breaking out over Europe.

4. Protestant Europe outraged

Léger had escaped to France on April 23, making straight for Paris. There, ten days later, he issued his famous "war communiqué," in which he described the fall of the Waldensian enclave and appealed for help for his defenseless people. As Protestants read his words they could arrive at only one conclusion: mob-like soldiers led by nobles and rendered fanatics by Catholic friars were the very essence of the Counter-Reformation, a menace to all of Europe. The reaction in England was immediate. On May 17 the Council of State took up the "Waldensian question," regarding it not as a simple political fact, but as a theological and spiritual issue. The massacre of the Waldensians was not seen merely as genocide in a secular sense, but as the annihilation of saints by the power of the anti-Christ. Puritan England stood in solidarity with her distant sisters and brothers beyond the Alps, taking their martyrdom upon herself. There was a period of national fasting. Puritan preachers stirred up the rage and grief of their people as expressed in John Milton's famous sonnet, "On the Late Massacre in Piedmont":

> Avenge, O Lord, thy slaughtered saints, whose bones
> Lie scattered on the Alpine mountains cold;
> Even them, who kept thy truth so pure of old,
> When all our fathers worshipped stocks and stones,
> Forget not: in thy book record their groans,
> Who were thy sheep, and in their ancient fold
> Slain by the bloody Piemontese, that rolled
> Mother with infant down the rocks. Their moans
> The vales redoubled to the hills, and they
> To heaven. Their martyred blood and ashes sow
> O'er all the Italian fields, where still doth sway
> The triple Tyrant; that from these may grow
> An hundredfold, who having learnt thy way
> Early may fly the Babylonian woe.

Indignation was soon echoed over much of the European continent. Thanks to the indefatigable Dutch printers, the literature market was flooded by a stream of newspaper articles, tracts, pamphlets and special reports, in which the sadistic actions visited upon the Valleys people were depicted in horrifying detail.

The House of Savoy, through its ambassadors in the various capitals, tried to minimize what had taken place. To no avail. Public opinion in Europe had clearly made up its mind that violence against the Waldensians had made Savoy an outcast.

England dispatched a note of protest to Turin, while calling for the intervention of European powers from Denmark to Transylvania. A month later Cromwell took the further step of sending a special envoy of ambassadorial rank, Sir Samuel Morland, to make his case in Turin. As Morland read his text (in Latin, composed by John Milton) some of the courtiers may have tittered at his Anglo-Saxon accent, but they could not have failed to be impressed by the force of his words. It was clear that the "Waldensian question" could not be solved by the Irish mercenaries.

Europe had been aroused for the cause of a few thousand Protestant rustics in Piedmont, and Savoy's unstable regime was visibly shaken by the avalanche of protest.

The once "good Reformed subjects" had, in the meantime, become rebels like the English Puritans. Using guerrilla tactics, Janavel and Jahier, a leader from Pramollo, started to harass the Catholic villages on the plain; it was the French war of religion with an added Puritan touch. The Savoyards called them *barbetti*, rebels.

In the ensuing struggle, the Count of Marolles responded to Waldensian forays by a systematic round-up of the population. Plunder was met by plunder; soon neither side was taking any prisoners. Nor did the fighting end when Janavel was seriously wounded and Jahier killed. Guerrilla warfare became even more widespread. Volunteers arrived from Pragelato, including Huguenot commanders with cavalry. On July 26 a contingent of guerrillas raided and conquered Torre itself, where they burned down the monastery. It was an unmistakable message to the Holy Office: the Counter-Reformation would be resisted at all costs.

In the face of relentless partisan warfare at home and formidable international diplomatic pressure, Turin knew that some concessions were inevitable. Accordingly, the French ambassabor was asked to mediate a settlement in Pinerolo. With the Waldensian delegation stood the Swiss and English diplomats.

The document made public at the end of the negotiations (August 18, 1655) reaffirmed the Cavour agreement in recognizing the right of the Waldensian communities to exist. It did so, however, with an emphasis far different from its predecessor. Here was an edict concerning "grants of mercy" by a gracious ruler who offered pardon to his rebellious subjects. Rights no longer really figured in the document, only the generosity of the sovereign.

5. Outlaws

Insofar as the "pardons" document seemed to guarantee the continued existence of the Reformed communities it doubtless reassured the Protestant forces abroad, though in reality it was little more than an armistice. Nothing in it changed Janavel's intuition that although the Waldensian enclave remained intact the threat of Catholic aggression still hung over the land. The first sign appeared almost overnight — the new Fortress of S. Maria, begun barely two weeks after the "pardons" and finished in record time. Cannons now dominated the town of Torre and the Pellice Valley.

The fortress was not the only menace. The agreement itself was violated: requisitioned lands were not restored to their rightful owners; kidnapped children were not returned to their families. Fines and trials further pointed to a deliberate strategy of generating tension. This kind of cool and calculated pressure should be distinguished from the open conflict which took place earlier in the century. In this new climate Catholic absolutism sought to bend the resistance of one sector of the population — as in the case of Pragelato — and to sow provocation in the other — the lot of the Waldensian Valleys.

The situation deteriorated week by week. Pastor Léger, now returned to lead the community as moderator, found himself accused of all sorts of violations for which he had to appear in court, accusations ranging from having preached in San Giovanni (true) to that of having personally profitted from funds sent to the Waldensians from Holland (false). As for Janavel, not only was his vineyard not returned to him, but his son was kept a prisoner. Every effort was made to grind down the Waldensian ranks by impugning their leaders and inciting the people to protest. When at last repeated provocations led to a popular uprising the Savoyard diplomats played their trump card, claiming that this was the act of an incorrigible people, the kind of warfare carried on by "outlaws."
. Guerrilla warfare was rekindled. Hit-and-run attacks against Catholic villages were common. Janavel and his men, more cunning as a result of their previous experiences, gave no quarter to the Marquis of Fleury. Normal civil life became paralyzed; the Waldensian men took to the mountains while the Savoyard courts tried the partisans in their absence, pronouncing death sentences in rapid-fire succession.

Léger, accused of conniving with the rebels and sentenced to death, had to flee, denying the Valleys their international contact. The Waldensians, who had been regarded as victims of oppression and as defenseless martyrs, came to be looked upon as insatiable rebels.

The Valleys folk, weary and disappointed, gradually began to disassociate themselves from the partisans and to long for a more normal life. During a stormy synod, a group seeking reconciliation gained the upper hand, asking Janavel and his men to withdraw and to cease operations so that terms could be sought with the authorities at the negotiating table. Using Swiss delegates as arbitrators, a series of conferences took place in Turin in December 1663 and January 1664 in which various open questions were resolved, concluding with another "pardon" document dated February 14, 1664. This one provided for a general amnesty (except for the rebels already condemned), and reaffirmation of the pardons of 1655, but withdrew the right to worship at San Giovanni and required that a delegate of the Savoyard court be present at all sessions of the synod. This last article, seemingly harmless in the face of the peace arrangements, was actually a devastating blow, for it signified the end of the Reformed communities' autonomy. Ten years of terrible crisis had left them outwardly safe; inwardly worn out and deprived of their leadership, they were resigned. In one horrible decade the Waldensian world had experienced in its own way the tragic drama of European Protestantism — the Puritan revolution overcome by Catholic absolutism and the victory of Louis XIV's policy over that of Cromwell.

The Valleys folk were now to live under the sign of exile. Léger, the intellectual who had been a real leader for his people, became a European refugee. Janavel, the free farmer, became the proprietor of a small tavern in Geneva. Of an evening in the silence of their homes, these two men, destined never again to see their native Valleys and having fought their last battles, were engaged in writing their memoirs — and their hopes. From each of them was to come a classic of Waldensian literature. Léger's was the monumental *Histoire générale des Eglises Evangéliques des Vallées du Piemont . . .* , published in 1669 in Leyden, where he was to remain a pastor to the end of his life. For his part, Janavel issued a manual of military tactics for his captive people.

Léger sought to delineate the evangelical character of the Waldensian churches on three grounds: their claim to antiquity as true descendants of the apostles; the purity of their doctrine as revealed in a review of Waldensian medieval theological literature; and the suffering his people endured as documented by his own personal testimony. Janavel's was a modest set of instructions, written in French and awkward Italian, giving practical advice on the way his people should defend themselves. Although poles apart in form and intended audience, the two works were one in lucidity of faith and religious passion.

123

15. CROMWELL'S LETTER TO THE DUKE OF SAVOY (1655)

Most Serene Prince,

We are informed by letters received from several places in the vicinity of your dominions, that the subjects of your royal highness, professing the Reformed religion, have been commanded by an edict, published by your authority, to quit their habitations and lands, within three days after the promulgation of the said edict, under pain of death, and for the confiscation of their property, unless they shall enter into an engagement to abjure their own, and to embrace the Roman Catholic faith, before the end of 20 days. We have learned also, that regardless of their humble petitions to your highness, praying that you would be pleased to revoke the said edict, and to grant the same privileges, which were anciently conceded by your serene ancestors, your army fell upon them, cruelly slaughtered great numbers, imprisoned others, and drove the rest to flee for refuge to desolate places, and to mountains covered with snow, where hundreds of families are reduced to such extremity, that, it is to be feared, they will all shortly perish with cold and hunger. Upon receiving intelligence of the melancholy condition of this most oppressed people, it was impossible not to feel the greatest commiseration and grief, for we not only consider ourselves linked to them by common ties of humanity, but by those of the same religion. Feeling therefore, that we are invoked by the sacred voice of brotherly love, we declare that we should fail in our duty to ourselves, to God, to our sisters and brothers, and to the religion we profess, if we did not employ every means in our power to obtain an alleviation of their unparalleled sufferings. It is on this account that we most earnestly entreat, and call upon your highness, in the first place, to call to mind the enactments of your serene ancestors, and the concessions which they made and confirmed from time to time in favor of the Waldensians — which concessions were granted, no doubt, in time of obedience to the will of God, who desires that liberty of conscience should be the inviolable right of everyone, and in consideration of the merits of these subjects, who have ever been found valiant and faithful in war, and obedient in time of peace. And as your serene highness has graciously and nobly trodden in the steps of you predecessors in all other things, we again and again beseech you, that you not depart from them in this instance, but that you revoke this edict, and any other that is oppressive to your subjects, in consequence of their professing the Reformed religion; that you restore to them their ancestral habitations and property; that you confirm their ancient rights and privileges; that you cause reparation to be made for their injuries; and that you order an end to all vexatious proceedings against them. If your highness will comply with this request, you will do what is most acceptable to God; you will comfort and support the minds of those unhappy sufferers, and you will be conferring a favor upon the neighboring Protestant states, and especially upon us, who will consider such clemency as the effect of our intercession, which will constrain us to do every kind office in return, and will be the means of not only strengthening, but of renewing and increasing the relations and friendship which have subsisted between this commonwealth and your dominions. Promising ourselves much from your justice and moderation, we heartily pray God to direct your mind and thoughts, and so to grant you and your people the blessings of peace and truth, and to prosper all your undertakings.

Given at our court at Westminster, May 25, 1655.

Oliver, Protector

—W.S. Gilly, *Narrative of an Excursion to the Mountains of Piedmont* ...(London, 1827), pp. 218-220.

16. JANAVEL'S MANUAL ON GUERRILLA WARFARE (1685)

Beloved friends in Christ, these few words express greetings with all my heart and testify to the love I have for you. I trust that you will accept some thoughts I want to share with you regarding the questions that concern you. If indeed God should decide to put your faith to the test, as it is said, and as I think will come to pass, I ask that you receive with ready minds these observations of mine, although I have not the slightest doubt concerning your good conduct and your trustworthiness.

The first duty to which you must pledge yourselves is to maintain unity; the pastors should accompany their flocks day and night, so that they may be surrounded with honor and respect as befits the Lord's servants on earth; they should not be permitted to expose themselves to danger in battle but should dedicate themselves to prayer toward God, to encourage the combatants, to comfort the dying, and to provide safety for the wounded and for the families in need. They should take care exclusively of the functions related to their office, with the exception of those who have the capacity and willingness sufficient to take part in the council of war and who do not fear the sight of blood.

The pastors should call an assembly of the people; after having given the necessary exhortation according to the word of God, they should lead young and old to pledge faithfulness to God, to their church and to their people, to the last drop of their blood . . .

You will absolutely refuse any encampment [of the ducal troops] in the countryside, for otherwise you will be lost. Let the massacre of 1655 serve as an example to you. If there should be an attack against you, defend yourselves as best you can on the first day, even without commanders. But afterwards see to it by day and night that you organize yourselves properly. If you think it right, follow the counsel that I give you: organize small squads of 20 men per unit, each with one sergeant, two corporals, one captain . . . The command should be entrusted to a mayor, if he can be found, who can give orders to the captain in each locality. You should have a secret council of war composed of one man from each Valley, a man who is faithful and a believer, one or two courageous pastors, and a general commander to supervise all the people of the Valleys.

All of this should be done in good order and in a popular assembly. If God grants you the time to do it, you should provide wheat to be set aside in a safe place in the mountains to help those in need and to provide for the mobile units.

If possible, you should order the Catholic population to leave the Valleys. However, those who join should be given a safe place along with all the others. Above all, keep the lines of communication between the various Valleys open at all times, even in winter.

When you attack the enemy always advance in two formations, the one in front and the other on the flank, in order not to fall into an ambush. Captains should not jeopardize the lives of their soldiers but should safeguard them, for the men belong to the church of God which must be conserved.

Strong and robust men as you are, do not spare yourselves the labor of building barricades where you think it necessary, and felling trees and digging ditches in the roads so that the enemy may not advance . . .

If you should see that the enemy is about to attack, order your men to eat before daybreak, so that they will have strength for the fight . . . The long rifles should be entrusted to expert hands who can use them effectively; above everything else, avoid shedding innocent blood, lest God be angered against you.

I add this: today the arsenal of the enemy includes bombs, cannons, grenades, and the fire of artillery and cavalry; yet the troops who appear as devils will be turned back by men who fear God and fight for God's cause . . .

I forgot to say: never sound a retreat, for your soldiers will lose heart and the enemy will be encouraged . . .

If, as I think, the enemy will encamp at Villar, take the roofs off the houses and leave the roof flagstones against the walls; the enemy will not be able to camp in the open . . . Do not leave intact any bridge or trestle across the Pellice stream . . .

Do not shoot until the enemy is clearly within the range of your weapon; direct your fire at the officers first . . . If a regiment loses its officers, it is already half defeated. May the Lord give you lucidity of spirit and hold you in awe of God's name. . .

—G. Janavel, "Memorie ed avvisi dati alli Religionari," in the *Bollettino della Società di Studi Valdesi*, n. 49, pp. 46ff.

VII.

EXILE

1. The shadow of Versailles

The year 1685 found the face of Europe greatly changed. In England, the Puritan republic had been replaced by the pro-Catholic Stuarts, while in Holland the self-confident, peaceful and tolerant Calvinist merchants seemed to be absorbed by their commercial affairs. In France, Loius XIV was on his way to becoming an absolute autocrat. His splendor was such that even the old pharaonic title of "son of the sun" could not do him justice, so that he had to be hailed as "Sun King!" The whole continent in reverential awe seemed to look up to Louis and his castle at Versailles, that grandiose theater where he was always the leading actor, parading around among prostrate dignitaries in ceremony which was almost a liturgy in itself.

France under Louis was not made up simply of courtiers, the music of Lully and the comedies of Molière. The vain Sun King commanded a powerful nation, a healthy and growing economy, and the latest in military equipment for his capable soldiers.

Within this vast empire the Protestant churches represented the last dissident element. In signing the Edict of Nantes (1598) Henry IV had given the Huguenots considerable autonomy. But in 1685, after years of legal compromises and violent pressure on the part of the infamous royal troops, the Edict was revoked. The Reformed religion was legally cancelled; henceforth France was to have but "one law, one faith, one king."

In defiance of the king's decree requiring all citizens to remain in the country, French Protestants took the path of exile by the hundreds of thousands, becoming refugees in Protestant Holland, Germany, and England. With them went their wealth, their remarkable technical skills and advanced education, their high culture and an unquenchable passion against Catholic rule.

Quite naturally the revocation decree impacted those territories east of the Alps along the Chisone and in the Val Pragelato. In the first half of the seventeenth century Val Pragelato had been entirely Protestant. On one occasion, in 1629, the Archbishop of Turin had ordered a search of the area in the hope of finding a single Catholic family. There was not one. The French sought to "reconquer" the area by sending in Jesuit missionaries in 1659. By the time of the revocation of the Edict of Nantes Reformed worship was completely outlawed, all but three Protestant churches were levelled, and even those three were consecrated as Catholic churches. Following the lead of their French counterparts, a number of Reformed families and their pastors became exiles in Germany.

2. The January edict

Understandably there was growing alarm in the Valleys at the beginning of 1686. In January the young Duke Vittorio Amedeo II, yielding to his uncle, Louis XIV, issued a decree which paralleled in Savoy Louis' action in revoking the Edict of Nantes. It was not long before pastors were expelled, Waldensian worship forbidden, and Catholic baptism ordered for all children. The fate of the mountain communities appeared to be sealed.

Remembering their past experiences, the Waldensians sought to gain time through affirming their loyalty to the duke and defending their rights based on the agreements signed at Cavour. Meanwhile they sought the intervention of the European Protestant powers.

Waldensian pastors, on the whole, viewed the situation as hopeless. Their reluctant counsel was for the Waldensian people to follow the Huguenot example and become a refugee community in foreign lands. But the pastors were opposed by some of their own people, stalwart resisters who felt that to abandon their homeland was to betray all that their communities had stood for in the past. Already some of the latter were organizing armed bands to begin guerrilla warfare.

A few weeks of quiet followed; as the duke's edict had directed, church services were suspended. But on March 6, in an act of open defiance, Waldensian worship was resumed in the churches and children were baptized. This did not make any easier the task of the

Swiss delegates who had come to Turin to intervene for the Waldensians, though after days of cooling their heels in the antechambers of the duke's court the delegates finally obtained permission to meet with the Waldensians. That meeting proved to be a tumultuous affair, with the Swiss insisting that the only course open was that of exile, an exile not foreseen in the edict and one which would have to be sought through negotiation.

The French, meanwhile, were impatient. Marshal Catinat had his orders, and in Pinerolo he ostentatiously paraded his troops as a warning to the Savoy court that it should immediately carry out the edict or he and his battalions would move in.

The last act of the drama was played out on March 12 at a meeting of the Valleys folk at Roccapiatta. The Swiss offers were generally supported by the pastors, who pointed to the unyielding facts: the silence of most of Protestant Europe, and the overwhelming force of Catinat's army ready to strike. The only other option was armed resistance. Passions were strong, but in the end, in deference to the women and children, those who advocated resistance gave in. Exile was affirmed for those who would elect it.

The assembly at Roccapiatta was notable in that Henri Arnaud, the militant pastor whose role in Waldensian history was to be so important in years ahead, emerged to play a leading part. Of French Dauphiné origin, like so many of his fellow pastors, Arnaud had prepared for the ministry by studies in Switzerland and in Holland. Recently he had had contacts with the Huguenot world, where perhaps he had received fresh inspiration. It was after his passionate plea that the assembly decided to opt for armed resistance. His arguments doubtless were based upon an appeal to Waldensian tradition and to the biblical promises.

Many Huguenots, and especially the exiles, nourished the hope that by miraculous intervention God would bring wrath down upon the oppressors. Not only the firebrands among French preachers, but also sober pastors readily identified the beast in the Book of Revelation with King Louis XIV. He who persecuted the saints would certainly be overthrown. Even the time when this would happen was calculated (from the mysterious "numbers" in Revelation) as falling in the year 1686. In the mind of Arnaud, victory would come after only a few weeks of Waldensian resistance against the beast.

Before leaving the area, the Swiss ambassadors tried in vain to reason with Arnaud and his men of apocalyptic vision. Nor were

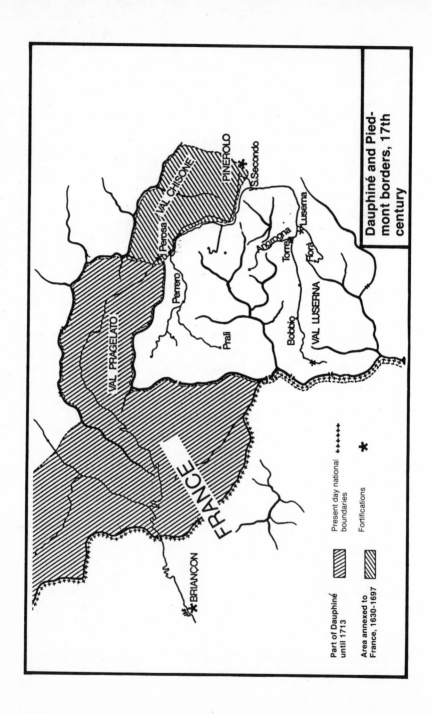

Dauphiné and Piedmont borders, 17th century

Present day national boundaries

Fortifications

Part of Dauphiné until 1713

Area annexed to France, 1630-1697

FRANCE

BRIANÇON

VAL PRAGELATO

VAL CHISONE

Perosa

Perrero

Prali

PINEROLO

S.Secondo

Angrogna

Torre

Bobbio

Fora

S.Luserna

VAL LUSERNA

they successful in persuading the duke for postponement of enforcement of the edict. With clear heads, the Waldensians held a last service on March 21, awaiting the end.

3. Three days with destiny

The combined French-Savoyard *blitzkrieg* against the hapless Waldensians lasted only three days. A pincer movement executed by Marshal Catinat and Gabriel of Savoy closed off access to the high ground and destroyed the Waldensians' improvised lines of defense. Hourly, it seemed, the smoke from the fires signalled the advance of the French and Piemontese troops. One by one the traditional strongholds of heroic Waldensian resistance and victories fell to the conquering armies, to become sites of indiscriminate slaughter.

At the head of a Reformed people in flight there was no longer a Lentolo, a Léger or a Janavel, only the village functionary, Forneron, frantically waving his white flag and seeking an audience for honorable surrender.

May 3 it was all but over. Long columns of prisoners were lined up in the Valleys and on the heights under an incessant rain. The victors began a systematic search of the woods and caves. The last to resist were hurled down ravines or hanged from the trees. At the Grande Guglia the Waldensian flag waved for a few days longer, but on May 7 even this last stronghold, which had resisted down to the last man, was taken.

The countryside was now formally re-Catholicized, even if it had been reduced to a wilderness like the Huguenot villages of Louis XIV's France. Of some 14,000 persons thought to have made up the Waldensian community before the onslaught, more than 2,000 perished, 8,500 were imprisoned in Piedmont, and the rest survived thanks only to the renunciation of their faith, an act which was more formal than substantive.

4. The "unconquerables"

After the troops had withdrawn, a small group of survivors began to come out into the open to reorganize themselves. There were attacks at night, hand-to-hand fighting, and plundering — the tactics of Janavel's guerrillas. Still remembered as "unconquerables," they did indeed constitute a thorny "law and order" problem during the summer.

131

The Savoyard answer to the partisans was a typically prudent one — behind-the-scenes mediation through the Swiss. As a result, the partisans were granted expatriation, their families were liberated, and a pledge of safety for the people taken hostage was given. By autumn this chapter was closed.

What the "unconquerables" left behind was a veritable wilderness — farmhouses destroyed, vines uprooted, trees cut down everywhere. The young duke and his courtiers saw in this ravaged earth the fulfillment of a dream. Having at long last rid themselves of the plague of the Reformed people, the wilderness would now blossom and become a garden of Catholic faith and culture.

This dream proved to be illusory. In spite of the combined efforts of the notaries and ducal officials, the best Waldensian land in the Valleys fell into the hands of rich Savoyards with plenty of capital, while the poor Catholic farmers could purchase only by going into debt to the state.

The duke's plan of repopulating the countryside with solid Catholic citizens proved to be equally problematic. There was always the disturbance caused by some fugitive Waldensian intent on returning to what had once been his home. The re-Catholicized families' trustworthiness was a question. The new Savoyard immigrants, having no roots in the Valleys, turned out to be drifters, accepting ducal subsidies and then disappearing into the night. After a year of determined effort the newly-settled did not number more than a thousand.

Despite the special and lavish attention that the Savoyard court paid to the area, sending in missionaries, creating new parishes and building new churches, this "final victory" of the Italian Counter-Reformation remained a disaster, for it had countenanced the destruction of a people.

5. From prison to exile

What of the Waldensian prisoners? After a few days in the round-up centers, they were marched off to Turin and to 14 other detention sites. For the most part these were military fortresses, prisons, and old castles, where the Waldensians were denied food and water and even straw for lying upon. Decimated by sickness and cold, they also had to endure almost constant pressure by the priests who promised freedom if they would renounce their faith and become Catholics. The pastors and their families, with some community leaders, were kept in special prisons, badgered day and night in an effort to break their will. As in Calabria a century before, every able-bodied man was soon up for sale as an oarsman in the royal galleys. Two thousand men were packed off to Venice, while others were sent to France. The records of the time tell the whole ghastly story: among a Waldensian contingent of 1,400 in the Piedmont dungeon at Carmagnola, only 400 survived after a few months; a group of 1,000 in another prison at Trino was reduced to a mere 46.

The Swiss cantons, meanwhile, once again set their diplomacy in motion for the cause of their Reformed friends. The first appeal made by the Diet of Baden was ignored. It was actually only after repeated and urgent requests that the court in Turin finally consented to look at the question of the prisoners.

There was only one way out and that was exile. The duke still hesitated, however, for economic and political reasons. It must be added that, in spite of their suffering, not all of the Waldensians wished to emigrate, hoping against hope for a miracle, some quite unforeseen change in the political situation.

In September the Swiss Canton of Aarau delegated Gaspar and Bernard de Muralt as its envoys for negotiations at the Savoyard court. By October the two brothers were moving well towards an agreement, complete with logistical preparations. But it was only in January of 1687, exactly a year after the edict which led to the Waldensians' imprisonment, that the duke gave his permission for an organized departure of those who wished to leave.

Even so, the duke insisted upon a proviso forbidding settlement of exiles in the Swiss cantons bordering on the duchy, specifying that the Waldensians be sent as far north as possible, to the Protestant provinces of Germany. Nor did he permit the pastors to be included in the exodus, keeping them hostage in Turin. As for those who renounced their faith and turned Catholic, they were sent to the duke's lands in the Vercelli area.

Thus was opened one of the most painful pages in Waldensian history, the long march of those hundreds of women, old people and children just out of prison, crossing the Susa Valley, Moncenisio and Savoy in the dead of winter. These were not warriors, but human spectres, moving northward toward freedom.

The first of 13 contingents left on January 17; the last group to reach Geneva arrived on March 10. Of 2,700 Waldesnians who began the trek, 2,490 actually made it to Geneva. Among those who died on the way was a whole group from Fossano, caught in a blizzard on Moncenisio. Others were simply lost, including children kidnapped to be raised as Catholics.

The Swiss who accompanied the march as guardians were tireless and methodical, encouraging the bewildered and weak, fending off as best they could the kidnappers, protesting vigorously to the Savoyard authorities whenever there were violations along the way. It must be acknowledged that the ducal officials who were charged with the transfer of this mass of refugees proved to be good Savoyard Catholics with a heart. They performed their duties faithfully and humanely, remembering that after all this long calvary was composed of human beings. How different from the brutal French.

Upon reaching the outskirts of Geneva, the Savoyards were set upon nonetheless by the angry Geneva folk, covered with insults and abusive language, and accused of every sort of abomination. Even more bewildering to the Savoyard guards must have been what they saw upon actually entering the city. Here was the whole population lined up under the leadership of the city council — plus the entire core of pastors in black robes. The 46 survivors from the prison of Trino were greeted by people almost on their knees, and the multitudes vied with each other for the sick and dying, embracing the tattered exiles as if they were sacred relics.

Perhaps by this time the astonished officers of the duke had begun to realize that the tumultuous demonstration was not a mere gesture of sympathy. These were Protestants receiving their very own martyrs. An entire world stretching from Scotland to Brandenburg to Geneva was represented there, one which for years had been smoldering in silent indignation and which now was exploding.

With the passing of the last column across the bridge, a phase of the five centuries of Waldensian history south of the Alps could be considered as coming to a close. The survivors in Piedmont were no longer a community but a sorrowful lot: "Catholicized," they were destined to die among the rice fields of Vercelli; others, wanderers, might try to make their way back to the mountains, while young boys, stolen from their parents, were likely to end up as valets in uniform.

VIII.

REPATRIATION

1. Alliances in search of new Europe

The Swiss, although they had saved the Waldensian refugees from death, were unable to persuade the survivors to settle down. Time after time the impatient exiles refused to cooperate with efforts to place them in the interior of the country, preferring to subsist in makeshift settlements near the frontier. Like refugee communities everywhere and at all times, the little Waldensian community was full of tensions between the merely nostalgic and the activists who vowed they would never give up hope of return. The women toiled so as to survive while the men clustered in taverns in the evenings, recalling the resistance of years gone by. The Waldensians were but a drop in the great human river of Protestant exiles in this period. A swollen stream of rejected European peoples moved ever northward in search of lands, homes and peace.

Brutal experience gave exiled Huguenots and Waldensians an understanding that most of Protestant Europe could as yet only dimly perceive — that the imperialism of Louis XIV would surely reduce the continent to whipped galley-slaves, bent over and chained to their oars. The community of exiles, in Holland as well as in Switzerland, seething with passion, dreamed of one anxiously-awaited day, that of victory over the beast of Versailles. Waldensians shared this dream, but somewhat more modestly, hoping for a return to their mountains no matter what.

In July of 1687 a first attempt to return ended in failure, as did a second a little later. At this point the worried Swiss exacted from their charges a declaration of submission to their authority and a pledge that the refugees would break up their camps near the border with Savoy. Hopes for repatriation having vanished, the few hundred remaining Waldensians had no alternative but to accept the offer of integration with Huguenot colonies in Germany.

This was the time, in the years immediately after the revocation of the Edict of Nantes, that Louis XIV's imperial power reached its apex in his own country and across Europe. The continent seemed headed for domination by a French dictator and his Jesuit advisors. The Protestant Europe which still existed could no longer offer a viable alternative form of civilization: it had become a collection of petty interests. The Low Countries, which had resisted the French battalions, had given up, England was moving towards Catholicism and Germany was divided.

But it was also in these very years that the formidable French machine showed some signs of infirmity. The myth of the invincible Sun King gradually lost its fascination and Europe began to say No. New alliances were in the making. A foment in public opinion consolidated into a definite anti-French movement, fed by indignation at the scandal of the revocation of the Edict of Nantes and by the subsequent massacre of the Huguenots.

When in 1688 revolution broke out in England, bringing William of Orange to succeed James II on the throne, the anti-French movement had sufficiently matured to make way for this Anglo-Dutch sovereign who proposed a radical change of direction.

William of Orange — like his forebearer, William the Silent, and like Coligny and Cromwell — belonged to that company of Protestant politicians whose first aim was not to achieve a balance of power or national triumph but to be true to an idea. In his eyes Louis XIV personified the type of imperialism which would snuff out political freedom in Holland and England and hasten the death of the Protestant world.

It is all the more remarkable that this tense and somewhat sickly nobleman should have been able to translate European indignation into effective political commitment, restraining France by weaving a network of new alliances through persuasion and well-placed funds. While Frederick William of Brandenburg planned "colonies of refuge," William was getting ready for intervention and real liberation.

The Waldensian story once again was tied to events in Europe as a whole, and in particular, this time, to action by the two great Protestant powers of England and Holland.

William knew that one of the weak spots on the European political map was Piedmont. His emissaries, accordingly, were not slow to contact the Waldensians with a project to mount a military expedition which would open a front for guerrilla war behind Catinat.

The expeditionary corps, 60 percent Waldensian, was organized in the minutest detail, providing for about 1,000 men, including officers, doctors, and chaplains. Preparations were made in absolute secrecy, awaiting the order to undertake operations, which came in the middle of August.

2. The long march

Thus began the epic journey by a Protestant commando force which has come to be known as the "Glorious Return," and which is one of the best-known episodes in all Waldensian history. On the night of August 17, 1689, the corps ferried across Lake Geneva to the village of Yvoire. From there they proceeded by forced marches, climbing hills and scaling mountains, across the 130 miles which separated them from the Waldensian Valleys.

Preceded and followed by hostages taken in the villages along the way so as to avert attacks, the commando column moved forward relentlessly, leaving the exhausted and wounded behind. The surprise element and sheer daring precluded an encounter with regular Savoyard troops. The only clash with French soldiers was at Salbertrand, in the Susa Valley, on the night of September 23. In spite of heavy losses the Waldensians moved on victoriously. Seeing this "foreign legion" descending upon them, the Catholic people in the Valleys abandoned their homes and took flight toward the plains to the east. The Germanasca Valley was freed without a struggle.

At Prali it was necessary to regroup and count losses. Casualties numbered 30 percent. The redoubtable pastor, Henri Arnaud, seized the occasion of the liberation of the former Waldensian church from the Catholics to preach on a text from Psalm 129. His point was that the Waldensians had reclaimed this Protestant outpost so that preaching of the gospel might once more go forward in Catholic Piedmont. Theirs was not a return of the homesick but of soldiers marching to God's drumbeat. One of the "returned" echoed as much in his diary:

> ... It is not possible to recount all that we suffered in the mountains; our zeal was rekindled by the thought of returning to our homeland, there to reestablish the rule of Jesus Christ and destroy that of the idols and the anti-Christ.

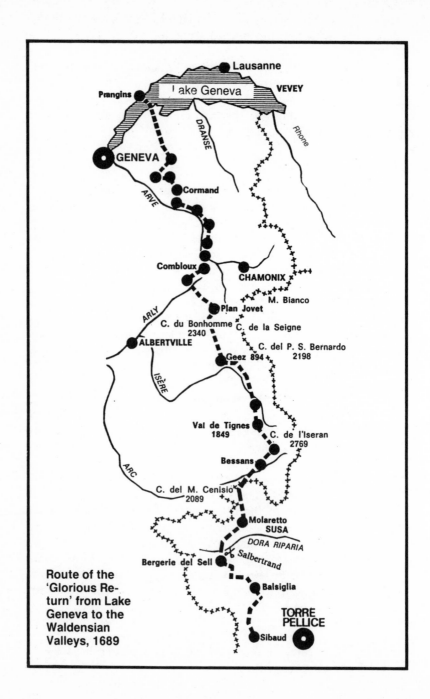

Route of the 'Glorious Return' from Lake Geneva to the Waldensian Valleys, 1689

This same determination was reaffirmed on the heights of Bobbio, at Sibaud, during the course of an assembly when a solemn covenant was made.

Here was a Protestant mini-army, carrying out its mission in the great anti-French battle. Outwardly, the soldiers were identified by orange ribbons on their caps and jackets, the color of the House of Orange, leader of the anti-French coalition. The exchange of vows between officers and men in this little army, however, was far from routine. In the context of the Protestant struggle, it was the intentional expression of the vocational solidarity which to this day characterizes Waldensian spirituality.

It was not by chance that of two texts which were the guiding lights of the undertaking, one was the Bible and the other the manual by Janavel. Militarily, this was an insurrectionist force, while on the ideological plane, it was an expedition with hearts fixed upon the vision that war was not to conquer land so much as to open the way for a new social purpose.

"Liquidate the Waldensians immediately!" was the cry from Catinat. Things did not turn out as he ordered, however, and by winter the guerrilla force was well established in Piedmont. Until the spring it was necessary to leave the Waldensian bands in their mountain trenches near the village of Balziglia in Val Germanasca.

3. The longest day

Months of cold, solitude and guerrilla raids took their toll; the Huguenot commander himself abandoned the undertaking. There were only 300 Waldensians who remained and even they were deprived of means of escape. At this point Henri Arnaud took over. He had already played a decisive role in organizing the expedition, but now he became both the religious and military leader of the little Waldensian band, as Janavel had been in 1665.

In a sense, these men symbolized two aspects of seventeenth century Waldensian spirituality; Janavel, the farmer, rooted in the soil; Arnaud, the cosmopolitan intellectual. Janavel recalled the Puritan armies engaged in battle for the Lord, while Arnaud was at home in the Anglo-Dutch world of the burghers and merchants, the world of Cromwell and of William III.

Arnaud was quite a remarkable figure. Not without pride and frequently authoritarian, he nonetheless accomplished his task, organizing his 300 men while maintaining contact with the Protestant world. If this little band of desperate men now buried under the snow, suffering from hunger and anxiety, was not turned into a band of plunderers, but grew in their sense of vocation as a true Reformed community, it was due to Arnaud and his hammer-like preaching, where there was no thought of uncertainty or of surrender. Everything was focused on the coming battle in the spring.

The fateful day arrived on May 2. Four thousand French troops under the command of the Marquis de Feuquière lined up along the valley in full battle array. On the heights above were 300 men, in rags, manning their trenches. In the pre-dawn silence the Waldensians held their last service. The hymn heard down in the valley had no churchy ring to it: it was the martial beat of Psalm 68, a Reformed hymn set to the music of Goudimel:

> Arise, O God, scatter your enemies:
> let them also that hate you flee before you.
> As smoke is driven away, so drive them away:
> as wax melts before the fire, so let the wicked perish.

The first assault of the French took place in a blinding snow storm among the trees of an overhanging slope. After a day of fierce fighting it was repulsed. Once again the Marquis attacked, this time having first commanded the militia to push his cannons up the steep inclines so that his artillery could get at the Waldensian defenses. After the artillery barrage the Balziglia trenches had to be abandoned, and the last survivors gathered on a buttress awaiting their death. Then the totally unexpected happened. During the night, while the attackers were tending the surrounding bivouac fires, a deep fog descended on the whole area, allowing the Waldensians to escape. Confident of his victory, de Feuquière had already dispatched word to Paris announcing the capture of the "bandits." Instead, the survivors had escaped and were out of reach.

Still another event — equally unforeseen but of far greater significance — took place just several days later. The unpredictable Vittorio Amedeo II broke his alliance with France and joined forces with England and Austria.

The Waldensians were saved! An order went out to free the prisoners and pastors in Piedmont. Exiles returned home from Germany and Switzerland. Around the surviving nucleus of the 300 soldiers the community could begin rebuilding. Decimated and exhausted, the Waldensian remnant had been miraculously saved.

With Piedmont's move into the camp of the English, a surprising new day dawned. His eastern flank no longer exposed, the duke could now deploy his troops along the Alps to keep a watchful eye on the French. There followed a marked change in the political and cultural picture. Vittorio Amedeo now took his cue from Parliament in London rather than from the castle in Versailles. The impact of the presence of English diplomats was so great that at Lord Galloway's headquarters in Avigliana a synod of the Reformed churches in Piedmont could be held, with six ministers and 24 elders present. A Protestant church was organized in Turin itself.

Quite naturally, "the Waldensian question" became a priority concern. In 1694 the duke was compelled by his new allies to issue an Edict of Toleration which guaranteed the right of the Waldensians to exist on their lands.

17. THE COVENANT OF SIBAUD (1689)

God, by his grace, having brought us happily back to the land of our forebears, to reestablish there the pure service of our holy religion, in continuation of and for accomplishment of the great enterprise which this great God of armies has hitherto carried on in our favor:

We pastors, captains, and other officers, swear and promise before God, and on the life of our souls, to keep union and order among ourselves and not to disunite ourselves from one another, while God shall preserve us in life, even if we should be reduced to three or four in number . . .

And we soldiers promise and swear this day before God to obey the orders of our officers, and to continue faithful to them, even to the last drop of our blood . . .

And in order that union, which is the soul of all our affairs, may remain always unbroken among us, the officers swear fidelity to the soldiers, and the soldiers to the officers, all together promising to our Lord and Saviour Jesus Christ to rescue, as far as it is possible for us, the dispersed remnants of our people from the yoke which oppresses them, that along with them we may reestablish and maintain Christ's rule, even unto death, observing in good faith this present engagement so long as we shall live.

—Ernesto Comba, *Storia dei Valdesi*, 3rd ed. (Torre Pellice, 1935), pp. 217-218.

Part Three

THE ALPINE GHETTO

(1689-1848)

According to God's promise we wait for new heavens and a new earth in which justice dwells.

—2 Peter 3

In the face of bondage, of pervasive injustice and of defeats visited upon those who seek a better ordering of the world, in the face of this we announce that struggle has purpose, that defeat is not the last word, because God has revealed to us in Jesus Christ a justice which is turning upside-down the way of this world.

—ministerial candidate Daniele Garrone, in his trial sermon before the synod assembly, Italy, 1983

I.

THE GHETTO IS BORN

1. The curtain falls

If the conflict between William III and Louis XIV can be seen as one which pitted the forces of the rising middle class against those of an absolute monarchy, in certain aspects it was also a war of religion — Anglo-Dutch, Protestant merchants against Catholics represented by the French nobility. The defeat of the French, therefore, signaled a major setback for the Counter-Reformation. What the Counter-Reformation had hoped would be a great Catholic offensive was shattered on the cliffs of Dover.

The Peace of Utrecht (1713) brought to a close the wars in which religion and politics had been intimately intertwined. Indeed, in its wake all religious passions seemed to have been spent, so that even if one retained a certain fervor, it was not of the kind to do battle for "the faith." Tolerance became a virtue; human reason assumed a place alongside the Bible as the guide to life.

For our story, this change in European outlook led to far-reaching developments. Piedmont withdrew from the French influence and entered that of England. She had finally turned her back upon medieval Catholic absolutism and had sided with the Protestant mercantile powers. It also meant that the little Waldensian world was now safe at last from military attack from Turin, protected by edicts imposed upon Piedmont by the Protestant powers in the 1690s.

There were, to be sure, some unfavorable consequences for the Valleys folk. In the climate of relaxation following the wars of religion the Waldensian minority in Piedmont was no longer considered to be in the frontline of the battlefield and soon became a half-forgotten enclave, a little Protestant island in an otherwise Catholic land. And when the backs of the Protestant powers were turned, Piedmont saw that she could once again undertake measures which would render the little island insecure. Vittorio Amedeo was able through his "peaceful" campaign to accomplish what he had failed to achieve militarily. His success was to be such that within a relatively few years Protestants were to lose half their territory and 60 percent of their population.

It all began in the Chisone Valley, where the Peace of Ryswick (1697) permitted the duke to reacquire control over the area, including Pinerolo. One of his first acts in the following year was to order the expulsion of all French subjects from his newly annexed lands.

His repressive measures hit not only the historic Waldensian population in the annexed territory, but also the Huguenots who had taken refuge there — altogether some 3,000 persons. Seven out of the 13 pastors were expelled, including Henri Arnaud himself.

The exodus was not a replay of the suffering of 1686, but it was still not without pain. In the uncultivated hills and marshes of Wuerttemberg in Germany, the exiles shared the typical lot of refugees; unfamiliar with local customs and German ways of making a living, they were looked down on by the local population and exploited by the blossoming economy of the principalities. Once again they patiently built up their communities, giving them the names of villages they had left behind in the mountains — Perouse, Gross-Villar, Pinache, etc. They also reorganized their churches, holding firm to the religious and linguistic traditions they had brought with them — a pattern which would continue until the early years of the nineteenth century.

At the head of the exiles was always the towering figure of Arnaud, the remarkable cosmopolitan pastor who committed his organizational skills to the building up of these diaspora communities.

Hardly had the forced exodus from the Chisone been concluded when the Protestants of the Pragelato region to the north suffered a similar fate. In the relative quiet of 1709 the Reformed inhabitants of Val Pragelato petitioned the synod for a union of their churches with those of the Waldensians to the south. They had, after all, the pledge from the duke (from the treaty imposed some years earlier by the Protestant powers) that their services according to Reformed rites would be protected and maintained. Four years later, however, came the treaty of Utrecht. At that time and bowing to French insistence, Vittorio Amedeo reactivated the old restrictions on political and religious freedom for the Pragelato Protestants. By an edict in 1716 the Reformed were forbidden to assemble more than 10 persons in any one place or to visit assemblies in the Waldensian Valleys, and in 1721 a decree announced that every new-born child was to be baptized Catholic. The final blow came in 1730, when the authorities ordained that "all inhabitants in that (Pragelato) Valley shall profess the Catholic religion, and no exercise, public or private, shall be permitted of the pretended Reformed religion."

In spite of initial attempts at resistance, the handwriting on the wall was clear. By the hundreds the Pragelato folk felt compelled to abandon their lands and villages, joining the refugee trek to Germany.

2. The ghetto

Forty years after the "Return" the Waldensian Valleys resembled more than anything else a Jewish ghetto in Europe, where the people lived a segregated and self-sufficient existence on the fringes of the larger society. It was a marginalized world but not an undeveloped one. The Waldensian ghetto may have been typically frail — a single crop failure or flood being enough to upset its delicate economic balance and to threaten starvation — but it had men and women of real spiritual strength.

No doubt strength above all was required to reconstitute their little world. Wars, exiles and deportations had reduced the country-side to a wilderness. There were families to be brought back together, villages to be rebuilt, fields to be reclaimed from neglect. If sheer strength was needed for survival, Reformed faith provided the fountain of inspiration for daily living.

This is not to say that the Waldensians of the mid-eighteenth century were a replica of the Varaglias and the Janavels of earlier times. They were not driven by a desire to build a new civilization nor did they live their faith with the same ethical-political passion as had their forebearers. Modest farmers with much common sense, they tilled their fields methodically, and enjoyed an occasional round of target practice or a game of cards of an evening at the *osteria*. They have since been accused by some nineteenth century romantics of giving inadequate attention to their historic Waldensian faith. It has been said that their piety was all in externals, without warmth, that they were Christians without conviction.

From a spiritual viewpoint the judgement may contain an element of truth, but in historical context it is certainly wide of the mark.

In the Piedmont of Carlo Emanuele III, one was either a Catholic or a "religionist," which is to say, of Reformed religion. What counted was not personal conviction but whether one was enrolled in the Catholic or Reformed world. What was recorded officially at the registrar's office was what mattered.

The little Waldensian ghetto now expressed itself more through its lifestyle or what can be called its "culture" than through its preaching and battles for the faith.

Synods of the time reflect this fact. They did indeed remain the high point in the life of the Waldensian communities, but one reads the records in vain for a meeting of minds on great issues or for a debate of real theological moment. Their concerns were mainly administrative, revealing the daily skills required to keep intact a Protestant culture. The 1745 synod held at San Germano can be taken as an example. The dates are February 24 and 25, and the synod is being held in the presence of the sovereign's magistrate from Pinerolo, one Giacinto Bernardino Castelli. The first order of business is a request by Captain Jean Freyrie, known popularly as "The Feather," who asks to be paid for work he had done on the minister's residence at Maniglia. This is followed by Barthélémy Appia's request for a scholarship for his son so that the latter might pursue his studies in Holland. The pastors and elders are urged to be vigilant in seeing that Sundays be properly observed, and that the ban on Sunday games and festive occasions be maintained. The moderator is reminded of his duty to keep "an accurate record of all papers that concern our church" and the synod underlines its rule that announcements of engagements or the celebration of marriages should not be made on Saturdays. Members are informed that tours of duty for chaplains will henceforth be for only six weeks, that a pastor has been assigned to Angrogna, and that two persons have complained that their family pews have been reassigned. The synod closes by fixing the first Sunday in April as a "day of thanksgiving for the blessing granted to the armies of . . . our sovereign, and a day of fasting to ask blessings on the armed forces of the king and to placate the wrath of heaven for our sins."

All this is surely rather modest for a Christian community, but it was what a church of "religionists" could and should do to survive. Every time the leaders of the little "ghetto church" met to order their affairs the refrain was similar. The record would mention perhaps a dozen pastors, 18 to 20 delegates with familiar names such as Grill or Frasche, elders, and the presence of the local mayors.

It was incumbent upon the pastors not only to provide for religious services, but also to be the leaders of the community as administrators, town counselors, and examples of good conduct.

The pastor in a little mountain village, after having made his rounds during the day and milked his cow in the evening, might very well be found in his study, writing to his acquaintances in Geneva or Leyden. In doing so he was not only responding to a personal need, but was also fulfilling a duty to his people by exchanging those ideas which were necessary for the renewal and survival of the Waldensian culture.

It was quite natural in this period that the *Tavola*, the Executive Board of the church, composed of the moderator and two other pastors, should assume an ever increasing importance; it is they who administered financial aid, saw to the proper functioning of the schools, ruled on the orthodoxy of the preachers, kept in touch with the young men who were pursuing studies abroad, and maintained communication with the other churches in Europe.

These were not entirely static times — far from it. If the order of the day was now for standing their ground, the ghetto people still had to be as alert and watchful as in the years of the wars of religion. After all, the Italian world of salons, learned abbots and masses of people in misery was irreconcilable with that of the mountaineers, say, of Bobbio, or the likes of a Pastor Peyran. The Kingdom of Sardinia was based on a system of servile obedience, while the Waldensian ghetto was founded on men and women schooled in personal responsibility.

Insofar as the struggle was a cultural one, the Waldensians had a significant resource in their books, their schools and scholarships provided by Protestant friends abroad. Behind Pomaretto and Prarostino, so to speak, stood London, Amsterdam, and Geneva.

Perhaps this bloodless contest between two unequal forces was most like a game of chess. The Savoyard court aimed at victory, "checkmate" so to say, which would cause the Waldensians to surrender. But, surprisingly enough, the ghetto folk were never cornered for long, so that the game went on and on. We cite some of the actions in a single generation.

In 1730 Turin's attack was on so-called "legal" grounds. All the edicts of previous times were codified in a single decree aimed at paralyzing any Waldensian mobility in a net of suffocating restrictions. After five years of endurance, however, the Huguenot communities in Holland came to the rescue, raising funds for

149

strengthening and enlarging existing Waldensian popular schooling. As one wag said, even if Savoyard law restricted attendance at a Waldensian funeral to six persons, at least those six would know how to read.

In 1739 "The Royal Society for loans . . . to benefit Catholics or converts to Catholicism in the mixed valleys" was instituted with the aim of purchasing land owned by Waldensians. In 1743 the Savoyard authorities directed the construction at Pinerolo of a large building for keeping Waldensian boys and girls who could be enticed at the "age of discretion" (14 for boys, 12 for girls) into Catholic surroundings. One can imagine the abuses this led to. In 1748 the diocese of Pinerolo was created and straightaway it was authorized to build new Catholic churches in each Waldensian locality.

To this was added the rule that all towns should have a Catholic mayor and a Catholic town council, even if there were only one or two token Catholics implanted in any given place. It was a lonely time for such settlers, symbolized by the obedient priest who often said mass without a single lay worshipper present.

A Dutch committee assisted the Waldensians in building a Latin School at the secondary level, so that Waldensian young people could acquire the necessary classical languages to prepare themselves for advanced studies abroad.

3. Farmers and the elite

These ghetto folk then, as now, were farmers, bound to a rocky and mountainous land which required regular terracing if it was to produce any crops. Then, as now, it was frequently necessary for the breadwinner to leave the land for shorter or longer periods of time in order that all of the mouths might be fed. Not a few of these "sons of the bandits" enlisted in the army where they were known by their battle names, such as "La Liberté," "Sans Chagrin," or "La Rose." There they were in their green coats — drummer boys, perhaps, or even quartermasters, but never officers, since they were Protestants. The wars of the century saw them die on the different battlefields in which Savoyard troops were engaged. More often that not, however, they would return home as pensioners, and would be found quietly cultivating their little gardens and passing the long winter evenings with their memories.

There was a certain cadre which became the intelligentsia of the communities — the pastors, the notaries, and a few school teachers.

As in the time of republican Rome, a few families became the elite, by the middle of the century constituting a local bourgeoisie.

The educated young men of this group must have all looked very much alike, in their long black coats and black stockings. Educated at the Latin School, they went off to Holland or to Switzerland for further studies, returning to take up ministry at Prali or Bobbio, often with a foreign wife and her spinet piano, and with many friendly contacts throughout Europe. Other sons similarly endowed might follow academic careers, study law or end up crisscrossing Europe as tutors. These are the types who put their stamp on the Waldensian community and conducted its affairs. Methodical, straightforward, they certainly were not Arnauds or Légers. Life in the ghetto did not so much demand charismatic as efficient leadership. There were a few interesting people, more notable for the singularity of their characters than for their accomplishments.

There was Pastor Brez, for example. Most of his short career was spent in Holland (he died at the age of 35) where he became an avid student of the natural sciences, a correspondent in some of the more important academies of Europe and author of a history of the Waldensians, in which he presented them as a tribe of good "children of nature" who worshipped God in truth and who lived essentially peaceful and serene lives. There was Pastor Rodolfo Peyran, of distinguished lineage, who was several times moderator and who filled stacks of notebooks which he declined to publish for fear of censorship. Popular tradition has it that in his youth he once served as secretary to Voltaire.

Out of this little elite there even emerged a very few who became modestly prosperous landholders and business people. Who could ever have imagined a century before, at the time of the "bandits," that a small group of Waldensians could have managed to establish themselves so successfully and serenely?

True, the glorious Ciabàs church, symbolic of the Reformation battle, by now had lost its roof in a storm and served only as a hay loft; not far away was the fine country residence of the Peyrot family, referred to as "from Holland" because of commercial ties with the Dutch. By the end of the 1700s the image of the Waldensian was no longer that of the itinerant bookseller prepared to die for his books, nor was it that of the "bandits" with Janavel's manual of battle tactics in their jerkins. It was more likely to be old Alberto Peyrot, seated in his easy chair and keeping track of his dynasty of children, in-laws, nieces and nephews who were scattered across Europe, from Leghorn to Edinburgh.

Yet it was this small, silent ghetto of farmers, half-hidden in the narrow-minded and drowsy Piedmont of the time, which represented in Italy the message of the Protestant Reformation. They amounted to just a dozen pastors, some businessmen and modest numbers of simple farmers, but they kept alive a spirit of free inquiry with their critical reading, intellectual curiosity, books, debates, newspapers and discussions. The Protestant Reformation for them stood for at least that much! Only a few may have read Voltaire and the *Encyclopedia* of Diderot, but all in some way breathed the air of modern Europe and none would be taken by surprise with the breaking out of the French Revolution (1789).

II.

THE REVOLUTION

1. Liberty's tree

... The tree of liberty was planted before the old Town Hall today
... in the seventh year of the French Republic and the first year of
Piemontese liberty. May God's grace make us worthy of this
precious temporal and spiritual freedom that our martyred forebearers so greatly longed for.

It takes little to imagine the gleam of joy that lit up Pastor
Peyran's eyes as he entered these words in his parish register at
Pramollo. The world of *L'Ancien Régime*, synonymous with au-
thoritarianism and bigotry, was finished. On the horizon of the little
Waldensian ghetto now beckoned the promise of the Revolution —
Liberté! Egalité! Fraternité! It was a little like leaving behind the
troubled waters of the Cape of Good Hope for a friendly port.

The Waldensian intelligentsia saw the Revolution as simply a
continuation of the talk on liberty already heard for decades in
Europe. To the common folk of the Valleys, however, it meant
something very real. It meant that they could acquire land on the
plain and that their children could be admitted to schools of higher
learning. In short, it was an end to the old segregation.

Piedmont did not seem to grasp what was at stake and was
terrified by the turn of events in France. Waldensians, on the other
hand, hailed the new direction. To become Jacobins meant for them
a clear choice, a decision for the new, for tomorrow, with no regrets.
As moderate Jacobins and still the king's subjects, they would
continue to do their duty honestly so long as the old Vittorio
Amedeo III remained on the throne. They certainly did not turn
their celebrating into a storming of the Bastille, though in the course
of much singing and hilarity something new did happen when
Count Rorengo was made to throw his credentials of nobility into

a bonfire. Thereafter, he was no longer "Don Rorengo," but just citizen Rorengo — like everyone else.

Jacobins they were, even if they were not boisterous and did not dress like French radicals. In the Valleys, the whole population was involved in the revolutionary cause — unlike other parts of Italy where it touched just a few university students, professionals, and here and there someone from the declining elite. It was perfectly logical that the moderator himself, Pietro Geymet, should assume a place in the provisional government at Turin. A portrait of him has been preserved through his family — a kindly and chubby church-man dressed in his sea green morning coat in the midst of those radicals and rationalists, perfectly at ease in his position because he was in support of his people's general political line of many years' standing.

The Waldensian elite — various Geymets, Peyrans, Appias — produced men who were remarkably skilled in the arts of politics and diplomacy. They succeeded in making their case with one seat of power after another — going from Amedeo III to republican France, thence to the Russian occupiers, back again to France, and finally returning once more as subjects of the good old Savoyard sovereign. They accomplished this continual round without com-promising the interests of their people and all the while managing to avoid gratuitous exploits or violent repression. With Napoleon they recalled the "Return;" with Suvaroff, the persecutions. Ap-pealing to the rule of reason or to historical continuity, to the integrity of tradition or to their record of loyalty, they played their cards wisely. The political events in these years can be read as proof of a formidable sense of solidarity born out of life in the ghetto and its immense inner strength.

2. The Napoleonic interlude

The French Revolution led to the Napoleonic Empire (1804-1815), and in that context the ghetto disappeared for good, both as a legal entity and as a social reality. New laws recognized the right of all citizens to profess the religion of their choice, freely and without discrimination. Lands which for centuries Waldensians had culti-vated only as hired hands could now be bought. Valleys merchants could at last think of expanding their commerce. Pastor Peyran could publish his notes without censorship. Pastor Geymet could be named a government functionary in Pinerolo!

The transformation was taking place in the full light of day, not as a gift from a sovereign, but as a right. The infamous "home for Waldensian children" was closed, and with it the pervading fear that children would be kidnapped and brought up as Catholics. Most significant of all, a Waldensian church was built in San Giovanni, the first outside the ghetto, a monument to redress the centuries of religious repression.

This was the brighter side. The Waldensians soon discovered, however, that the same French eagle which had wings for protection also possessed sharp claws to keep everything in Europe under strict control. It was not long before they read of an astounding decree: Paris had ordered the full integration of the Waldensian Church into that of French Protestantism. The Waldensian synod had to disappear, along with the Board and the office of moderator. The structure and ordered discipline so painstakingly worked out over the centuries as instruments of survival and identity were abolished. Now the Waldensians were to be but one minute corner within the French church.

That was not all. Since the Waldensians were now absorbed into French Protestantism, the English crown suspended its customary financial aid. How, then, were the pastors and teachers to be supported? The answer came from France with characteristic decisiveness. To begin with, all of those Catholic churches and related properties located in places where there were really no Catholic faithful were to be turned over to the Waldensians.

This was followed by a decree that all Waldensian "clergy" (to use the Napoleonic terminology) were to receive stipends from the state. Within a few short years the Valleys pastors thus passed from being outcast heretics to paid state functionaries.

Still more far-reaching was the cultural transformation in the Waldensian communities. Ghetto life and the issue of "religion," with all the isolation and oppression, had provided the people with a sense of identity and strong purpose. Now, one was no longer a "religionist" (a clear, if pejorative, distinction) but one among many "citizens." To be "Waldensian" was no longer a social or countercultural statement, but just a private matter.

The new climate of freedom and equality suited the leading Waldensian families; it often meant that they could mix with their peers in the larger Piemontese society, send their children to school and follow careers of their own choosing. The Waldensian mountain folk followed rather more cautiously.

Actually, the Napoleonic period was too brief to leave any lasting impact on Waldensian life other than that of strengthening views on the separation of church and state. It would be interesting to speculate as to what might have happened if the Waldensians indeed had been swallowed up indefinitely in French Protestantism. But the Waldensians were not destined to be a people merely of common sense and reason. The Age of Enlightenment was to give way (in the 1830s) to a new awakening in the form of an evangelical revival. In a sense, the varied experiences that the church went through in passing from ghetto to revolution and thence to liberation may have prepared their hearts for the Great Revival.

There is one other aspect of the brief Napoleonic era which must be noted. Behind the ghetto had been the protecting hand of the Protestant powers, with their friendly embassies and regular financial aid. After liberation the Valleys folk had to stand on their own.

Colonel Marauda's militia and Pastor Geymet at his functionary's desk were examples of this new state of affairs. Napoleon would treat the Waldensian areas as an appendix to France, annexing them to the Dauphiné, but the Waldensians could not forget that the Piedmont plain lay open before them.

18. THE TREE OF LIBERTY (1800)

Citizens and Friends:
The ceremony in which we have just participated seems like a wonderful dream, doesn't it? Who would have dared to hope for it?

... We have had to suffer the constant nightmare of being wiped out by a horde of fanatics, driven by an eternal hatred for the peaceful inhabitants of these valleys for their way of praying and adoring God, and driven by the hope of pillaging our homes, egged on by the cruellest and vilest aristocracy that has ever been seen ...

My friends, I have recalled this horrible situation with the sole aim of making you even more aware that the protection which Heaven has granted us has been something very particular; our salvation is not the work of any people, who are mere instruments of the One whose hands hold the destiny of all nations. Citizens, I wish to remind you of the dangerous and terrible days we have come through for the sole aim of encouraging you to celebrate this day with thankfulness to the Supreme Being.

May this moment never be cancelled from the annals of Waldensian history and even less from the heart of every good Waldensian; let us transmit this memory down to our descendants, because we know that the unexpected happiness which we enjoy today is due to the One without whose knowledge not even one hair of our heads shall fall; after this One our thanks go to the French nation, and to the immortal Bonaparte and his comrades-in-arms.

Waldensians, may our virtues make us worthy of the august title of republicans which from now on we bear, because a republican by definition must be the most honest of people; this thought has won over many hearts to the cause of freedom.

Joyful Waldensians, may you be truly aware of the dimensions of your happiness . . . Yes, citizens, you are free; from now on it will no longer be necessary to grovel, trembling before those in power, who threatened and insulted you, not in the name of the law, but on the account of a whim of an insolent authority, who never knew his subjects. You will have none but the law above you and if you keep within its precepts, you will be able freely to present yourself before a magistrate, whatever his position, or before an officer, whatever his rank, for this is one of the advantages that this joyful revolution offers us.

Citizens, every time we look at this tree, may we remember our responsibility as free people. Will we ever be able to discharge in full our responsibility? If so, our happiness will overflow . . .Waldensians, in gratitude to those who have set us free, let us raise a salute: Long live the Republic!

—"Speech of Citizen Paolo Appia on the occasion of the second Tree of Liberty Celebration in Torre," in *Bollettino della Società di Studi Valdesi,* n. 62 (1934), p. 75.

III.

RESTORATION

1. Back to 1730?

When in 1815 the Napoleonic era had ended and Waldensian delegates were ushered into the Royal Palace at Turin to pay their respects to the King of Sardinia, recently returned from exile and placed on the throne, they must have thought they were dreaming. In the same hall where they had talked with the unpredictable Suvaroff and the authoritarian Bonaparte they were presented to a little dandy of a man in royal attire, topped by a white wig, pointing with delight to the beautiful way his wife had mended his trousers! Restoration — Piedmont style — had replaced the Revolution! It was as if years had been cancelled in a single wink of the eye. This was not even 1790 — it was more like 1730!

Unhappily, the dream was all too real. Before long, the notorious "home for Waldensian children" at Pinerolo once more opened its doors, a prohibition on the importing and printing of Bibles was again in force and there were to be no new Waldensian schools. Pastor Alexis Muston, prosecuted for having written a dissertation on the Waldensians without the approval of the censor, had to flee to France. Most typical of all was what befell the fine new church at San Giovanni. While spared from the hands of a wrecking crew, it was nevertheless ordered to be hidden behind a high barricade so as not to offend the eyes of Catholics as they went to mass.

The whole Waldensian community, in fact, was supposed to assume a role similar to that of their church in San Giovanni — hidden, out of sight, so as not to cause offense, a people who should not really exist in a Catholic country like the Kingdom of Sardinia.

So it remained for the Waldensians to undertake their own kind of restoration — to reestablish relations with the Protestant powers, to seek scholarships abroad for their children, to import Bibles by surreptitious means, and to take up once more the old struggle against a stifling bureaucracy. The synod of 1823 was decisive in this regard. The new regulations and Discipline transformed the Waldensian ghetto of the eighteenth century into a small but well-organized republic, complete with precise directions regarding pastors and teachers, and the conduct of worship. In this way the Waldensian Church prepared itself to resist clerical assault for decades, if need be.

Of course it was only Europe's old conservatives who harbored the illusion that the continent could return to the age of wigs and minuets. The young men who had fought against Napoleon at Leipzig were looking ahead; they had read Fichte rather than Voltaire. Convinced romantics, they held that the heart speaks more truly than the mind.

Albeit slowly, Italy was also beginning to feel the winds of change. The curtain of silence which throughout the eighteenth century had isolated her from Europe could not much longer keep out the new ideas or forbid the circulation of new books, often of Protestant inspiration. Furthermore, some Protestant families from northern Europe, attracted either by the climate or by business opportunities, began to settle in the cities. They were not numerous, but the significance of this migration was not lost on the Waldensians, who knew that after the foreigners had settled into their fine town houses and started up their factories, they would begin speaking of chapels that should be built and of chaplains to serve them.

2. A bishop's challenge

These years also saw the emergence of a new climate in Piemontese Catholicism — reactionary, certainly, but dynamic and rich in piety. This applied particularly to the new bishop in the Diocese of Pinerolo, Andrea Charvaz, a man of real stature. Like his predecessors, he kept the Waldensian minority in check, trying at the same time to win it back into the Catholic fold. He left no legal stone unturned in his efforts to repress Waldensian liberties. At one point, with the backing of King Carlo Alberto, he arranged to install Mauritian missionaries in Torre Pellice itself, turning the village Catholic church into a grandiose complex, complete with schools.

A few years later Charvaz initiated a similar program in Luserna San Giovanni.

But the bishop will be remembered mostly for the attack he made in his writing and speaking on the traditional Waldensian claim to be in direct line from the apostles themselves. Laying hold of some solid historical research, the bishop called this cornerstone of Waldensian apologetics nonsense, declaring that the Waldensian movement was of relatively recent origin. It was, he said, simply a deviation from Catholicism which needed only to be corrected and returned to the true Church. Although he was wrong theologically, historically speaking he was right — though the Waldensians stoutly refused to admit it.

3. Friendly pilgrims and diplomats

It was, indeed, the myth of the Waldensian experience running uncontaminated from apostolic times which generated such an irresistible fascination among a new generation of European Protestants, and most of all, the English. World travelers, armed with their diaries and sketch books, they were often drawn to the Valleys to confirm their vision of a pristine enclave which had preserved a pure and authentic faith. Of a number of such friendly visitors who might well merit a full portrait — the Sims', Allens, Gillys and Plenderleaths — we can recall here briefly only Allen and Gilly as two examples of a wider company.

Restless nobleman, William Allen was a Quaker and thus a pacifist and readily available to those in need. He first visited the Waldensian Valleys during an interlude in the Congress of the Holy Alliance which he was attending in 1821 at Verona. Overcome with compassion as he observed the quiet dignity of the pastors and the poverty of the people, he returned to Verona to throw the meeting into confusion by his revelations, so much so that his friend Czar Alexander I was moved to give a large sum of money for the construction of a hospital at Torre Pellice — to the great embarrassment of the ambassador from the Kingdom of Sardinia.

The Reverend W. Stephen Gilly was a high church Anglican, an erudite canon and friend of the Archbishop of Canterbury. When he set off for the continent to find traces of Valdesius' disciples he quite naturally thought at first he would find them in Lyon. In that city there wasn't even a shadow of a Waldensian; someone advised him to go across the Alps. As a result of his discoveries in this and other visits he was eventually to write an account of the Valleys people, always with a deep attachment to that little Protestant world so different from his own. The book, dedicated to George IV, met with considerable success. As an Anglican, Gilly was ever on the lookout for evidence of apostolic succession, so that the chronicle he set down was that of a fragment of true primitive Christianity which had been preserved in the Valleys. He also was concerned for the practical needs of the church, and Waldensians owe to him the founding of the *collegio* (junior college) in Torre Pellice. That institution was destined to be the center of Waldensian culture for more than a century.

This was also a time of renewed activity on the diplomatic front in Turin. For years Waldensians had been able to count unfailingly on English and Dutch interventions on their behalf. Now another Protestant power began to make its influence felt. The Prussian ambassador, Count Waldburg Truchsess, was not only an efficient diplomat who diligently carried out the policy of the government of Berlin in favor of the Waldensians, but also a man of faith and culture, a special friend of the Valleys. Whether it was gathering help for the construction of the church at Pomaretto, getting hymnals out of customs at the frontier, or demanding that a kidnapped Waldensian child be returned to its mother, he was always on hand to offer help.

All told, the "Waldensian ghetto" was highly regarded by Protestants of nearly every tradition. Those of a more traditional bent idealized it and hoped to see it conserved as it was; the romantics tended to be critical, and sought to encourage new forces at work. All who knew the Waldensian story acknowledged the whole church's indebtedness for the Waldensians' long history of faithfulness and they were anxious to generate acts of solidarity.

4. The Great Revival

In 1825 the quiet Valleys countryside was interrupted by the coming of a former Genevan soldier who had given up his military career to become a pastor and evangelist. After a time spent in the south of France, Felix Neff went to work in the isolated Protestant valleys of the Dauphiné, which, in a few years of intense activity, went through radical social and religious transformation. At the age of only 31, Neff died from sheer fatigue and privation, but it was through his work that the European evangelical revival burst upon the Waldensian ghetto.

Neff came into contact with the Waldensians quite by chance and was invited by Antonio Blanc of S. Giovanni to visit the Valleys. Warmly welcomed by the moderator, Pietro Bert, and by Pastor Mondon, he held meetings in the Pellice Valley for a month in 1825, managing to get away before Carlo Alberto's police could arrest him for subversion. Though brief, his visit sparked off a revolution. His preaching, like that of the revivalists, stressed some of the classic themes of Reformed theology, but with a romantic and individualistic emphasis. Sin, the fall and salvation in the cross of Christ alone were the keynotes of his preaching.

The movement triggered off by Neff's preaching was centered around S. Giovanni. At first it involved only a few families who kept their ideas to themselves, but in a short whole it expanded to include leading members of the Valleys churches. Evening and Sunday meetings in homes were organized for Bible study, singing, and spontaneous prayer — quite different from the traditional, rather formal Reformed services; it was more personal, more free in style, more engaging.

Leaders were country folk like Davide Lantaret and Antonio Blanc; what was even more unusual was the involvement of women who came with ideas and organizational gifts. After a couple of years a crisis arose: the Waldensian population at large reacted negatively to this religious fervor, seeing it as a betrayal of their tradition, while the leaders, the pastors in particular, felt that the theology of the revivalists was dangerously close to that of Catholic piety.

There were clashes over minor issues, such as forms of entertainment (shooting, dancing and singing) for the young. The revivalists held that these were mundane activities which betrayed and debased the authentic spirit of Waldensian culture, leading it to ruin. Groups of hotheads disturbed the revivalists and there were fistfights. The police began to suspect that there might be subversive elements in these groups. The Waldensian Board, fearing schism, decided to intervene, indirectly, backing Pastor Mondon. Disciplinary action was taken against the S. Giovanni consistory and Lantaret was removed from his post as elder.

In 1831 a dissident church was formed, led by a young minister trained at Geneva and backed by the Swiss and English revivalist movements. There was risk that this would really destroy the Waldensian ghetto, already hard-pressed by Catholic and Savoyard forces. Within a few years, however, partly on account of disagreement within the group, the breakaway faction was gradually reabsorbed into the mainstream, but the possibility of tension remained. As at other times in Waldensian history, opposing positions had forced the question of alternatives: should the church conserve the heritage of the past, or take up new ways of being "Waldensian?"

Even though it had formally survived, the enclave of the 1700s was finished; the struggle was no longer between "religionists" and "papists," but between "traditionalists" and the "converted," between people bound to past forms of Protestant life and those open to renewal. In this instance the tension was not as dramatic as at other times; between the years 1825-1840 a page in the Waldensian Church's story was turned, not so much in terms of events, as in terms of the church's changing sense of vocation.

The turning point was the work of a new generation, influenced more by the Genevan Bible schools than by the first generation of revivalists. Gradually it took over and adopted many of the aspects of the Great Revival movement. It encouraged new levels of lay participation in an array of new activity centered upon Bible study and prayer meetings, missionary work and education which would lead to the development of Sunday schools.

5. The general

For the "something new" the Waldensian people are indebted above all to one person who was not even a Waldensian, but an Englishman who spent all of his later years among them, General Charles Beckwith. It was he who was able to bring life to a new synthesis of tradition and renewal.

General Beckwith's portrait, showing him leaning on the cane which supported his wooden leg, has been displayed for generations in Waldensian schools and homes. No one, not even Janavel, succeeded in penetrating so deeply the spirit of the Waldensian people.

Like Gilly, the general was an Anglican, though more influenced by the Great Revival than was Gilly. An officer in Wellington's army at Waterloo, Beckwith sustained a severe battle wound which cost him a leg and finished his military career. Culturally he was the product of an Anglo-American upbringing, combining sentiment and pride with a gift for getting things done. He was, in short, a member of that English governing class which made the British Empire in the nineteenth century so renowned for its accomplishments.

It was Gilly's book, read as a convalescent, that engraved on

Beckwith's mind an indelible picture of the Waldensians as a beleaguered apostolic people and that led to his choice to tie his destiny with theirs in an unusual bond of love and authority. Spending the rest of his days in the Valleys, he disdained the role of a colonial viceroy, respecting the little autonomous and independent "nation" of Waldensians with its own particular contribution to the mosaic of Protestant Europe.

Early on, Beckwith saw clearly that the time for the ghetto was over and that the Waldensians must look to the future; improving and updating an eighteenth century experience was not enough. It was not sufficient, he argued, just to renew one's faith, while retaining a ghetto mentality, as was happening among many revivalists. Both the church and people, he insisted, needed a new direction.

While the Waldensians were preoccupied by questions of personal freedom, the upkeep of their churches, and piety, Beckwith was looking out on *Italy!* The great poet Lamartine had characterized Italy in this time as the land of the dead, culturally, politically, and spiritually. In his larger vision Beckwith asked if a vital Christian faith could not rise again in this land. His question challenged the Waldensians to the core, and their response would require fundamental rethinking and farsighted planning.

What was needed was a new *culture* — schools throughout the Valleys, not just for the elite, but for all. While Gilly had envisioned an English-style college on the outskirts of Torre Pellice — complete with campus and green lawns — Beckwith's eye was on those hamlets clustered on the rocky slopes, little dwellings with unsanitary stables and without light, where children ran about barefooted and ill-nourished. Right there, in those hills and among the very poor, Beckwith determined to build his "dominion" of schools.

The task required much patient and methodical effort, but by the year 1848, every Waldensian hamlet — some 169 in all — had its own one-room school!

Beckwith entered the picture only after local villagers had raised the money for the purchase of the land, often at exorbitantly inflated prices. At his insistence the buildings had to be structurally sound, solid, spacious and modern. The cultural revolution which he foresaw must come in like the sun through actual windows, no longer to be like vents in a bunker, as in the Valleys homes up to that time, and on whose size the state had imposed a tax. The windows were to let the light shine in!

Day after day, the general could be found at one work site or another, hobbling determinedly on his peg leg, white silk scarf flowing in the wind and battle decorations gleaming; any local supervisor who was not getting on with the job according to the timetable could be sure of being upbraided, and any church consistory which hadn't mobilized its people could expected to be reminded of its duty.

Schools needed books, teachers, and instructional material, and so an integrated system was set up from the hamlet schools through the junior college at Torre Pellice. The old system of the 1700s — tutoring in the hands of a few pastors and elders — was replaced by a dynamic system of qualified lay teachers. Beckwith's influence went even further and affected the future leaders of the church who, sent to study abroad at the new revivalist schools, came back full of new ideas and ready to shoulder new responsibilities.

6. The fateful year of 1848

Piedmont in Carlo Alberto's time bore the image not only of conservatives like Bishop Charvaz, but also of such men as Roberto d'Azeglio and Cavour, liberals for whom the deplorable condition of the Waldensian and Jewish minorities in the realm posed a serious problem of conscience. The plight of the two small minorities was generally considered insignificant in comparison to the "major" social and economic questions this generation had to face; still, it had to be dealt with. Here were islands of people forced to live on the margins of society, just a few miles from the cities which saw themselves playing a major role in a modernized Italy. And within places like Turin, Cuneo, and Casale, the stark ghettos stood out as relics of another age.

The struggle for civil liberties for the Waldensians and Jews became a testing point in the struggle for a new constitution and a new Piedmont. The climate of expectation was so great during the weeks of that "liberal springtime" of 1848 that the Waldensian Board decided to risk a petition to the king, requesting that he revoke all the repressive edicts. A public referendum soon afterwards confirmed the climate for change. On February 8 the new constitution itself was made public and on February 17 the now-celebrated Declaration was issued, at last granting to the Waldensians civil and political liberties and putting all citizens in the kingdom on an equal footing. The Declaration guaranteed the right of admission to higher education, the free exercise of the profession of one's choice and the right to acquire land. As for religious freedom, the Declaration brought no relief from the old restrictions. "Nothing herein is new regarding the exercise of their worship…" Thus, civil liberty was assured but not religious freedom.

Still, after centuries of abuse, the very fact of the Declaration was of such importance that one can understand the enthusiastic reception given to the news in the Valleys. From Turin in the night came two young couriers who had galloped on horseback at full speed to bring the word. As the news spread, the Valleys folk hurriedly gathered at their churches, just as in the difficult years of the persecutions. This time, however, it was not to implore the Lord's help in their extremity of need. It was a time for hymns of praise and for impromptu speeches expressing very simply gratitude to God and thanks to the king.

Great bonfires blazed all over the heights that night. And on February 27, a delegation of Waldensians headed a parade in the streets of Turin, amid applause and shouting of "Long live the Waldensians! Down with the Jesuits!"

The ghetto was finished for good. At last it was possible to leave one's house without at every turn encountering the infamous epithet "barbetto." It would take over a century for Waldensian civil rights to be fully implemented in the practical fabric of national life,[5] but at least it was possible to think of buying that little farm on the plain, contemplated so wistfully in the mountains. One might now start a business — or enroll in the university.

19."EITHER YOU ARE MISSIONARIES, OR YOU ARE NOTHING . . ." (1848)

. . . Although your fate is far from being decided, you are emancipated, and you can participate in all that is going on. With energy, sense of responsibility, and a determined will, you may do great things; it depends entirely on yourselves. If every Waldensian had the entire English nation at his or her side, nothing would change . . .

If you have independent force of will, you will succeed; if not, you will remain lost in the crowd, and nothing more will be heard of you. Your career — if your sluggish existence since the Reformation deserves such a name — will be closed. The old ways are over, and new ones are beginning to break forth. Henceforth either you are missionaries, or you are nothing. Your first duty is to assert you civil rights; your future depends upon the realization of them. Your future depends upon the place which you will take in Piemontese society, and on the moral and religious practice which you will be able to realize in that society.

Do not deceive yourselves; the foreigner will no longer aid you. Either you will remain hidden in your obscurity, or you will draw the eyes of the world upon you. You must get moving, or you will not be able to bear the light of your own candle . . . There is no middle road. Either act efficiently, struggle, persist, arrive at the goal, or be altogether set aside. The travails of the past have lodged in your people bad habits in their thinking and action, and they've got to get beyond them.

Your people have got to get stirred up by their cause and find courage and perseverence to keep their eyes fixed on the prize of religious and civil freedom. It's that, or it's all over for you.

Stand up for something, or be nothing — that's what it comes to. I'm not hiding my concerns here. There are bright people in your midst, but they have no influence on the rank and file of your people. They just aren't up to it — they couldn't muster Gideon's 300, nor Janavel's band . . . Put the past behind you so as to have some hope of making a difference in the future.

—Beckwith's January 4, 1848 letter to vice-moderator Lantaret, in J. P. Meille, *General Beckwith, His Life and Labours Amongst the Waldensians of Piedmont* (London, 1873), pp. 198-200.

20. DECLARATION OF EMANCIPATION (1848)

Carlo Alberto, by the grace of God, King of Sardinia, Cyprus and Jerusalem, Duke of Savoy, Genoa, etc., Prince of Piedmont, etc.: Taking into consideration the loyalty and good sentiments of the Waldensian people, our royal predecessors have, of their own accord, and by successive measures, in part abrogated and mitigated the laws which anciently limited their civil and political rights; and we, following the same course, have also granted them gradual extensions of rights. The reasons of the ancient restrictions having now ceased, and the way now being open for the system gradually adopted in their favor, we have, of our own free will and accord, resolved to make the Waldensians partakers of every advantage compatible with the general principles of our government. We, therefore, by these presents, of our certain knowledge and royal authority, and by the advice of our council, have ordained, and do ordain as follows:
1. The Waldensians are admitted to the enjoyment of all the civil and political rights of our other subjects, and may freely attend our schools, both within and without the university, and obtain academic degrees.
2. No change, however, is made as to the exercise of their worship and their own schools. . .
Turin, February 17, 1848

—E. Comba, *Storia dei Valdesi*, 3rd ed. (Torre Pellice, 1935), pp. 293-294.

Part Four

ACROSS ITALY!

(1848-1945)

The Lord our God said to us in Horeb, "You have stayed long enough at this mountain; turn and take your journey. I have set the land before you." Hear, O Israel, what I speak in your hearing this day: Not with our forebears did the Lord make this covenant, but with us, who are all of us here alive this day.

— Deuteronomy 5

The name "Waldensian" does not come from the Historic Valleys: it belongs to the story of men and women all over Europe who took up a common faith commitment, and a common struggle for freedom and the primacy of the gospel of Christ. . .A Waldensian is not someone who can claim a mere tie to an historic family name or locality. A Waldensian is one who has made a distinct faith decision to go down that road of resistance to evil, of struggle and faithfulness, whose motor is the freedom of the gospel. . .Historic Valleys traditions and ties have their place. But we are saved by grace, not by tradition.

The centering point is not some Waldensian "doctrine" (which doesn't exist!), but the gospel for all which can never be made "Waldensian." To be sure, there can be a "Waldensian" way of reading and living the gospel, but even this comes under continuing searching examination, and is never dogmatized, never imposed on anyone.

Sisters and brothers who recently have become members of our church communities, or who belong to communities beyond the Historic Valleys: don't consider yourselves "outsiders." Because of your decision to follow Christ, you are full participants in a reality God is still working on—a reality which in the past has had its "glorious" bursts of light, as well as shadows "less glorious." By God's grace our church faces a future which involves your and others' struggle to act in faithfulness to the good news of Jesus Christ in the concreteness of the human situation.

— Pastor Alberto Taccia, Italy, 1988

169

I.

ITALY, MY COUNTRY

1. The quest for full liberty

It was more than legitimate for the Waldensians to celebrate the Declaration of February 17 with their bonfires and parades, but to associate this event with real liberty was, to say the least, naive. The hesitant and introverted Carlo Alberto really belonged to the eighteenth century, and his tolerance owed more to the Enlightenment than it did to constitutional liberty, more to a paternalistic vision of power than to a democratic conception of government. It became clear that any authentic liberty would come to the Valleys folk only by determined struggle, so that first and foremost they knew they had to wage an all-out public campaign.

The text of the Constitution itself was unmistakable: "The Roman Catholic Apostolic Religion is the Religion of the State. The other confessions now existing are tolerated in conformity to the laws." The wording in the king's Declaration of 1848 concerning Waldensians was, if anything, even more explicit: "No change . . . is to be made as to the exercise of their own worship and their own schools."

As the Waldensians had decided that their horizons now extended to the whole of Italy and were not confined to their own Valleys, inevitably they clashed with Carlo Alberto's policy which contemplated a benign Protestantism, legal, but held within its own orbit, a purely private affair.

The government in 1849 proposed that the "Waldensian Society" and the Jews be accorded certain advantages in return for the state's supervision — a supervision involving all sorts of minute regulations. The Waldensian Board replied by insisting on the church's full freedom of worship, rejecting any privilege that implied state supervision.

In this struggle the Waldensians were supported by progressive elements in Piemontese society, personified by Cavour, the statesman with whom they had maintained a rather prudent collaboration across the years. Cavour had been greatly influenced by English and Swiss Protestant contacts; indeed, his famous formula of "a free church in a free state," which for many years prevailed in government policy, was of liberal inspiration, very much like that in the Swiss Reformed churches.

Cavour's was a calculated sort of liberty, serving to convince the British and Americans that Piedmont was the only truly liberal state in the Italian peninsula, thus meriting their support in the cause of national unity. In actual practice, however, there was very little liberty for colporteurs and evangelists not directly associated with a church, and certainly not for anyone the Piemontese police suspected of harboring republican ideas associated with the name of Mazzini. The Cereghini family in Liguria, for instance, was found guilty of the charge of free-lance preaching and sentenced to prison. It was against this kind of political and governmental notion of contained religious liberty that the Waldensians had to wage a continuous battle. Their calling was clear: to graft into the Piemontese conscience and then into that of all Italy the conviction that *all* faiths should stand on an *equal footing*.

2. "Either you are missionaries, or . . ."

The year 1848 marked a fundamental turning point in Waldensian history, comparable to Bergamo, Chanforan and the "Return." As such it was also a time of crisis, the importance of which may have been underestimated by both contemporary and subsequent historians. When the euphoria of the first few months of that year evaporated, the church found herself face-to-face with problems which reached far into the future.

Coming to the synod for the last time, the king's representative in 1848 said that from this point on the Waldensians would become part of "the great Italian family." But how would they be taken into a family from which they had been excluded for centuries? How would they live as free citizens after centuries of persecution and segregation? Besides, in this case as at other times in the past, there seemed to be two tendencies confronting each other in the Waldensian communities themselves, two conceptions of what it meant to be faithful. Representing the one were those who were schooled in the general climate of the Enlightenment, while in the other were those deeply influenced by the Great Revival — Amedeo Bert, chaplain at the Prussian embassy, and Pastor Jean-Pierre Meille, to take an example of each.

Quite a few of the Waldensians, now that they could live their religion without fear, were indeed content to settle down in all tranquility, their goal being to create in Piedmont a Reformed enclave patterned after the Protestant cantons in Switzerland. There were others who wanted to move onto the plain and to live the gospel there as a church in sharp contrast to Catholicism. The latter were a minority, perhaps, but they had clear views.

And Beckwith, lucid as usual, had already foreseen the advent of this crisis. Addressing himself to the Waldensian Board on the eve of the watershed events of 1848, he had stated, "Either you will be missionaries, or you will be nothing." That declaration would be long remembered as both a challenge and a judgement. It meant that the hour had now come for Waldensians to become deeply involved in the great adventure of national renewal. It also meant that they had to discover Italy.

In the following years, the synods may have resembled those of the eighteenth century in outward appearance, but they were actually greatly changed. New ideas began to take hold; no longer could the synod be mistaken for a little parliament in a little world closed off to itself. The Discipline was not changed, but the spiritual climate changed. Small signs of a new day: the old Osterwald Catechism gave way to a new text, the old Psalter was replaced by a hymnal, and the liturgy was renewed.

Other decisions were of greater weight: to study Italian, so as to facilitate communication within the new Italian reality; to set up in Torre Pellice itself a theological seminary for the preparation of ministers (without, however, cutting ties with universities abroad); to create a publishing house for the diffusion of Bibles, tracts and books. It was not by chance that the publishing house was given the name Claudiana, in memory of Claudio of Turin, the bishop who sought reform in the Church in the ninth century.

In all these developments there can be detected the influence of the Great Revival at its best, overcoming a privatized and introverted religious life. The most lively part of the church was discovering the vast dimensions of the missionary challenge — a rediscovery of the mainspring experience of the Poor seven centuries earlier. The little Waldensian world of the Valleys was about to explode like Lyon in the twelfth century, creating once again a new diaspora, last ventured in Piedmont in the first half of the sixteenth century.

3. The discovery of Italy

Earlier in the 1840s a few Waldensians had experienced something of the broader aspects of Italian life through contacts with Protestant groups in Tuscany, the region which was the heart of the cultural and religious renewal of the time. There the fervent Reformed witness from Geneva created one of the most dynamic outposts of Protestantism in Italy. The region was also the home of a more liberal Catholicism, whose best representatives, people like the Lambruschinis and the Ricasolis, evidenced real love for the gospel and a desire to root it in the lives of their people.

This was the Italy that four Waldensian pastors had found when they were sent to Tuscany to learn Italian. It was a marvelous discovery for them, even as students. How much more, then, was the euphoria of 1848, when Bartolomeo Malan and Paolo Geymonat set out to serve emerging communities in Tuscany. They found families ranging from the common folk to the upper classes, who were willing to risk prison in their desire to meet together and study the Bible. It was as if these people were the tip of a spiritual iceberg emerging from the depths of the Italian soul. Beyond them was the world of the exiles in Switzerland or England — with their own Protestant paper, the first in Italian, *L'Eco di Savonarola*, printed in London — looking to the day when religion in Italy would be a force for renewal and no longer a sign of servitude.

A period of repression unfortunately closed the springtime of 1848, putting an end to the brief Tuscan experience. Malan was summarily banished and Geymonat, charged in Rome with having violated the grand duchy's laws regarding the dissemination of religious propaganda, was led handcuffed to the frontier.

The second encounter with the larger Italian reality took place in Turin, home of the friendly embassies of the Protestant powers, where for decades the Waldensians had been able to live under international protection. By now Turin was not only the capital of the little Sardinian kingdom, but potentially the capital of all Italy. Turin was becoming the rallying point for some of the best elements in the emerging Italian *Risorgimento* (national unification).

More and more Waldensians headed for Turin. It was, after all, their own regional capital; moreover, they were conscious that here a great struggle was about to take place which could lead to a reborn Italy.

In 1850 Pastor Jean-Pierre Meille moved from Torre Pellice to Turin, leaving his posts as a *collegio* professor and editor of the Waldensian newspaper. Upon arriving in Turin he did not join forces with Pastor Amedeo Bert, finding that the latter's congregation, because of its language and makeup, did not meet the challenge of the times. Instead, Meille began to hold services in Italian, organized various meetings and debates, and published a weekly paper, *La Buona Novella* (The Good News).

Within a short time, Meille had organized the first Waldensian Italian language congregation. To it came refugees from all over Italy, including such personages as Bonaventura Mazzarella, the fromer professor of theology in the Salesian Order who later became a deputy in Parliament, and Luigi De Sanctis, a former priest.

By 1853, just five years after emancipation, Meille's congregation was ready to inaugurate an imposing new church, built in a prominent place on one of Turin's main boulevards. The project had the full support of General Beckwith and of Giuseppe Malan, the prominent Waldensian banker and first Waldensian delegate to Parliament, who perhaps more than anyone else embodied the spirit of his generation.

Of course it was only natural that the various reactionary elements in Piedmont should have raised their voices against the building — and that they should have been opposed by the liberals who favored it. On the day of the actual inauguration, with the full diplomatic corps present, as Pastor Meille placed the Bible on the pulpit the whole assembly was aware that something new had taken place: after 300 years the Reformation was back on the map as a promise for renewal in Italy. Indeed, the same sentiments were echoed for Italian exiles by their spokesperson, Gabriele Rosetti, in London.

Fanning out from Turin, Waldensian activity radiated in several directions — up the Aosta Valley, to Alessandria and Genoa. In this latter city, which was livelier and more open than Turin, Pastor Geymonat organized the city's first group of Protestants and from there he carried his preaching into Liguria.

For a few years the Waldensian Church was the focal point for all Protestants in Italy, concerting the energies of the historic Reformed parishes of the Valleys with those of new groups of believers, farmers and intellectuals alike. Unfortunately, this period of unity lasted only until 1854 when trouble broke out within the family on the occasion of the Waldensians' aquisition in Genoa of a deconsecrated Catholic church building. Cavour, the prominent liberal, opposed the move and brought pressure on the Waldensians, who then abandoned the project. Some, including Mazzarella and De Sanctis, perceiving in this back down what they considered a serious infirmity in Waldensian will, embarked upon a course of their own, forming what they called "Protestant Societies" which later became the Free Church. It seems evident from hindsight, though, that the real reason for the break stemmed from differences in religious sensibilities, basic divergences in theology, and from certain cultural disparities.

4. The heroic decade

The years between the Second War of Independence (1859) and the fall of papal Rome in 1870 saw an astonishingly rapid extension of Waldensian work. Its stages followed those of the *Risorgimento* in general: in 1859, Lombardy and Tuscany; in 1860 Sicily and Naples; in 1866, Veneto.

The first problem confronting the church was organizational in character. The inherited structures clearly were not appropriate for the present situation; Piedmont was too far away from the new communities which needed freer structures.

The solution was the creation of a quasi-autonomous body called the Committee on Evangelization. Though responsible to the synod, it would have its own headquarters, budget, authority to publish and the freedom to send out pastors and teachers wherever it deemed best. It is worth noting that in calling into being a Committee on Evangelization the church was introducing terminology new to itself and to Italy in general.

To evangelize did not (and does not) mean for Waldensians to seek to convert people to a sectarian confession. The aim was (and is) *to arouse interest in the gospel, to generate the critical reflection* which the Protestant Reformation for three centuries had woven into the cultural fabric of the Protestant nations, and *to penetrate the Italian conscience and Counter-Reformation mentality.*

On the facades of the churches and chapels built in those years there appeared neither the name of the Waldensian Church nor its emblem; the churches were simply identified as "Protestant" or "Protestant Christian" churches.[6]

The work of evangelization was not organized and directed from an office desk; the Committee acted with complete freedom as circumstances and as opportunities required. Evangelists and pastors under the Committee's direction were encouraged to take their own risks and assume responsibility for their own actions.

During the Second War of Independence, for example, Pastor Giorgio Appia and his brother, Luigi, a medical doctor, joined forces with Henri Dunant, a Swiss doctor, in organizing a hospital field service on the battlefield at Solferino. This volunteer aid to the wounded, quite apart from military auspices, was the origin of the Italian Red Cross. Following that campaign Appia made his way to Brescia and Peschiera, there to gather Waldensian soldiers and their comrades for Bible study and to distribute Bibles and tracts. In 1860 the same Appia landed with Garibaldi at Palermo. With a few foreign Protestants, some local residents and students, he proceeded to form the first nucleus of a Protestant congregation in the city. When he moved on to Naples a few months later he gathered a similar group.

Or again, Pastor Giovanni Ribetti moved to Tuscany soon after the banishment of the grand duke, ready to resume the work begun by his colleague, Geymonat, some ten years earlier. In Leghorn Ribetti's debates with Catholics attracted a great deal of attention, drawing violent protests from the clergy and causing a considerable stir among the people. Likewise, Pastor Davide Turino, at the outbreak of the Third War of Independence (1866) did not hesitate to leave his church in Milan for Venice, where, within a year, he founded the first nucleus of Waldensian believers.

In addition to those whose works are well known, an extended band of laypeople spent time and energy spreading the knowledge of the gospel. There was Captain Cignoni, the secret night courier who brought Bibles from Nice to his native Rio Marina. There were the Andreetti and Bellenci families, who helped draw together the first nuclei for future congregations in San Fedele and Catania.

But surely the most characteristic figures of this evangelical penetration across Italy were the colporteurs. Loaded with their New Testaments and popular reading matter they seized on the opening given them as booksellers to talk about the wonders of the gospel. To a great extent the change in religious conscience on the part of many people was due to the colporteurs' persistence and dedication. How many Protestant communities in the remote corners of Italy arose from those who listened to the colporteurs and read the books they offered! How many polemical battles with a fanatical priest or a superstitious crowd in the market place did these humble messengers of the Good News engage in! How many foul epithets, shouted at them from one village to another as they made their rounds, did they endure! Their monthly reports and personal accounts are no less profoundly moving than manuscripts written by the medieval Waldensians. The reality which comes through these pages is analogous to that of medieval times: fatigue, isolation — and incredible tenacity.

It is already evident that this kind of evangelism came in the wake of the church's wise decision to address itself, first of all, to the common folk rather than to an intellectual elite. When the decision was made to move the theological seminary from the "capital" of the Valleys in Torre Pellice to Florence, the heart of Italy, it was not for political and cultural reasons, but for reasons in keeping with the church's sense of vocation: assuring that its future pastors and evangelists would be trained in the heart of the country, ready for the demands that *Italy* would make upon them.

When it was decided that the church's publishing house also should move to Florence, it was not so that erudite treatises could be produced, but rather that a priority could be given to popular publications such as *L'Amico di Casa*, the illustrated household almanac which included all sorts of practical advice and *L'Amico dei Fanciulli*, perhaps the first paper ever to appear in Italy intended uniquely for children.

Rome itself was the last stage in the evangelical journey. Only a few days after the Piemontese troops had breached the Porta Pia in 1870, Pastor Prochet was there, holding a worship service in a hotel room. He had actually been preceded by a colporteur, whose faithful dog drew a cart full of books.

Prochet's first sermon was taken from Romans 1: "For I am not ashamed of the gospel of Christ: it is the power of God unto salvation to everyone who believes . . ." It was a challenge to a living faith and a Protestant reply to the Vatican Council which had just proclaimed the Pope's infallibility in limited areas.

Of course the work of evangelization was not the work of Waldensians alone. There were Mazzerella, mentioned above; Gavazzi, who became the chaplain to Garibaldi's "red shirts;" and others of different backgrounds.

All of these different Protestants shared the same faith even when they were diverse in their spiritual formation. For their part, the Waldensians saw their work as linked with Protestant churches in Europe. Others, probably in rejection of their Roman Catholic origin, refused any organization which they considered too rigid, and shied away from such things as a written confession of faith, an ordained ministry — anything which seemed to smack too much of church organization.

The debate between the two schools was not always on the level of ideas, but sometimes degenerated to personal attacks. Waldensians were accused of being too much tied to Piedmont, of being more at home speaking French than Italian, of clinging too closely to their traditions. And Waldensians replied that the other Protestants were too Italian, too superficial, too much permeated by a remnant Catholic mentality.

Alongside the Waldensian witness there gradually emerged two movements which sought to be independent of historic Protestantism: the Church of the Brethren spoke for those of pietist and revivalist tendencies, while a nationalist and activist movement of Garibaldian inspiration streamed into the Free Church.

21. NO PRIVILEGE, NO CONTAINMENT ... (1849)

I. The religious society of the Waldensians must be recognized as a moral body under the name it has acquired in history and which is given in its Constitution, that of the Evangelical Waldensian Church; this is a right which has been won by centuries of severe trials, and which has been confirmed by the Statutes and by the Declaration of Emancipation, and which is indispensable for its existence and for the free development of its life.

II. The Waldensian Church, which is a part of the Christian church, must be considered by itself and quite independent from the Jewish society, which has its own principles, organization and needs.

III. The Waldensian Church, being such by virtue of its practice of faith and its Constitution, must administer itself in an absolutely independent manner according to its principles, within the limits of the common law; all impediments or limitations by the state to its activity and to the development of its internal life would compromise its character as a church, and would represent an attempt to destroy it.

IV. The Waldensian Church, having its own permanent legal representative, is answerable only to the Minister for Internal Affairs.

V. The Waldensians, being called to enjoy fully their civil and political rights, must be admitted into all state institutions of assistance and education, and the law will formally exempt them from the practices and exercises of the state religion, according them the freedom to look to their own ministers for their necessities in matters of religion.

VI. The Waldensian Church has its own order by which it has up to now sustained the expenses for its services . . .

VII. The Waldensian Board, as the permanent legal representative of the Waldensian Church, is authorized to present its own comments on proposed legislation.

—Declaration of the Waldensian Board, September 27, 1849, in G. Peyrot, *Rapporti tra stato e chiesa in Piemonte nel triennio 1849-51* (Milano, 1955), p. 97.

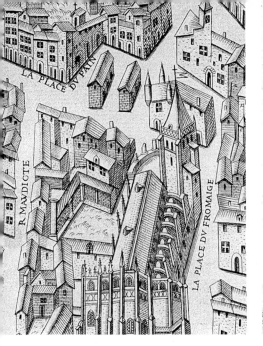

1. In St. Nizier quarter of Lyons, 'Street of the Accursed', so called after Valdesius' expulsion from the city (from a 1548 map)
2. First page of earliest known Waldensian theological treatise, *Liber Antiheresis,* by Durand of Huesca, 1192
3. The 'Waldensian Lord's Supper,' Naumburg Cathedral, 13th century

5. Preacher stands accused before tribunal (Nicola da Dresda, 15th century)

7. 'Coulège dei barba' at Pra del Torno, Val Angrogna, site of pre-Reformation school for itinerant Waldensian preachers

4. Waldensians at the stake, near Toulouse, 1251 (J. Luyken, 17th century)

6. Cattaneo's armed men accost mountain rustic, 15th century

8. First lines of most widely known Waldensian poem, the *Nobla Leyczon*, 15th century
9. Waldensian preaching at clandestine cave gathering (from *Amico dei Fanciulli*, 1910)
10. Waldensians at worship (from a Flemish miniature, 15th century)

11. Frontispiece of the Olivetan Bible, first in the French language, commissioned by the Waldensians, Neuchâtel, 1535

12. Confession of Faith of the radical Hussite Bohemian Brethren (in which they are called 'Waldensians'), published by the reformers at Wittenberg, 1538

13. Val Angrogna (Serre Church in background) and monument at Chanforan, site of 1532 synod which committed the Waldensians to the Reformation

14. Ciabas Church, Val Pellice, one of the first Waldensian churches built (1555) after adhesion to the Reformation
15. Frontispiece of New Testament in Italian, translated by G.L. Pascale, Geneva, 1555
16. Earliest known Waldensian history, anonymous, 1556
17. 'Gate of Blood' (center) at Guardia Piemontese (Calabria), site of 1561 massacre of Waldensians; left: G.L. Pascale cultural center, 1980s

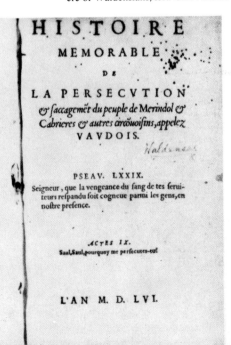

19. Pastor H. Arnaud in command of 1689 'Return' march (German, 19th century)

18. Waldensian resistance in the Valleys during the 1686 extermination campaign (S. Allason, 19th century)

20-21. Ex-Church at Ghigo di Prali (1556), where H. Arnaud preached upon reaching the Valleys, 1689
22. Ghigo di Prali, Val Germanasca (W.G. Bartlett, 1836)

LVCERNA SACRA:

cioè,

BREVE SOMMARIO DI PROVE
Della Fede Christiana,
Per paſſi eſpreſſi della S. Scrittura.
Per **VALERIO GROSSO**
Miniſtro della parola di Dio
nella Chieſa del Villaro.

*La tua parola è vna Lucerna à i miei piedi & vn lume
ài miei ſentieri.* Salmo. 119.105.

IN GENEVA.
Stampato per Giovan. di Tornes.
M. DC. XL.

LA

LITURGIE VAUDOISE,

OU LA

MANIÈRE DE CÉLÉBRER

LE SERVICE DIVIN,

COMME ELLE EST ÉTABLIE DANS L'ÉGLISE ÉVANGÉLIQUE

DES

VALLÉES DU PIÉMONT.

PAR ORDRE DU SYNODE.

Lausanne,
IMPRIMERIE DE J.-S. BLANCHARD AÎNÉ.
1842.

---

23. Frontispiece of exposition on the faith by Pastor Valerio Grosso, with earliest
known Waldensian emblem, Geneva, 1640
24. Frontispiece of earliest published Waldensian liturgy, Lausanne, 1842
25. Dourmillouse in Val Freyssinières (W.G. Bartlett, 1836)

26. 'Conscience,' periodical of the Free Churches, 1860s
27. First issue of Wesleyan Methodist periodical, 'Protestant Civilization,' Naples, 1874
28-29. Methodist Episcopal periodicals, 'The Torch' (Florence) and 'The Evangelist' (Rome), 1880s

31-33. Waldensian Church at Grotte (Sicily), early 1900s: interior, school, 'Protestant Philharmonic'

30. Laying of cornerstone for Waldensian Church in Colonia Valdense, Uruguay, 1892

34. Sales-distribution of Bibles and religious tracts by colporteur, Rome, 1870s
35. Exit from service at Rodoretto, Val Germanasca, early 1900s
36. Street evangelist, Italy, 1920s

38. Bible reading at home, Val Angrogna, 1950s

40. Centennial service at Via Spezio Waldensian Church, Palermo, 1960s

37. Waldensian Pastor A. Deodato leads prayer in V-E Day services, Naples, 1945

39. Waldensian women in traditional dress, Historic Valleys, 1950s

41. Inauguration of Waldensian Church at Campobasso (Molise), with Moderator E. Rostan, 1960s

42. Conference of Methodist-Waldensian federation, Methodist Church in Bologna, 1970s

43. Breaking bread in the town square, Orsara di Puglia (Puglia), 1980s

44. Pentecost service, Pomaretto, Val Germanasca, 1980s

45-46. Waldensian Churches at Torre Pellice (upper) and Prali (Historic Valleys), 1950s and 1980s

47-50. Historic Valleys-area churches (clockwise from upper left): S. Secondo, Luserna S. Giovanni (1970s); Pomaretto (installation of pastor, 1960s); Pinerolo (at worship, 1980s)

51-52. S. Lorenzo Church, Val Angrogna, 1980s

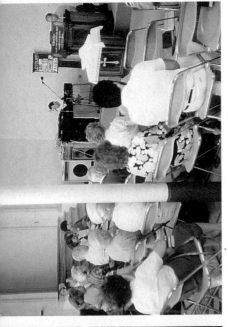

53-54a,b. (upper) Methodist Churches in Gorizia and Trieste (at worship and *Radio Trieste Evangelica*) (Friuli-Venezia Giulia), 1980s
55-56a,b. Methodist-Waldensian Church in Venice, 1980s; Waldensian Church in Turin (central and periphery facilities), 1960s and 1980s

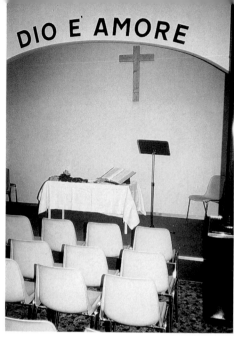

57. Via F. Sforza Waldensian Church in Milan, 1980s
58. Chapel-cultural center in Rovereto (Trentino), 1980s
59. (lower) Via P. Lambertenghi Methodist Church in Milan, 1980s

60-63. (clockwise from upper left) Piazza Cavour Waldensian Church in Rome, 1980s;
Waldensian Churches in Grottaglie (Puglia) and Vittoria (Sicily), 1980s

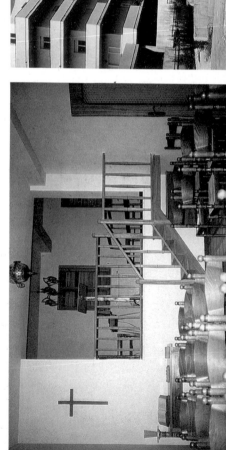

64-67. (clockwise from upper left) Waldensian Churches at Grottaglie (Puglia), S. Giovanni Lipioni (Abruzzo), Vasto (Abruzzo), and Dipignano (Calabria), 1980s

68-69. (upper) Waldensian Churches at Carunchio (Abruzzo) and Riesi (Sicily), 1980s

70-71. Via G.E. Di Blasi Methodist and Waldensian Church in Palermo, and Waldensian Church in Trapani (Sicily), 1980s

72-75. (clockwise from upper left) Via Spezio Waldensian Church and teens class, Palermo, 1980s; church school class at pastor's home, Marsala (Sicily), and Waldensian Church in Catania (Sicily), 1980s

76-79. (clockwise from upper left) Waldensian Churches in Valdense (exterior and interior) and Paysandu, Uruguay, 1980s; poster ('missing children' of dictatorship years) in pastor's study, La Paz, Argentina, 1980s

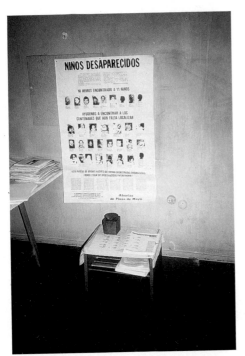

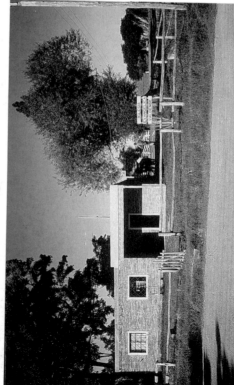

80-83. Waldensian Churches in Paysandu cluster—Chapicuy (upper), Pietras Coloradas (lower left)—and Montevideo, Uruguay, 1980s

84. College of pastors, Argentina-Uruguay, late 1980s

85. Break at Argentina-Uruguay synod session, San Gustavo (Entre Rios), Argentina, 1980s

86-87. Waldensian National Boards (*Mesa Valdense, Tavola Valdese*), in Argentina-Uruguay and in Italy (at Torre Pellice hostel), late 1980s

89. Review Commission reporting at synod in Italy, 1980s
91. Ordination during opening service in Italy, 1980s

88. District conference, S. Secondo (Historic Valleys), 1980s
90. Synod opening service recessional, Italy, 1950s

92-93. Senior former moderator and current moderator, Pastors A. Deodato and F. Giampiccoli, addressing 1988 synod in Italy

94. Synod Hall, Torre Pellice (Historic Valleys), during synod session, 1980s

Church-state confrontation in Italy:
95. Draft by V. Subilia, Waldensian Seminary professor, of 1943 synod declaration of the church's having failed to proclaim 'at whatever risk the message of Christ in all its implications'
96. Hanging of Valdo Jalla, Waldensian partisan, S. Germano (Historic Valleys), 1944

97. Moderator G. Bouchard on behalf of Waldensian-Methodist churches signs Agreement with Prime Minister B. Craxi in Rome, 1984, pursuant to Italian Constitution article on religious freedom (1948).
98. Francesco Cossiga, President of the Republic, makes first-ever presidential visit to a Waldensian institution (Theological Seminary, Rome) on Waldensian Freedom Day, 17 February 1986 (center to right: Pastor Tullio Vinay, former senator; Mod. G. Bouchard; Dean B. Corsani)

15. August rallies in the Historic Valleys:

99. Methodist professor and lay preacher (later, chaplain to partisans and martyr at Mauthausen) J. Lombardini, preaching at Inverso Pinasca, 1940

100-103. Gatherings at Bagnóou (upper right) and Pramollo, 1980s

104-106. (left) Federation of Protestant Churches in Italy (FCEI), 1980s: 'Eboli and Beyond' conference on Italy's deep south at Monteforte, and eighth general assembly at Florence

107-108. Federation of Protestant Youth-Young Adults in Italy (FGEI) congresses at S. Severa and Agape, 1980s

109-112. Waldensian Theological Seminary, Rome: exterior; library; group of students, 1970s; conference with S. African church and liberation leaders, 1988

113-116. Conference centers, 1980s (upper left and clockwise): Casa Cares (Tuscany), Ecumene (Rome), Adelfia (Sicily), Bethel (Calabria)

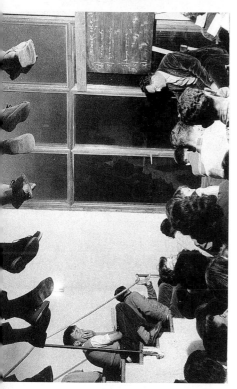

117-119. Agape Conference Center (Historic Valleys) in 1950s (upper left) and 1970s

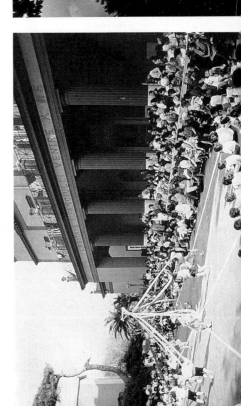

120-123   Homes-schools for children (upper left and clockwise); Hogar Nimmo (Colonia, Uruguay, 1980s); Centro Noce (Palermo, 1960s); Istituto Ferretti (Florence, 1980s); Casa Materna (Naples, 1980s)

124-125. (upper) Hospitals at Torre Pellice (Historic Valleys) and Naples, 1980s
126-127. Gould home-school for youth and hostel, Florence, and Waldensian hostel, Rome, 1980s

128-131. Homes for the aging (clockwise from upper left): Valdense, Uruguay, 1980s; Historic Valleys—L'Uliveto, Luserna S. Giovanni (Russian refugees), 1950s; S. Germano (under construction), 1980s; S. Giovanni (under construction, Waldensian Church in background), 1970s

132. Protestants in national march for disarmament, Rome, early 1980s. 133. International staff, peace research center (CEDIP) at Catania (Sicily), 1980s.
134. Waldensian Book Store, Milan, 1980s. 135. Cultural center, Udine Methodist Church (Friuli), 1980s

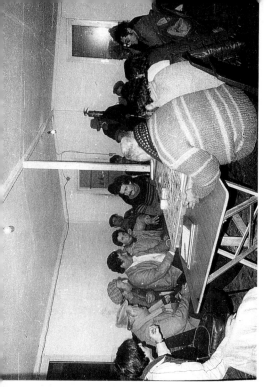

136-139. Ministries at times of national distress (clockwise from upper left): Pastor distributes Church World Service food supplies, S. Giacomo (Molise), 1950s; formation of agricultural cooperative at Senerchia (Campania) following earthquake, early 1980s; Speranza (Sicily) and Monteforte (Campania) Villages sponsored by Protestant churches for families displaced by earthquakes, 1970s and 1980s

XVII febbraio 1985   Settimana della Libertà

GIUSTIZIA
SENZA BARRIERE

Di fronte alla presenza di centinaia di migliaia
di lavoratori africani ed asiatici in Italia

Le Chiese Evangeliche

Riconoscono in questi fratelli il prossimo
con il quale Gesù Cristo si è identificato quando disse:
"fui forestiero e mi accoglieste" (Evangelo di Matteo cap. 25:35).

Denunciano le condizioni di discriminazione e di ingiustizia
in cui questi fratelli sono costretti a vivere.

Chiedono al Parlamento Italiano
una rapida approvazione di adeguate misure legislative
che tutelino i diritti di questi lavoratori.

Propongono a tutti gli italiani ed ai credenti di mobilitarsi
affinché si apra nel nostro Paese
anche questo spazio di libertà e di giustizia.

Federazione delle Chiese Evangeliche in Italia

140. Gignoro home for aging, Florence, 1980s
141. 1980s major mission motif ('justice without barriers') poster: caring and advocacy for third world immigrants and refugees in Italy
142. Catania (Sicily) Waldensian 'sanctuary church,' 1980s

143-146. Community development ministries, 1980s (clockwise from upper left): El Pastoreo Center, Rosario, Uruguay; J. Lombardini Center, Milan-Cinisello; Servizio Cristiano, Riesi (Sicily) (lower)

II.

THE PROTESTANT FACTOR

1. In step with liberals and Masons

The "heroic" period associated with the *Risorgimento* came to a close with the capture of Rome in 1870. Italy was confronted with the task of building a nation. It was an undertaking rendered more difficult by the legacy of problems inherited from her religious history.

In the following years the country found itself almost equally divided into two camps. The liberals were bent on creating a modern European lay state; opposing them were the Roman Church forces, who had already fiercely resisted the *Risorgimento* on the grounds that it meant the end of papal power and traditional Catholic culture. Each had its own organization, newpapers and banks; each was up against the other with no holds barred.

The liberals and the Masons were passionately anti-Catholic. On one occasion, at the death of Pope Pius IX, they even went so far as to disrupt the funeral procession, attempting to dump the casket into the Tiber River. In their eyes, religion was authoritarian, anachronistic, superstitious, given to magic and deserving of being replaced by modern science.

"Atheists, unbelieving subverters of the faithful, corrupters of the people," were the charges hurled back by the Catholic forces in defense of the Church's schools, its charities and inherited privileges. Politically, the Catholics were staging an anti-Italian general strike; culturally, they were out of the game entirely, their only guide being the *Syllabus* of Pius IX, which condemned everything in the modern world from Bible societies to socialism.

In this context the Italian Protestants had to make their witness.

Of course they had already differed from the Catholics in their attitude toward the *Risorgimento*; their choice was clear and was made with conviction. They had chosen the future, not the past; renewal, not restoration. They thus had found themselves side by side with liberals, radicals, and, a little later, with socialists, in combatting papal obscurantism. They were a component of the progressive forces. Indeed, they looked upon themselves as the religious counterparts of modern nations like England, Germany and the United States, nations to whom Italy looked for inspiration in its aim to create a renewed society. In the middle of the nineteenth century any forward-looking person who wished to participate in public life as a Christian, the Protestants argued, could not fail to be drawn to their way.

And this proved to be true not only among the Italian middle class, but among the lower classes as well. The history still remains to be written of those Italians from the south who emigrated to the United States for a time, discovered the Bible there, and then returned to their native country, Bibles in hand, and possessing a new awareness of their own dignity. Preaching the gospel with fidelity, they also utilized the experience they gained in the New World to become a force for renewal. Their solitary battles against great odds deserve a place in the history of popular militancy in Italy.

Because of a certain affinity of language and spirit, the emigrants on their return worked well with Protestant mission groups, which some years earlier had begun to operate in Italy. The British Wesleyan Mission had already arrived in 1861, the British Baptists in 1863, and Baptists from America shortly afterwards. The American Methodist Episcopal Mission was established in 1871 and the Salvation Army came in 1887.

Toward the end of the century a cadre of responsible leaders made an effort to gather the various Protestant groups into an *Alleanza Evangelica* (Protestant Alliance), a generous ecumenical experiment which was unfortunately short-lived. Protestants cooperated, however, in a fine weekly which they called *L'Italia Evangelica* (Protestant Italy). The journal succeeded in expressing a common Protestant voice from 1881 to 1907.

2. Evangelization's hour

For the Waldensian Church, the 30 years between 1870 and 1900 were a time for consolidation. Having sown widely in hope, it was now a question of organizing what had been done, and the situation required even greater steadfastness and persistence than before. Two elements distinguished Waldensian work from that of the other Protestant denominations: a popular constituency and a well-defined theological heritage. All Italian Protestant communities had working-class constituencies, but in the Waldensian case the bond was more intense. Under the Waldensian Board's leadership the Valleys churches nourished their rapport with the larger Reformed family, while the communities throughout the rest of Italy continued to expand under the direction of the Committee on Evangelization.

In the second half of the nineteenth century there coexisted two Waldensian nuclei: a church in the Valleys, embracing a local people with its specific educational, social, and cultural commitments; and a diaspora of believers within the field of evangelization.

Valleys churches furnished the teachers, pastors, and other leaders for missionary work, while the newer "Italian" communities provided stimulus, critical ferment and evangelistic sensibility. Without the former, the evangelists would probably not have had effective organization; without the latter, the Valleys churches might well have become ingrown, stagnant.

The second distinctive characteristic lay in the Waldensians' long theological tradition. Even if they lived their faith in a way which was quite similar to other Protestants, Waldensians could not forget their past as Reformed Christians. They were not merely a dissident movement but a church, one which had endured for centuries, with a Discipline, trained ministers and deliberative assemblies.

Waldensian evangelistic work was conducted on several different levels during the last three decades of the century. The public conference or debate on some timely topic played a major role (even to this day, frequently in church-related "cultural centers") whether it was held in a church, a community hall, or on the premises of a secular club. The tone of the meetings was in general strongly against the Catholic religion and its more characteristic expressions, such as the papacy, the cult of saints, and the like.

A notable event for this particular kind of evangelization occurred in Rome in 1872, when a great debate took place at the Tiberine Academy on the topic "Peter at Rome and his Episcopate." The hall was filled to the rafters, and it seemed as if half of Europe's journalists was there.

Little by little, however, meetings of this sort began to lose their impact, being too boisterous and superficial. They may have helped to make the Waldensians better known among the wider public, but served little other purpose. Quite different was the deeper and more methodical work of the pastors and evangelists in the neighborhoods and small towns, where the Reformed pattern included regular church services, Bible studies, etc.

The slow but steady pace of this more solidly organized work is evidenced by the dates of church buildings constructed or acquired during the time: Coazze (Piedmont) in 1879; Verona in 1880; Milan, 1881; Naples, 1881; Vittoria (Sicily), 1887.

Of course the major cities were not the only places to attract Waldensian congregations. Groups in small towns like Coazze (Piedmont), Felonica Po (Lombardy), Riesi (Sicily) and Rio Marina (Tuscany) were the result of the work of dedicated individuals, operating in different ways, some almost accidently. Often they were formed in the face of fierce opposition by the local clergy, and the local authorities often failed to safeguard the most fundamental rights of the non-Catholic population.

After political unification, the Waldensians saw that Italy's first need was in the field of public education, so they very wisely decided to make this the first priority in their outreach. In every village or town where permission was granted they undertook to organize a one-room school. The building of chapels was a second priority.

The teacher-evangelists had a minimum of training in education and theology, but it proved sufficient for the task of holding meetings of the faithful, teaching children, and assisting the elderly. The little centers in the Protestant communities for information, education, and community services played a significant role in the civic renewal of the nation; they were the fruit of the Waldensians' persuasion that Italy's first needs were *schools*, not cathedrals; *books*, not sacred images; *clear thinking*, not processions.

As soon as the municipal and governmental agencies were in a position to assure adequate instruction, Waldensians closed down their schools. This followed the principle on which they were founded in the first place, namely, that they were to be means of provisional assistance, not instruments of indefinite power, to be supplanted by "public sector" institutions when the latter were fit for the job.

With the elementary schools there came important initiatives in specialized education and social service — vocational schools in Turin and Rome, an orphanage at Vallecrosia, and a hospital in Turin.

3. Cultural life

The Waldensian Church made an effort to convey its message in cultural terms, though without great success, partly because not enough people could be assigned to this work, but more significantly because of lack of interest on the part of the public.

Italians in the nineteenth century were quite insensitive to religious topics, because for centuries they had been deprived of anything original in this field and also because they were accustomed to considering theological questions the private preserve of priests. On the other hand, if there was one thing on which embattled clerics and secularists were agreed, it was just this: religion was essentially a political question, not a cultural one. Both felt the great problem of the day was the "Roman question." Preoccupation with that rendered all other discussions uninteresting.

The Waldensians' rather modest cultural research followed the lines of traditional Reformed piety — Biblical studies and a reexamination of their history. In the former, Professors Alberto Revel and Enrico Bosio distinguished themselves by their commentaries and critical studies of Biblical texts, and Professor Emilio Comba was the outstanding Italian scholar of the time in Reformation and Waldensian studies.

The Waldensian Theological Seminary, having been transferred to Florence in 1860, quite naturally played a major role in this research, all the while preparing pastors and evangelists for their tasks. The most important theological journal of the period was *Rivista Cristiana* (Christian Review); Comba was the editor of the first series, from 1873 to 1887.

These studies were not undertaken for cultural interest alone, but for an evangelistic purpose as well. They were an essential part of the Waldensian Church's rethinking of its mission. Above all, Biblical research had to provide future evangelists with the sort of preparation which would enable them to preach the gospel in an effective way and provide the young communities with Christian studies which would undergird real alternatives to Catholicism.

The idea was not that of "clericalizing" culture or of making it an instrument of ecclesiastical designs; what the Waldensians had in mind was equipping a people for a *searching examination of society through the prism of critical Christian thought.*

When Emilio Comba recaptured for his readers the sixteenth century dissidents — "our Protestants" as he called them — he not only accomplished a work of undoubted historical value, but above all he gave to Italian Protestants an awareness of their history, a fresh consciousness of who they were. Now Protestants could assert that they were not a secondary, foreign, and disturbing element in the history of Italian religious life, as the Catholic polemics constantly asserted, but an essential component of it. Italy was Catholic, specifically because the Reformation had been cut short by murderous violence. Italian Protestants were "at home," and therefore were entirely within their rights to raise their deep-running questions which had been previously suffocated in blood.

The Church of the Counter-Reformation, the *Syllabus* and Vatican I was not "the Church of Italy" but only "a" church, that of the papacy, the one which had been victorious in numbers. The other church, continued the Protestant scholars, that of faithful and authentic believers and martyrs, was also Italian.

4. To the Americas

In the second half of the nineteenth century, an increase in the population and economic misery struck hard across all of rural Italy, including the little world of the Waldensian Valleys. The result was that many people emigrated. The first outlets for Valleys folk, quite naturally, were the nearby French cities and Geneva, where the language was no problem. A good many young men flocked to Lyon, Geneva and the French Riviera to take jobs as apprentices or waiters, intending to return home after a certain period. Such emigration gradually became permanent, however, involving whole families.

An even more important and striking development was the Waldensian emigration overseas beginning in the 1850s. The story of settlement in Argentina and Uruguay is taken up in Part Six.

Small numbers of Waldensians had made their way to North America since the 1600s, largely to escape persecution in Europe. In 1875, a splinter group left Uruguay for New York, and at length settled in Monett, Missouri. Economic privations led some 200 persons to emigrate in 1893 to North Carolina, where they gave their settlement the name of Valdese. Other groups, smaller, settled all across the United States, most notably in Texas, Utah, Illinois, and New York. With the exception of a congregation in New York City, which to this day remains a member congregation of the Waldensian Church overseas (so many immigrants came through the port of New York that, all things considered, it seemed wise to have a little piece of the Waldensian world at hand . . .), the Waldensian groups within a decade or so affiliated with denominations (usually within the Reformed family of denominations) already well established in the United States.[7]

5. The little world of "educated farmers"

Half a century after Neff's visit one could begin to see in the Valleys the profound changes which had been wrought as a result of Beckwith's work in the field of popular education. Now the area no longer resembled a little ghetto hemmed in by its mountains, but a small Protestant world which reflected on a small scale the features of European Protestantism, its virtues and its defects alike.

In the last decades of the century the church's promotion of education reached its zenith. At the turn of the century, Waldensians sponsored scores of one-room elementary schools, two middle schools and a junior college in the Valleys.

This school system was notable not only because it practically eliminated illiteracy in Waldensian constituencies, but because it provided the framework for Waldensian culture. At the local level, it was the school teachers who brought inspiration to many dimensions of Waldensian culture. They held Sunday worship services and gave religious instruction to the children; they were also the ones who promoted the development of libraries, available to all, gave classes in general cultural subjects and taught local choral or instrumental groups.

The teachers at the Torre Pellice junior college were responsible for the training of the local elementary school teachers. They also edited the church's weekly paper, called at first *Le Témoin* and later *L'Echo des Vallées*. This same group created a small and significant learned society which originally went by the name of *La Société d'Histoire Vaudiose*, (now *Società di Studi Valdesi*, Society for Waldensian Studies) whose aim was to promote knowledge of Waldensian history.

The creation of young people's groups, *Unioni dei Giovani*, after the Swiss model, was certainly the most coherent expression of this little Protestant world of "educated farmers," people who were accustomed to thinking in a critical and ordered way, trained, as they were, by the preaching of their ministers to a life of serious moral discipline and active participation. The young folk were an arresting example of life in the Waldensian churches of that time. In the evenings, even in deep snow, they would meet in the local Waldensian school, to read the paper by lamp light and to work on assignments. Meanwhile, the secretary of the group diligently kept a record of the proceedings, writing down everything in his or her notebook with impeccable handwriting.

And all this was by no means a closed world. Thanks to a knowledge of French and to contacts in the nearby countries, the Valleys folk could follow closely what was happening outside their little world. It was from these Valleys schools and villages that the Committee on Evangelization recruited the pastors who served as evangelists elsewhere in Italy; here also was the source of those women teachers who, without fanfare but with perseverance, took up their posts in the Waldensian schools of central and southern Italy.

Young people enlisted with the Paris Missionary Society for service in Asia, the South Pacific and Africa. Of the latter, for example, there was the Jalla family which pioneered the first churches along the Zambesi River.

The same missionary and revival spirit led the young to organize institutions which provided invaluable service among the poor of the land. In addition to the two hospitals at Torre Pellice and Pomaretto, founded at an earlier time and now equipped to offer full hospital service, Valleys homes for the aging at San Germano in 1894 and at Luserna San Giovanni in 1895 were built, followed by the Rifugio Carlo Alberto for incurables in 1898.

Perhaps no one better than the writer Edmondo De Amicis in his *Alle Porte d'Italia* (At the Gates of Italy) expresses the admiration of the liberal middle class for what the Waldensians stood for in public life.

The path the church had trod in the nineteenth century was symbolized by the inauguration Torre Pellice in 1889 of the Casa Valdese, the headquarters building which, with its theological library, its assembly hall for synod meetings and its offices for the Waldensian Board, reflected the church's alertness. From being barely tolerated citizens 40 years before, Waldensians had become a reality to be reckoned with, a small one, to be sure, but well-organized. Here was a group of churches with many specialized ministries, slowly but surely making its impact on the national scene.

22. THE WALDENSIAN THERMOPYLAE (1884)

... It seemed as if we were walking in one of those marvellous, unknown valleys, which is to be found in the Arabian Nights ... Oh, what a beautiful hermitage, just the right place to come and write a great story! There is one day in the year when the Angrogna Valley is all astir: it is the anniversary of the Declaration of Emancipation for the Waldensians. It is a day dear to them all ... From all around the Valley dwellers hurry to the church; the children from the 16 schools also gather there. Carrying the national flag and accompanied by the roll of drums, they are led by their teachers, while their families follow after them. They meet in a church, where the minister makes a special speech for the occasion. They sing, recite poetry, and receive gifts of white bread, which is a treat, and of an orange, which is a treasure. The teachers and all the local dignitaries feast together. In the evening bonfires are lit on the mountain heights, and the children return home along the very same paths on which their forebearers fought and died. Everyone is happy holding a little book, also a gift, usually relating to an episode in Waldensian history, written and published for the occasion. It will be read time and again during the long winter evenings in the little cottages half buried under the snow ...

We continued our journey and reached Pra del Torno. It seemed as if we were entering an immense fortress. It reminded me of that terrible *défilé de la Hache*, which, in his novel, *Salammbó*, Flaubert chose as the place where 20,000 barbarians perished of hunger. The huge rocks take on strange shapes, towers, the facade of cathedrals, great arches of galleries; some, like palaces in the sky, stand upright in the clouds, where vultures and eagles soar around them. Here and there high up in the mountains, small green carpets could be seen, where goats grazed; even to look at them made one's head reel. And there were little cottages that miraculously clung to the rocks like bird's nests. Lower down, clusters of rough black huts nestled close to the mountains' sides, under the continual threat of landslides and rock falls that occasionally bury them, crumbling them like glass trinkets ...

After walking for half an hour in silence we reached a rock, where there was a new church built in a mixture of gothic and arabesque styles and painted white and red like a garden shelter ... The valley seemed to be shut in on all sides, on the left by the mountains which form the Balfero gorge, on the right by the mountains of Soiran and Infernet, incredibly steep, bare and grey, all rocks piercing the blue sky. It was as if we had fallen into a trap in the mountains, imprisoned, cut off from the world, at the bottom of an enormous, concave tomb, open to the sky. And all around there was neither noise nor human voice. Only a girl of 12 or 13, a little cowherd, barefooted, dressed in rags, sitting on the ground in front of the church, reading a book. I glanced at the title; it was a *Histoire* of the Waldensian

Church, a large and elegant volume, published in Paris. I made note of the scene in my diary, joyfully, for she was the first country girl in Italy I had ever seen reading . . .

— E. De Amicis, *Alle Porte d'Italia*, 2d ed. (Roma, 1884), pp. 224, 244.

The Waldensian Church at Rorà (Historic Valleys, built 1845);
drawing by P. Paschetto.

The village of Rorà (Historic Valleys); drawing by P. Paschetto.

III.

THE NEW ITALY

1. Falling behind in new times

The years from the end of the last century to WWI were decisive in Italy in both the political arena and the Protestant world. For a period of several decades after the unification of the country in 1870, successive Italian governments had been dominated by anticlerical forces, Masons, and "positivists" in philosophy. When Giovanni Giolitti came to power all this was replaced by a policy which sought to balance three well-defined positions, each with a considerable constituency. On the right were the ruling class conservatives, people used to wielding power; on the left, socialist forces, drawn from a popular base; and in between, the complicated Catholic situation, also with a popular following, but conservative in outlook.

Perhaps no less important was a certain change in the intellectual and cultural climate, with authors like Gabriele D'Annunzio expressing a new form of idealism to combat the older scientific positivism. New fashions and interests in religion led some to embrace spiritism and theosophy.

How did Protestants and Waldensians in particular react to these new currents in political and cultural life? Taking advantage of greater liberty, they attempted to become more a part of cultural life in the country, as they did through *Bylichnis*, a journal published by the Baptist Theological Seminary, beginning in 1912.

On the whole, however, it must be said that although Protestants of the time succeeded to some extent in overcoming their isolation, they did not seem to grasp the deeper meaning of what was happening. They were not fully attentive to the issues which the socialists were grappling with, nor did they appreciate the stand of the Catholic "modernists" as they struggled to obtain a hearing within the Roman Church. There were notable individual exceptions, but Protestants generally were still so tied to nineteenth century revivalist categories that they missed the importance of the "great debates" which were going on in socialist circles and the significance of the encyclical *Pascendi* (1905) which was directed against the Catholic modernists.

Various reasons for this inattentiveness can be found. The pastors, trained largely in the school of pietism, sought to serve little flocks under constant social pressure, so that the attention of Protestant leadership was centered upon the local scene, rather than on the struggle for shaping national life.

This was also a time of regrouping and of new arrivals on the Protestant scene. The Pentecostal movement was beginning to take hold, thanks to emigrants returning from America. The Free Church of Italy ceased to exist in 1903 after half of a century of struggle and its members joined either the Waldensian or Methodist churches.

The Waldensian program of evangelization moved ahead, opening new churches in cities, like Milan, and in small towns, like Riesi (Sicily) and Corato (Puglia). The Waldensian Seminary continued its important publishing efforts, notably in the *Rivista Cristiana* (Christian Review). In 1908 *La Luce* (The Light), the weekly Waldensian paper which continues to this day, was successfully launched.

A period which should have been one of thoughtful reassessment and reorganization for new initiatives remained one of watchful waiting. In contrast to previous generations, the Waldensian Church now found itself more and more oriented to an individualistic, "petit bourgeois" mentality, in close touch with its own constituency, but hardly sensitive to the collective forces which were shaping the nation's life.

Of particular moment was the decline of the school program which had been such a notable part of the Waldensian evangelistic effort. New and stringent government regulations for schools in 1911 led the Valleys congregations to abandon altogether the task of opening new schools and to close many older ones; the pattern was repeated elsewhere as it became more difficult to recruit teachers who were swept increasingly into public schools.

The Waldensian Seminary, too, lost much of its momentum. Studies were pursued under the influence of the liberal theologian,

Giovanni Luzzi, responsible for an enduring translation of the Bible. The faculty were exponents of a sensitive and believing generation, certainly aware of the spiritual needs of the time; they failed, however, to fully understand the era through which they were living.

The year 1915 was notable for two events. That year saw the inauguration in Rome of the Waldensian Church in Piazza Cavour, the most impressive edifice in all Protestant Italy. The presence of so many people on the inauguration day, including an unusually large representation of Italian authorities, recalled a similar occasion in Turin some 60 years before. It seemed that at last the Protestants had secured their place in Italy's national life. Here, only a few hundred yards from the Vatican, and in the same city in which Valdesius' first disciples had sought in vain to be heard, Waldensians at last had an impressive new facility. At the inauguration in Turin, 60 years before, a prophetic word had been uttered concerning the entrance of the Protestant Reformation into Italy. Piazza Cavour marked the end of the nineteenth century evangelistic drive.

Of greater importance, however, was the decision taken in 1915 to bring together in a single entity[8] the Waldensian Board and the Committee on Evangelization. After 55 years of separate life, the two administrative arms of the Waldensian Church were now joined. From the Historic Valleys to Sicily, Waldensians in Italy were now unified administratively.

2. In the wake of WWI

Italy's entry into the World War in 1915 appeared to Waldensians, as to many Italians, the necessary complement to national *Risorgimento*. In the nationalistic atmosphere of the day, they were totally convinced that it was right to enlist. It was as if they wished to give final proof to Italian patriots of their fidelity to national goals. The war was a disaster for the whole nation, bringing on an interminable postwar crisis and the advent of Fascism.

As far as our story is concerned, two international facts were of major relevance: an end to predominance in world affairs by Protestant nations and the rise of national Catholic movements. To Italians, the war which locked the Protestant powers of Great Britain and Germany in battle also foretold the decline of a certain liberal-bourgeois ideology associated with Protestantism, with the result that Protestants and their values were called into question.

Other ideologies, in particular Marxism, were destined to move to center stage.

The breakdown of a civilization which went by the name Protestant also marked the resumption of Catholic claims and its old dreams of a conservative and popular humanism. The Catholic party once again entered as a major protagonist in Italian history.

In the climate of confusion and apparent vitality of the postwar period Italian Protestants thought mistakenly that they were playing a vital part in their country's affairs when they held a large congress of all denominations in Rome in 1920. Waldensians, too, deluded themselves by pointing to the transfer of the Waldensian Seminary from Florence to the nation's capital, Rome, and to the inauguration in Torre Pellice of two large educational buildings in memory of their war dead. In actual fact, they were marginal events. If the Protestants were not immediately aware of the portent of the fascist shadow overtaking the nation, they were to make the discovery in 1929, on that infamous February 11, when Mussolini and Cardinal Gasparri signed the Concordat between the Catholic Church and the state.

3. In the dark night of the Concordat

By signing the Lateran Pacts and thereby accepting the Vatican as its counterpart, Fascism repudiated the *Risorgimento* and its struggle for a free state. The Condordat not only assigned Catholics a privileged place in the nation, but revealed Catholicism's true face: that of a mass of people inextricably tied to a political power and bereft of any theological reflection. Catholicism paid dearly for this political entanglement — the most narrow conformism and cultural mediocrity prevailed right up to Vatican II.

In the dark night of the Concordat, Protestants now found themselves on the periphery of the nation, outcasts. The 1929-1930 laws spoke of them as "permitted" churches. Unfortunately, some well-placed people, certain Waldensians among them, deceived themselves into thinking that this amounted to legal recognition. After 1848, Waldensians had been "tolerated" but to be "tolerated" by the liberal governments of the nineteenth century meant a good deal more than to be "permitted" under the Fascists.

The regime sought by every means to control the Protestant churches, first of all, by approving the assignment of pastors to churches. It also attempted to circumscribe and monitor church activities, for in the eyes of the fascist police the Protestants were dangerous and suspect, given their many contacts abroad, their innate penchant for liberty and their spirit of autonomy. The fascist mentality harbored a perception that would have been unthinkable 50 years before: an Italian is by definition a good Catholic; a Protestant, likewise by definition is a foreigner, virtually a traitor to the national cause.

This judgement was professed in public speeches and implemented by police actions. Pentecostal groups, especially, were victims of the latter, persecuted by the decree which prohibited Pentecostal meetings in deference to "the integrity of the race." Pentecostals, the Salvation Army, and all Protestants were dubbed as people who had been "sold to the foreigner."

Italian Protestants also suffered a certain isolation internationally. The Waldensian congregations in Latin America were still an integral part of the Waldensian Church, sending delegates to the synod and receiving pastors from Italy, though in reality they were becoming more and more autonomous and drawn away from the "mother country." The same isolation was taking place with regard to Protestant Europe. Contacts were not completely cut off — these were the years of the beginning of the ecumenical movement and Waldensians got on board immediately — nonetheless, relationships suffered.

The fascist era brought retrenchment of program, but it also released wide-ranging reassessments within the churches as to the shape of ministry, sense of vocation, etc. Two lines emerged: to "recreate an evangelistic spirit" and to "advance a Protestant conscience." The Waldensian Youth Federation supported the former, while the second had the backing of the Waldensian Youth Groups, the Italian YMCA and a group of pastors and intellectuals led by Giovanni Miegge. The first group envisaged work along traditional and confessional lines. The second group sought to rethink Christian responsibility afresh in the light of the ecumenical movement and recent Protestant thought — the theology of Karl Barth and the struggle of the Confessing Church in Germany against National Socialism.

The vehicles of the first organization were seminars and youth camps, while those of the "Barthians" were the publication *Gioventù Cristiana* (Young Christians) and intense meetings on theology held at the Ciabàs.

The first theme harkened back to the nineteenth century tradition of personal faith and apolitical evangelism. It was aimed at strengthening internal cohesion in the communities. The second, inspired by the rethinking of Italian Protestantism undertaken by Giuseppe Gangale, sought to awaken in believers a faith which would be open to and face up to the social problems of the time.

The work of Gangale, a Calabrian scholar, member of the Baptist Church and editor of the weekly paper, *Conscientia*, had a decisive influence in the field of publications. From him a good many Protestants learned to address social issues head-on, which steeled them to be active in the antifascist camp.

Even though the two movements joined in 1938, the two currents remained distinct. When Fascism fell on September 8, 1943 laypeople associated with *Gioventù Cristiana* found themselves drawn by their theological orientation to assume responsibilities in the Resistance movement in the Valleys and elsewhere. The Waldensian Valleys, in fact, became especially well-known for widespread support of partisan activities. Given the political conscience of the Barthians and the Waldensians' traditional commitment to the cause of freedom, it is not suprising that the Resistance had such a popular following in the Valleys. The Waldensian Church as such made no corporate declaration on the partisan movement (nor earlier, on Fascism), but a number of its people surrendered their lives in faith's commitment to the struggle for freedom.

23. FASCISM VIEWS THE PROTESTANTS (1930s, 1940s)

...Italy has the privilege of being a nation with a most distinct individuality geographically. She has the most complete homogeneity from ethnic, linguistic and moral points of view. Her religious unity is a great strength of her people. To compromise it or even to allow the slightest fissure in it is to commit a crime against her national greatness.

— Benito Mussolini, address at the Opera House in Rome, March 18, 1934.

...Finally, it is necessary to underscore the point already made on the basis of investigations conducted by our staff: these Protestants in general, though they do not admit it, harbor a deep-seated hostility against Fascism, one which stems from their fundamental religious principles. It is necessary, therefore, to pay the most vigilant attention to their activities.

— Circular from the Ministry of the Interior to local functionaries, n. 441/02977, of March 13, 1940.

24. THE CHURCH AND THE STATE (1943)

The synod, recalling the principles contained in the Declaration of the Waldensian Board to the government of the Kingdom of Sardinia in 1849, makes the following declaration:

The Waldensian Church, *mater reformationis*, founded on the principles of the gospel, faithful to its Confession of Faith and its Constitution, confident of interpreting Christian conscience in the present situation, reaffirms the following principles:

1. This Christian church must rule its own affairs on an absolutely independent basis, according to its own principles.

2. This Christian church must not look to the state for advantages.

3. This Christian church advances complete freedom of conscience, of worship and of witness for all.

4. This Christian church reaffirms that any state interference or restriction of its activity, or development of its life in reliance upon privilege vis-a-vis the state, would undermine its autonomy, distort its nature, and compromise the integrity of its ministry.

5. The Waldensian Church considers that independence from the state and complete civil liberty are indispensable for fulfillment of its mandate from God.

— *Acts of the Waldensian Synod,* Italy,1943, n. 13.

'Be faithful unto death...': mural at the Synod Hall, Torre Pellice, painted by P. Paschetto on the eve of WW II, on the occasion of the 250th anniversary of the 'Return' of exiled Waldensians to Italy.

200

Part Five

A THOUSAND TONGUES TO SING:
THE METHODIST EXPERIENCE IN ITALY

(1859 ONWARD)

*I will make a way in the wilderness and pour water on the thirsty land—
you are my witnesses.
. . .When the Spirit is poured on us from on high, there will dwell in the
wilderness the justice which makes for peace.*

— Isaiah 32, 43, 44

*I believe in the power of God, and that Jesus Christ is the manifestation
of the will of God. I believe that the Spirit of God and of Christ works
among all people to encourage them and to call them to responsibility. I
believe deeply that God is a God of love and justice. I therefore believe in
Jesus Christ, the bearer of true love and justice, teacher of forgiveness
and freedom, and messenger of hope.*

— Teenager's confession of faith, Methodist Church in Udine, 1987

THE METHODIST EXPERIENCE IN ITALY

1. *Risorgimento* and the Great Revival

The name "Methodist" was already known in Italy in the early nineteenth century, long before any Methodist actually appeared in flesh and blood. The nickname "Methodist" had been used to make fun of any followers of the Great Revival, even if they were of the Reformed tradition and not followers of Wesley at all. Among the Waldensians themselves, not a few had been described as "Methodists" in the early 1800s.

It was not until 1859 — the *annus mirabilis* of Italian Independence — that the British Methodist Missionary Society sent its secretary, William Arthur, to sound out whether Italy offered opportunities for missionary work. His visit led him to the conclusion that Italy was already moving toward a religious revitalization, biblically inspired, that went parallel to the national *Risorgimento* (Unification). He expounded these ideas in his book, *Italy in Transition*, published in 1860, on his return to London. In it he advocated that English Methodists should help the Italian reform movement. Another survey was carried out by a young minister, Richard Green, who went as far as Naples, recently freed by Garibaldi. A year later, in 1861, Green and another minister, Henry James Piggott, were sent as missionaries to Italy, accompanied by Benedetto Lissolo (a former Catholic seminarian who had emigrated to England, where he had been converted and joined the evangelistic work). Green, though, shortly thereafter returned home for health reasons. From then on, the mission was led by Piggott, who was to stamp his vigorous personality on the work for the next 40 years.

By the mid-1800s, the advance of Methodism in the British Isles had almost come to a standstill. John Wesley's model of an itinerant ministry — evangelists travelling on horseback from one place to another — had declined. To compensate, Methodism had thrown itself with enthusiasm into a new form of itinerancy: missionary ventures in far-off and unfamiliar countries. Piggott was the son of a missionary family and at first it was planned to send him to Asia. It was his personal choice, however, to work in Italy.

Many well-meaning people in England were convinced that Italian "papists" were poor pagans to be converted. Others, including Piggott, knew that Catholic Italy was no pagan country. But it was just this that attracted him to the idea of struggle for the Protestant way in Italy.

From the time of John Wesley himself, Methodists had not been on affirmative terms with Catholicism. The father of Methodism was a man of the Enlightenment, although of the school of Locke, and not of Voltaire. Wesley's optimism was based on Arminian theology (the foundation of which is the repudiation of the Calvinist doctrine of election and the assertion of human responsibility in the process of salvation). His trust in experience; his conception of universal salvation; his horror of intolerance, fanaticism and slavery; and his generous humanitarianism all were a marvelous actualization of the spirit of the eighteenth century in Christian terms. Wesley also shared a decided lack of sympathy for papal Rome and its intolerant dogmatism; his negative views were by no means mitigated by the bitter experience of Methodist preachers in Catholic Ireland.

During the first half of the nineteenth century, Methodists had been led by Jabez Bunting's iron rule. Bunting had given his unqualified backing to the Tory party, the implacable enemy of the extension of political rights to Roman Catholics. When Bunting died in 1858, the Methodists shifted from the Tory position to Lord John Russell's Liberal Party. Lord Russell, however, was a passionate enemy of "papism" and an ardent supporter of the Italian *Risorgimento*. The result was that Methodists came to Italy to give the *Risorgimento* spiritual support and to help Italians free themselves from "Romanism."

Piggott, however, had no intention of forcing a foreign model, like British Methodism, on the Italians. He was an intelligent and generous man, who wanted to help Italians create a renewed church on their own, not dominated by foreign models. A reform movement had already developed in Italy under French-Swiss influence, and Piggott tried to get in contact with it. The movement ran in two currents — the Waldensians on the one hand, and the Free Church on the other. A part of the latter, in turn, looked to l'Eglise Libre of Geneva as its model; another part followed the example of the English Plymouth Brethren. All shared the same faith, nurtured by the burning piety and strict adherence to the Bible of the Great Revival. All shared a pronounced hostility towards Catholicism, thought to be the undoing of Italy. Anxious to return to the pure Christianity of the apostles, all rejected any form of mediation between God and God's people. All avowed their desire to be completely independent of foreign models; for this reason, even the Waldensians often refused to be called "Protestants," preferring the term "Evangelicals" or just "Christians."

Piggott went to Ivrea with Lissolo, and thence on to Milan. There he tried to work with preachers from the Free Church, already working in northern Italy, but the collaboration proved to be so unsuccessful that he advised the Methodist Missionary Society to create a new organization in Italy, entirely apart from the Free Church. Piggott complained of the Free Church's sectarianism, but there likely were ideological differences, too. The English Wesleyans had always refused to follow the way of the Free Church, more Calvinistic in its theology than the Wesleyans. The Italian Protestants did pattern themselves after the Presbyterians of Geneva and Scotland as well as the Plymouth Brethren, despite their rhetoric of aversion to foreign models. If the spiritual heirs of John Wesley, that champion of Arminian theology, could not find the Calvinistic theology of Geneva and Scotland to their taste, they could even less bear the libertarian radicalism of the Plymouth Brethren, poles apart from that methodical discipline which earned the Methodists their name.

After the break from the Free Church, the Wesleyan mission kept or created churches in Milan (where Piggott also set up a school for girls), Cremona, Intra, Parma (where the mission put its headquarters), Mezzano Inferiore, and in other towns in the region of Emilia. In 1863 an appeal was sent from Naples and another English missionary, Thomas W. S. Jones, was sent over. Piggott realized that southern Italy was quite different from the north and so left the mission in Naples considerable autonomy. From there the work spread in a short while to Salerno, S. Maria Capua Vetere, Cosenza, and Aquila. In the late '60s, Piggott extended his Wesleyan mission to the region around Venice, transferring the headquarters and girls' school to Padua, where he published a magazine with the rather odd title, *Il Museo Cristiano* (The Christian Museum). This shortly gave way to another publication, *Il Corriere Evangelico* (1869-77). Piggott employed a small staff of helpers, four from the north and three from the south, most of whom were ex-Catholic clergy; two (Francesco Sciarelli from the Abruzzo region, and Antonio Moreno from Sicily) had been friars and had fought with Garibaldi in 1860.

Piggott was convinced that the leadership of the religious reform movement in Italy should be the responsibility of the clergy in the main. Perhaps he had in mind the prophetic role which members of the Anglican clergy, like Wesley and his friends, had had in the Methodist movement. Wesley and his friends had remained on friendly terms with the Church of England, while the ex-friars and priests who joined Piggott did so largely because they loathed the Church of Rome. It was thus inevitable that there should be imprinted on Italian Methodism an anti-Catholicism which was more in keeping with the Italian anticlerical traditions than with those of the Anglo-Saxon revival movement. Anyway, Piggott always had at heart the training of ministers; their spiritual fruits were often really noble.

These first efforts were made amid tremendous trials and tribulations. Commonly the launching of a Protestant ministry in towns was "welcomed" by fanatical crowds who beat up or stoned the early evangelists. Those who dared to take part in the "heretics'" services risked reprisals — often losing their employment. The police often failed to intervene and protect against the perpetrators of violence. Sometimes, in fact, it was those who had been beaten who were arrested and charged with disturbing the peace!

Many Italians were both poor and illiterate, so the Methodists, like other Protestants, founded schools along with their chapels in a large number of places. The Wesleyan schools were particularly important in Naples where the need for education was extreme.

Despite numerous difficulties, the missionary effort succeeded in setting up a notable organization. The first Methodist Conference in Italy was held in 1868. A little later, in 1870, Rome was freed and Francesco Sciarelli was among the first to bring Protestant preaching to the Eternal City. In 1872 he teamed up with Alessandro Gavazzi and the local Waldensian minister, Ribetti, and took on three leading Catholics in a memorable public debate on whether the tradition that Peter had been in Rome was true. Not long after, the headquarters of the Wesleyan Church was transferred from

Padua to Rome.

The fall of the pope's temporal power led many to think that his spiritual domain would also collapse. In September of 1870 the Italian soldiers opened a breach in the Roman walls at Porta Pia. Within weeks, the General Missionary Committee of the Methodist Episcopal Church in the United States decided to send a mission to Italy to contribute to the spiritual transformation of the country; Leroy M. Vernon was named missionary and superintendent of the Methodist Episcopal mission in Italy by Bishop E. R. Ames. In August of the following year, he landed in Genoa with his family.

Vernon was born in Indiana and grew up in Iowa, where he began his ministry. He was a typical product of the Methodist stronghold in the American rural west. He worked first as a pastor, then as the principal of a high school in Missouri, likewise in the heart of the American Protestant landscape. But he was by no means a country bumpkin. He was described as an "urbane, cosmopolitan gentleman and scholar." He returned to America after his stay in Italy, and for the last three years of his life was the Dean of Syracuse University in New York State. A well-educated liberal, he was convinced, like Piggott, that it was imperative to help Italians achieve their own religious reform without imposing on them any foreign model. Vernon had none of Piggott's prejudice against Waldensian Calvinism. In fact, on his arrival he recruited as a helper, Enrico Borelli, an ex-friar who had worked as an evangelist and teacher with the Waldensians. In December of 1872 Vernon moved to the Emilia region and in the following months gathered together groups of converts in Modena and Bologna. Moving his headquarters to Bologna, he extended his work to Forlì and other centers in Romagna. He then founded a church in Rome and in October of 1874 transferred his headquarters to the Eternal City.

An intellectual, Vernon showed particular talent in recruiting people with considerable cultural gifts as his helpers in the Methodist Episcopal mission in Italy. There were, for example, Teofilo Gay, a Waldensian pastor who had received his training in the prestigious school of l'Eglise Libre of Geneva; Alceste Lanna, a Catholic priest and former teacher in one of the pontifical colleges in Rome; Enrico Caporali, a philosopher who was just as intellectually gifted as he was bizarre and who published the magazine *La Scienza Nuova*. Later, another philosopher, an ex-Giobertian friar from Naples and follower of Garibaldi, Pietro Taglialatela, joined Vernon. Thus was formed Vernon's first group of ministers, increased later by others, many of whom were of Waldensian origin.

In just a few years Vernon built up churches in several of Italy's main cities — Bologna, Rome, Milan, Turin, Venice and Naples — and in other smaller cities like Forlì and Terni. It is odd that a product of the rural midwest of America should have concentrated his work in urban areas: perhaps it was because Vernon found it easier to mix with educated people found more in the cities than in the country.

From a sociological point of view, the churches founded by Piggott and Vernon were not unlike most of the other Protestant churches in Italy: the majority of their members came from humble backgrounds (workers, artisans, small shopkeepers) and thus were linked politically to democratic radicalism, of which Mazzini and Garibaldi were the most famous representatives.

2. In pursuit of "Christian Civilization"

Unfortunately, the Piggott-Vernon Methodist missions were launched in Italy with an idea — that the *Risorgimento* in Italy would trigger religious reform — which proved to be illusory. The opposition of Pius IX to Italy's patriotic aspirations did cause many to leave the Roman Catholic Church. This, however, benefitted only an anticlerical secularism, which, as far as religion was concerned, went no further than the generic profession of faith in God as expressed by Mazzini and Garibaldi, or the humanitarian creed of the masonic lodges. Often Pius' resistance simply turned people to materialistic atheism.

During the *Risorgimento* there had been a considerable liberal Catholic trend, which included many among the more educated members of the priesthood and not a few political leaders from the liberal party. In general, the liberal Catholics were convinced that a political victory of liberalism would change Catholicism and that reform of the Church would be the inevitable result. Usually such liberals were not fond of Protestantism because they considered it alien to Italian traditions. Some did, however, sympathize with the fervent piety of the Great Revival and believed it was possible to reconcile the spirit of "evangelicalism" with Catholic tradition. The two largest Italian parties of that time were, on the right, the moderate liberals, and, on the left, the radical democrats. As a rule, the liberal Catholics supported the former, while the other party identified itself with an antireligious or at least irreligious anticlericalism. Pius IX and his Jesuit advisors had fiercely opposed the liberal Catholics by a series of acts from which there was no return (the declaration of the dogma of the Immaculate Conception of the Virgin Mary [1854]; the condemnation of liberalism and of the idea of a possible reconciliation between Catholicism and modern society, laid down in the *Syllabus* [1864]; the First Vatican Council [1870], which proclaimed the dogma of the infallibility of the pope and the subordination of the bishops to the authority of the pontificate). It became obvious that within the Roman Church there was no place for anyone who dared to disagree with this theological line. The liberal Catholics had no alternative but to leave the Catholic Church or to submit, repudiating their own convictions. The fate of the liberal Catholic priests was particularly severe, because they were vulnerable to the reprisals of their superiors, while their political allies, the right-wing moderate liberals, failed to lift a finger to help them.

The moderates' fear of the democratic left, and of its leaning towards republicanism, got the upper hand over their hostility towards the pope. After all, the pope, after 1870, was virtually powerless, while democracy was a tangible danger — and if that were not enough, the "red" of socialism began to appear on the horizon in Italy. Understandably, the wealthier classes forgot their sympathies for Protestant Christianity and started down the path which would culminate in the signing of the 1929 Mussolini-Holy See Concordat.

Before 1870 Italy had experienced a period of relative prosperity. The economic crisis which hit the world in 1873 initiated a period of stress which lasted until the end of the century. The suffering of ordinary people was aggravated by the taxes levied by the House of Savoy to cover military expenses; King Umberto I was convinced that only a strong army and an alliance with the reactionary dynasties of the Hapsburgs and Hohenzollerns could save him from a republican revolution. The exasperated masses were divided; some responded to the appeal of the clergy, an implacable enemy of liberal Italy, while others answered the call to socialism, even in its anarchic form. The priests incited the crowds to violence against the Protestant "heretics." The socialists preached that religion is the "opiate of the masses," and made no distinction between Catholic priests and Protestant pastors. In such a climate there was no room for a Protestant movement which proposed reform in Christian terms. There was no use hoping that in Italy popular revivalist movements like English Methodism would be possible. Neither the deep spirituality of Piggott nor the American dynamism of Vernon could change this harsh reality.

Though it appeared that little could be done by the two Methodist missions in King Umberto's Italy, work did go forward with admirable zeal. It was necessary to provide a spiritual refuge for those who did not feel at home in either Catholicism or secularism. The U.S. and British Methodists founded a modest number of small churches, and despite hostility or local indifference, these churches managed to survive. When Vernon ended his missionary work in 1888, the Italian Conference of the Methodist Episcopal Church (U. S.) included some 25 churches throughout Italy: in Emilia (Bologna, Modena, Faenza, Forlì, Dovadola); in Piedmont (Turin, S. Marzano Oliveto); in Milan and Genoa; in Veneto (Venice, Adria); in Tuscany (Florence, Pisa, Pontedera, Arezzo); in Umbria (Perugia, Terni); in Rome, Naples and Palermo; in Lucania (Melfi, Venosa) and in Foggia. The Wesleyan Methodist Conference (British Isles) had an almost identical number of churches: in Lombardy (Milan, Cremona, Vico Bellignano, Pavia, Intra); in Emilia (Bologna, Reggio Emilia, Parma, Mezzano Inferiore); in Veneto (Padua, Vicenza); in Liguria (Genoa, La Spezia); in Florence and Rome; in Campania (Naples, Salerno, S. Maria Capua Vetere); in Abruzzo (L'Aquila, Sulmona); in Cosenza and in Sicily (Palermo, Messina, Catania, Syracuse, Marsala). Each conference had just over a thousand members — a meager harvest, after many years of arduous work. Piggott and Vernon were right, nevertheless, to report these figures as successes, in the light of the extremely hostile environment in which both they and their Italian colleagues had worked.

In 1885 one of the great nineteenth century Italian novelists, Antonio Fogazzaro, published *Daniele Cortis*. In it a funny character is introduced, a certain Carnesecca (meaning "country-cured meat"), who is given this name by the country folk because he goes around the countryside near Vicenza, speaking of a martyr of the sixteenth century Italian Reformation, Pietro Carnesecchi, about whom no one knows much at all. For his pains Carnesecca is reviled and sometimes violently beaten. Carnesecca, no invention of Fogazzaro, actually existed. His name was Antonio Dalla Fontana and he was a Methodist preacher. That condescending attitude of Fogazzaro's is very telling: it shows that Fogazzaro was convinced that Protestants were poor imbeciles, worthy only of pity. He was no fanatical reactionary, but a moderate Catholic, a senator of the Kingdom of Italy, gifted with lofty spiritual sensitivity. One can imagine just how those who did not have Fogazzaro's sensibilities welcomed Protestant preaching!

A kind of authentic heroism was needed to continue evangelization in this environment. The work did continue and sometimes produced really striking results, as was the case of the Methodist minister Cappellini's "Military Church." In theory, all Italian citizens had to do compulsory military service; in practice, the wealthier managed to avoid it. So military service weighed especially heavily on the farm population: it was harsh and kept young people away from home for many years. As illiteracy was very common in the Italian countryside, soldiers found it very difficult to communicate with their families. In many cases, it was as if their kin were lost to them for years. Cappellini, with his "Military Church," offered not only a word of Christian faith to the young country folk in the Rome barracks, but also concrete assistance, especially in the form of correspondence with their families. He began to work within the Methodist Episcopal mission; in 1877, for practical reasons, he went over to the Wesleyans. Surely they were not far wrong if, in their reports, the Methodists spoke of Cappellini's work as a miracle of the Lord.

It was necessary to hold out a hand to those priests and friars who found it impossible to remain within the Catholic Church, because of their search for a form of Christianity lived out in the spirit of freedom. Among others whom Vernon welcomed in 1881 was the Count of Campello, a canon of St. Peter's Basilica, a Roman patrician and a leader of a group of prelates who had in vain dreamed of Catholic reform. Later, Count Campello tried to found in Italy a church along the lines of the Anglican Church. It proved to be a failure; only a small number of people, led by a religious thinker, Ugo Janni, survived. Methodists were among the most active Italian Protestants to concern themselves about former members of the Roman Catholic clergy. Some of those clergy, of course, were disappointing. An example was an ex-Cappucin from Sicily, Vincenzo Ravì, who joined the Methodist Episcopal Church in 1875, bringing with him an independent congregation which he had founded in the preceding years in Rome. He proved to be so quarrelsome that Vernon had him expelled in 1882, after which he took Vernon to court; although Vernon was fully cleared, it was not a good experience. By and large, however, the difference that the ex-Catholic clergy made was far more positive than negative.

In the '80s, another opportunity arose following the mass emigration of Italian workers, especially to Switzerland, the United States and Canada. In 1886 a church of Italian immigrants in Geneva joined the Methodist Episcopal Conference, along with its minister, Teofilo Malan, of Waldensian origin. An Italian Methodist mission began, which extended to several other Swiss cantons. Far more numerous were the Italian churches in the United States, where the Methodist Episcopal Church played a major support role. Often the preaching of the gospel was linked to various social projects, such as centers to provide education, recreation and assistance, all aimed at making the lot of the immigrants less bleak and at helping them to integrate into an environment totally different from that into which they had been born.

The effects of the emigrant experience abroad were felt in Italy, sometimes dramatically so. From the turn of the century onward, many small towns and villages in southern Italy were exposed to the preaching of the gospel by the witness of emigrants returning from their years abroad, where they had discovered the Bible and the Protestant way. In other cases, local initiative was the triggering event. The already-mentioned philosopher, Pietro Taglialatela, while minister at Foggia, was approached by some shepherds who had come down with their flocks from the Abruzzo mountains. Upon their conversion, they invited him to preach in the village of Pescasseroli. In 1886 a Methodist church was founded in the village; some years later the church disappeared, because its members emigrated to Buffalo, New York, where they set up a new church. The Protestants of Pescasseroli were immortalized by the most famous native of that village, the philosopher Benedetto Croce. Not without a certain good-natured sympathy, Croce wrote of them in an essay on his native village which appears in the appendix of his *History of the Kingdom of Naples*.

From the '90s onward the Methodist Episcopal churches in Italy followed a peculiar strategy, derived from the situation in the United States. The years following the American Civil War had seen a spectacular increase in the power and wealth of the United States. Max Weber had yet to formulate his celebrated theory on the relationship between the Protestant ethic and the spirit of capitalism, but even without it, some Americans had reached similar conclusions. That is, they attributed the successes of the United States to the beneficial effect of the spirit of Protestantism. Thus the terms "Christianity" and "civilization" were routinely linked together: all advancement of "Christianity" — understood to mean Protestantism — meant progress for civilization.

The Methodist Episcopal Church was one of the American churches which worked the hardest to promote "Christian Civilization." Its very growth was considered proof of the theory which holds that success is a sign of God's blessing. The philosophy of the "Christian Civilization" presupposed that the United States was solidly a "Christian" ("Protestant") nation, even though there were millions of Jews, Roman Catholics, Greek and Russian Orthodox Catholics as well as smaller groups of non-Protestants. Important to the story of the Italian Protestants, however, were the millions of Catholics, who, in growing numbers, were emigrating from Poland, Ireland, Italy and the Austro-Hungarian Empire. These "papist" masses broke the supposed spiritual unity of the United States; they brought in customs which were alien to the Protestant ones; they put in danger, it was thought, the moral level and very prosperity of the nation. To save the genuine spirit of "America" (and American business) and "Christian Civilization" it was necessary to defeat Catholicism in its Roman "den." Once papism was defeated in Italy, it was reasoned, Catholic priests would certainly be reduced to silence in America. So if the hopes of Vernon for religious reform in Italy had been dashed, it was necessary to start afresh, bringing to Italians the light of an authentically American Methodism.

Vernon's mission to Italy ended in an atmosphere of bitter criticism on the part of other American Methodist missionaries. One of them, William Burt, declared he was upset and "almost overwhelmed with discouragement" to discover that Italian Methodist ministers shared the habit of their fellow citizens of drinking a little wine at meals, and that even Vernon, lunching with Italians, "took the social glass." Moreover, he was scandalized by the fact that Italian Methodists preferred their Waldensian compatriots' ordered liturgy to the American revivalists' emotionalism. Vernon was removed with dispatch and Burt took over the leadership of the Italian mission in 1889.

William Burt was born in Cornwall, England; at the age of 16 he emigrated to the United States, where he worked as a manual laborer. In 1881 he was ordained a minister and appointed to work in the State of New York. After five years' service, which revealed that he had good organizational skills, he was sent to Italy. Unlike Vernon, he was no intellectual, but a hard-working organizer and an *homme à poing*, determined to correct the errors of his predecessor. He corrected them so well that within a few years most of the ministers, including Teofilo Gay, Alceste Lanna and Enrico Caporali, had left the Methodist Episcopal Church! To fill in the gaps, Burt opened a theological school (to add to the Waldensian and Wesleyan schools), first housed in Florence and later in Rome. He

213

recalled Vincenzo Ravì, whom Vernon had fired, and made him lecturer of the History of Christianity. Unfortunately, once again quarrels broke out and in 1895 Ravì left, this time for America and for good.

The strategic goal of the new Methodist Episcopal president in Italy was the destruction of papal power. In his judgement, most Italians were hostile to the papacy. What was needed was a strategy to convince them to dissociate completely with Catholicism and become Protestants. This, he felt, would complete the work of the national *Risorgimento* and bring Italy into the sphere of "Christian Civilization." To reach these goals, he thought, it was necessary to start from the top, in other words, from the liberal upper class and possibly from the royal family itself, convincing them that the Kingdom of Italy would never have peaceful times as long as the Vatican continued to plot and stir up the ignorant populace.

The relationship with the Freemasons took on considerable importance. The masonic lodges were among the few places in Italy where the harassed Protestant minority could find an open door, instead of hostility and contempt. In the case of the Methodist Episcopal mission, such an intimate relationship was reached that it was difficult to distinguish the one from the other. It was, after all, an American mission, and Italian Masonry looked to it for inspiration.

In its weekly paper, the *Evangelista*, the Methodist Episcopal mission conducted a virulent and tireless campaign against Catholicism. It also ran a publishing house and its churches were well situated in the centers of various Italian towns. The most imposing of all was the church in Rome, facing Via XX Settembre, half-way between the Royal Palace — the Quirinale — and Porta Pia, as Burt pointed out rather smugly. Consecrated in 1895, it was indeed an antipapal center.

In comparison with other Protestant denominations, the Methodist Episcopal Church had few elementary schools — half a dozen in all. There was also an orphanage. In Rome it opened a junior college for boys, and another for girls, with the stated aim of educating children from the higher ranks of society. The girls' junior college — called Istituto Crandon after the wealthy American woman who had financed it — was housed in the most elegant street in the capital, Via Veneto. In its reports, the Methodist Episcopal Church could boast that its schools were attended by the sons and daughters of government ministers, senators, members of Parliament, and also by the children of General Menotti Garibaldi, the eldest son of the national hero.

Burt's antipapal strategy might seem justified by the fact that at the head of King Umberto I's government was the strongly anti-clerical Mason, Francesco Crispi, and that other important Masons had posts in various ministries. However, the Masons failed to embrace Protestantism, even if they preferred to send their children to Methodist schools rather than ones run by Jesuits. The number of churches increased in proportion to the considerable sums spent on the crusade against the Vatican. The way in which American Methodists responded to Burt's appeals for ever larger contributions was certainly admirable. When the years of prosperity came to an end and lean times set in, it was the small churches that the two Methodist pioneers had founded in Italy that stood the test, while the more ambitious enterprises crumbled disastrously.

These vicissitudes should not obscure the point that the two Methodist denominations in Britain and the U.S. made a precious contribution to the safeguarding of Italian Protestantism in a time of real difficulty. The Protestant churches in Italy, except for those in the Waldensian Valleys, were founded in the main during the *Risorgimento* era. There was, therefore, a risk that when the enthusiasm of that era died, they, too, would disappear. To make things worse, all the best leaders of Italian Protestantism — such as Garibaldi's chaplain, Alessandro Gavazzi; or the Waldensians, Luigi de Sanctis and Paolo Gaymonat; and the Brethren, Piero Guicciardini and Bonaventura Mazzarella — died during the '80s. The two Methodist missions played a crucial role in preventing Italian Protestants from becoming discouraged and stagnating. They helped keep the issue of Italy's spiritual renewal alive. They made the point that the small Italian Protestant churches were not isolated, but represented the Italian branch of a great Protestant family whose role in history was by no means at an end.

3. The Free Church and "masonic evangelism"

Above all, the Methodists were instrumental in saving those "free churches" to whom Piggott, on his arrival in Italy, had in vain offered his cooperation. These churches were born by the spreading beyond the Alps of the Great Revival of Geneva and Lausanne, and of the ideas of the French-Swiss thinker, Alexandre Vinet, concerning mutual independence of church and state. In the first half of the nineteenth century these ideas reached the Waldensian Valleys and brought about a profound spiritual renewal of their people. Shortly

215

afterwards, in the Grand Duchy of Tuscany and in the Kingdom of Savoy, especially in Piedmont and Liguria, other Italians, who had been brought up as Catholics, were moved by the same ideas. In these regions, small groups of believers began to meet in the years between the late 1840s and 1860.

The absolutist government of Tuscany persecuted these Protestants, many of whom were imprisoned or exiled for their faith. Although the government of Turin was a constitutional one, it was by no means a model of liberalism as far as Protestant activity was concerned. As it needed, however, for political reasons to cultivate its friendship with England, it could not afford to ignore the pressure brought to bear by the English in favor of religious freedom. Thus, it had to resign itself to the fact that Protestant churches were being opened within its boundaries.

The Protestant movement in Tuscany was largely the fruit of a direct relationship between Florence and Geneva. Further to the north, in Piedmont and Liguria, the Swiss Revival's influence reached Italians through Waldensian missionary work. Soon, however, there broke out a fracture between the Waldensians and a number of their converts. It was said that the latter could not accept the Calvinist (Reformed) model on which the Waldensian Church's order was based. The libertarian radicalism of the Plymouth Brethren, instead, was then gaining ground. Another problem, not verbalized, but nevertheless true, was that many of the new converts were followers of the democratic views of Mazzini and Garibaldi, whereas the Waldensians preferred the moderate liberalism of Cavour, who held that democracy was but the gateway to a socialist revolution.

Each group of separatists defined itself as a free church, to show that in spirit it was united to the free churches of Geneva, Vaud and Scotland. Whereas the Waldensians had ministers who received rigorous training at a high academic level, the free churches saw themselves as having "laborers of the Lord" or "evangelists," generally coming from the working and lower classes, long on enthusiasm and short on formal training. They were people of great faith and impeccable moral austerity, tempered by the hard school of persecution, by their underground struggles and their battles for Italian Independence. In the years immediately after the Unification of Italy, they managed to plant free churches all over the peninsula, facing the violent reaction of Catholic clergy with great courage. The threats they endured were by no means so much rhetoric: in 1866 there was the massacre of Barletta, in which several Protestants were lynched by a crowd stirred up by fanatical priests.

Soon the difference between the followers of Plymouth radicalism and of those who desired more compact organization surfaced — a disagreement which enabled a colorful personality, Alessandro Gavazzi, to emerge. A Bolognese by birth, and a former member of the Barnabite order of friars, Gavazzi was famous for his uncommon eloquence. He was no disciple of revivalism. He was one of the many friars and priests who had acclaimed Pius IX when the pope had blessed the patriotic movement and who later had covered the pope with insults when he had betrayed the hopes of the Italians. Gavazzi, too, wanted religious reform in Italy, but above all he wanted to free Italians from the papal yoke. He was concerned with neither evangelical piety nor theological problems. He was a brave man of action who had been a chaplain to volunteers in the war of 1848 against the Austrians and who in 1849 and taken part in the defense of Rome, along with Garibaldi. Subsequently, he took part in the Garibaldi campaigns of the 1860s, encouraging, with his spell-binding oratory, the general's "red shirts." Between campaigns, he visited Britain, the United States and Canada, enlisting sympathy for the Italian cause. It is a mystery how, with the poorest of English, he managed to raise so much enthusiasm for his cause; wherever he went, he ignited fires. In 1853, in Montreal, he was nearly lynched by a mob of ferocious Irish — troops were called in and in the ensuing battle, 16 people were killed and 36 wounded.

It was during the periods between campaigns that Gavazzi launched a program to set up tighter organization among the confused galaxy of free churches. This meant a declaration of hostility towards those who sympathized with the Plymouth trend. There was a split and in 1870 about 30 free churches decided to accept Gavazzi's proposal and founded the Christian Free Church in Italy. The others kept apart, gradually dropping the name "free churches" and adopting the designation of Assemblies of Brethren from the Plymouth Brethren.

The life of the Christian Free Church in Italy lasted for a little more than 30 years and continually see-sawed between reality and wishful thinking. The reality consisted of a number small churches, whose members were very humble people with a burning spirit of ardent popular Protestantism. Proof of their vitality is the fact that many of these churches survive to this day, although they are now called Methodist churches. The wishful thinking was that of a great antipapal reform movement, which with the political backing of the democratic left and the masonic lodges, would galvanize Italians into action. It was, however, just a dream. Even though the political backing of the democratic left and the Masons could ensure that whenever Gavazzi took the floor there would be a full house, few of the crowd would actually convert to Protestant Christianity. In 1876 the liberal left came to power in Italy, but there were no dramatic changes in the religious situation. Gavazzi and his friends followed the evolution of the Italian political scene with anxious hope. They were to be once more disillusioned. In the early 1880s an attempt was made to unite the existing Protestant churches in Italy into one ecclesiastical whole. It was believed that one relatively large organization could wield greater influence on Italian life than several small and weak groups. But the project foundered in the face of the conservative stance of the Waldensian Valleys people and of the total unwillingness of American and British missionaries to relinquish the helm.

There were serious financial impediments, too. The Christian Free Church could make only meager contributions because its members were poor folk. A costly organization was beyond their means. Above all it needed far more pastors, so more and more ex-friars and priests were recruited as ministers, rather than the fervent, simple people of humble origin. The Christian Free Church had to depend on aid from abroad. John MacDougall, minister in Florence of the Free Church of Scotland, proved to be an extremely helpful fund-raiser. At the beginning, the Christian Free Church also received considerable financial support from the American and Foreign Christian Union, an interdenominational organization in the United States, which had sent various missionaries to Italy during the *Risorgimento*. Unfortunately, during the international economic crisis of 1874, the Americans hurriedly withdrew, and MacDougall was left on his own to find financial backing for the Italian churches. Understandably, this meant a growing conformity to the Scottish model. In Italy a cousin of Scottish Presbyterianism already existed in the Waldensian Church. The Christian Free Church began to emulate the Waldensian Church, although it was not in the same league in many respects.

After Gavazzi's death, MacDougall handed over the leadership in 1890 to a rather unreliable character, Saverio Fera. Fera was born in Calabria and while still a youth had fought with Garibaldi. He was converted and joined the Wesleyan Methodist Church. He became a pastor of the church in Palermo, but in 1888 he went over to the Free Church, taking all his congregation with him. Fera was a high-ranking dignitary of the Masons, and it is possible that his status with the Masons dazzled the now elderly MacDougall, who failed to see Fera's lack of integrity in dealing with the Wesleyans and Piggott.

Francesco Crispi became Prime Minister in 1887. He ranked high in Masonry, and at the time, Masons played a considerable role in Italian life. Many in the Christian Free Church were deceived, and thought that Fera would be able to leverage power, thanks to his close links with Crispi.

In 1890 Fera managed to change the name Christian Free Church in Italy to the Italian Evangelical Church, in deference to Crispi's vociferous nationalism. From then on, Fera's arrogant and boisterous leadership of the church had little in common with the gospel. Several communities, including those in Milan and Forano Sabino, with their ministers, went over to the Waldensians. Others affiliated with Burt's Methodists. The excesses of the boastful line of Fera brought the church to its knees; the advancing senility and, at length, death of MacDougall completed its ruin.

Fera, now desperate, implored the two Methodist organizations to help him, and it was the Methodists who forgave his many sins and saved the ex-Free Church from outright disaster. In 1903 the Italian Evangelical Church was dissolved and its communities with their ministers and their properties went in part to the Methodist Episcopal Church and in part to the Methodist Wesleyan Church .

The Methodist Episcopal Church inherited the churches of Bassignana, Sondrio, Savona, Udine, and Venice in northern Italy (along with a boys' school, also at Venice, for the training of the poor for industrial work); Pisa, Pistoia, and Leghorn in Tuscany; Mottola in Puglia; and Scicli in Sicily. The Wesleyan Church received the churches of Ponte S. Angelo in Rome, S. Jacopo fra i Fossi in Florence, S. Simeone in Milan, other smaller groups in Lombardy, and Carrara. The church of Palermo once again became part of the Wesleyan Church. All in all, the two Methodist bodies gained about a thousand members. The streaming of the former members of the Christian Free Church in Italy into the Methodist ranks had a far greater importance that statistics show. These people came straight from the fiercely anti-Catholic and strongly democratic tradition of Garibaldi's "red shirts," and they brought this heritage into the two Methodist bodies where the tradition was already very much alive. Quite a number of the Italian Methodists were radical democrats, Masons, and zealots of the Mazzini and

Garibaldi traditions. The incorporation of Alessandro Gavazzi's spiritual children strengthened Italian Methodism's radical democratic character which was to distinguish it in the larger family of British and American Methodism for years to come.

4. Into the new century: democracy under fire

When the Christian Free Church was absorbed into the two Italian Methodist Churches, Burt and Piggott were no longer at the helm. Piggott had retired in 1902 and Burt had become a bishop in 1904. The former, however, continued to teach in the school for the training of Wesleyan ministers and so continued to wield considerable influence for many years. The latter was given the superintendency of Methodist Episcopal work throughout Europe and so continued to deal with Italy. In 1912 Burt returned to America to serve as bishop in the Buffalo, New York area. Right up to his retirement in 1924, Burt continued to stay close to Italian affairs, as superintendent of Italian language Methodist churches in the United States. Italy and the Italians had truly conquered the hearts of both the Englishman and the American.

Piggott was succeeded by William Burgess, a missionary who had spent 30 or more years in India — rather clear evidence that by then Italy held only a minor place in the worldwide strategy of British Methodism. On the other hand, American Methodism continued to support generously the work in Italy. Unfortunately, there just was no one abroad with quite the same energies for work in Italy as Burt — for all his shortcomings. Happily, new Italian lay and pastoral leadership emerged among the Wesleyans. Piggott's ever-expectant hope for signs of a new religious awakening in Italy lived again in Emanuele Sbaffi and in Giovanni Ferreri. The former took on the administrative leadership of the Wesleyan churches, while the latter was the author of works of profound Christian devotion and, with Ugo Janni, founded the pan-Christian movement, a forerunner of present ecumenism. Among the Episcopal Methodists, the children of Pietro Taglialatela came to the fore. Alfredo showed brilliant intellectual gifts as a writer and lecturer in theology; Edoardo was a professor of education at the University of Genoa. Carlo Ferreri, Giovanni's brother, became prominent in the administration of the Methodist Episcopal Church, while laypeople, like the Wesleyan businessman Bossi of Milan and the Episcopal lawyer Salvatore Mastrogiovanni of Rome, showed remarkable talents in the same field.

The American historian, A. William Salomone, has characterized Italy at the beginning of the twentieth century as a "democracy in the making." The new king, Vittorio Emanuele III and his astute prime minister, Giovanni Giolitti, seemed to favor progress. Bishop Burt was given an audience by the king and took the opportunity to exhort him to free Italy from the ominous papal power. The last thing that a Savoyard monarch wanted to do was to imitate England's Henry VIII, but all the same, Vittorio Emanuele III delighted his American visitor by conferring upon him a high decoration.

The Italian Socialist Party was by now the cutting edge of democracy in Italy. It often resorted to a type of tactics called "the popular front," that is, an electoral alliance with the radical democrats and republicans to win power in local governments. One of these alliances actually managed to win power in Rome, and chose a Jew, a former grandmaster of Italian Masonry, Ernesto Nathan, to be its mayor. These years were full of hope for the supporters of the "masonic evangelism" strategy. They were the years of the Dreyfus affair in France, which caused an uproar also in Italy, and the years of Pope Pius X's condemnation of the Catholic modernists, dramatically underlining the unbridgeable abyss that divided the Vatican and modern civilization. Protestants in general and Methodists in particular threw themselves with enthusiasm into the battle against reactionary and antisemiticc clericalism.

The struggle shifted from the position of Crispi, who was a bitter enemy as much of the "red" socialists as of the "black" clerics, to the "popular front," which had socialists and republicans in the forefront. If one reads the *Evangelista* of those years, one realizes how much the Italian Methodists opened up to ever more progressive social views.

In the atmosphere of the democratic progress of the new century, the Italian Protestant churches grew considerably in numbers. Once more, much of this increase was due to emigration to the United States in the main and, to a lesser extent, to Switzerland and Canada. Methodists, more and more, had to tackle problems of Italy's rural south, whence the bulk of the emigration came. Methodists reached villages such as Perano and Palombaro in the Abruzzo region and Albanella, south of Naples. The Wesleyans evangelized the miners who were working on the Sempione tunnel, and so strengthened the Methodist presence in the area, especially at Domodossola, Omegna, Luino, and Intra. In the meantime, the Episcopal Methodists worked among the Italian emigrants at

Vevey, Lausanne and other Swiss cities. It was at Lausanne that Alfredo Taglialatela got involved in a debate with a socialist agitator, who flaunted atheism with an aggressive arrogance. That noisy atheist was none other than Benito Mussolini who, one day, would sign the Concordat between the Italian Government and the Vatican.

An Italian Methodist minister, Felice Dardi, founded a Methodist Church at Trieste, which, at that time, was still a part of the Austrian Hapsburg Empire, Catholic and reactionary. Presumably, its church members were democratic radicals or perhaps republicans. Anyway, the Methodist Church in Trieste soon became the object of the hardly benevolent attention of the police, and in 1905, Pastor Dardi was tried for having held unauthorized meetings. The Empire tolerated the "historical" Protestant denominations, like the Lutherans and Calvinists, but this tolerance did not include the "new" churches like those of the Italian Methodists. Pastor Dardi thus had no little trouble in disentangling himself from hassles with the authorities.

In the meanwhile, Dardi's Neapolitan colleague, Riccardo Santi, moved by the tragic lot of the city's waifs abandoned on the streets, began to take some of them into his home, and bring them up as his own. His family accepted the newcomers enthusiastically. Thus Casa Materna was born, destined in time to become a major ministry at the very forefront of social and educational work in Italy.

In 1906 the Italian Conference of the Methodist Episcopal Church numbered 2,700 members, 45 communities and 48 ministers. Undeniably much progress had been made, even taking into account the inclusion of a considerable number of members of the former Free Church. In the following years, an ambitious project was launched, the Methodist junior college on Monte Mario, a commanding hill in Rome. An imposing building, it was large enough to challenge the nearby St. Peter's cupola — a triumph of the "masonic evangelism" strategy.

It was at this very point, however, that Italian Masonry suffered a serious setback — its division in 1908 into two branches, the larger one, with its headquarters in Palazzo Giustiniani, which shared French Masonry's intransigent secularism, and a small branch, named after the Scottish Rite, with its headquarters in Piazza del Gesù, which professed to share the pro-religious views of American Masonry. The leader of the schismatics was Saverio Fera, now a Methodist minister. A not particularly edifying show, of course. Giolitti, wanting to rid himself of the "popular front," capitalized on the weakening of Masonry and pulled the diplomatic strings of the Kingdom of Italy so as to obtain for the schismatics the blessings of American Masonry. The masonic potentate appealed to Bishop Burt to get his support in the squabble. When American Masonry did not side with Fera, the potentate heaved a sigh of relief. Nevertheless, Giolitti felt strong enough to promote a liberal-Catholic electoral alliance directed against the republican and socialist "subversives." In the 1913 elections, this alliance won and the "masonic evangelism" strategy sustained a deadly blow.

Giolitti, however, like the magician's apprentice of the fable, had called up demons over which he had no control. He was himself overcome by ultraconservative forces. A new government was formed which threw Italy into the Great War (WWI) without Parliamentary consent. Giolitti was against this, but dared not offer opposition for fear of finding himself encamped with the "reds" and against the king. There ensued a tragic split within the democratic forces in Italy. The socialists were against Italy's declaring war, while the radicals, republicans, and most of the masonic lodges were in favor of Italy's allying with republican France and liberal England against the reactionary empires of Austro-Hungary and Germany. Protestants, including the Methodists, shared in the general suffering on the home front and in losses in the trenches. They also went through moral anguish in the conflict between their horror of war as Christians and their intense patriotic loyalty — between their conviction, on the one hand, that this was a war to save the Mazzini-Garibaldi principles and the fear, on the other hand, that a conflict which had Germans fighting against the English, and later the Americans, was in fact a sort of civil war between Protestants, from which "Christian Civilization" could only emerge broken to pieces. Hope was rekindled in 1917 through President Wilson — a practicing Protestant, a minister's son — and his "Fourteen Points." The triumph of Wilson's America augured well for the victory of "Christian Civilization" over the Catholic empire of the Hapsburgs. Italian Protestants were passionate Wilsonians, and the most ardent of all were the Methodists. Alas, those hopes were soon to be dashed: the failure of the American president's policy looked like a Protestant defeat. The reactionary and nationalistic forces which had trembled at the possibility that Italy might enjoy a democratic evolution could raise their heads once more with Wilson's failure.

In the wake of WWI, the Episcopal Methodists exploited the

defeat of Austria by opening churches at Gorizia and on the Istrian peninsula. As a sign of the desire for unity within Italian Protestantism, both branches of Methodism took an active part in the Congress of Italian Protestants which met in Rome in 1920. Before long, though, hope for progress was arrested by ominous political developments in Italy.

The factory workers and farmers, who had been thrown into the crucible of war, returned home elated by news of the Russian Revolution, and decided to put an end to the social injustices which had weighed upon them for centuries. In violent and bloody reaction, the fascist squads soon curbed the workers' movement. In 1922 the fascist leader, Benito Mussolini, called by the king to head the government, set out to destroy the freedom of Italian citizens, with the consent and backing of generals, landowners, industrialists and the Holy See.

At Scicli, in the heart of the poorest and most underdeveloped part of Sicily, farmers, led by the local Methodist minister, rose in the name of socialism against feudal oppression. Pastor Schirò was elected mayor and in this post he worked unflinchingly in favor of the poor until fascist violence wiped out his socialist administration. Driven from his post as mayor, Schirò, with his family, for years suffered harsh persecution.

At first, no specific measures were taken against Protestant churches, perhaps because Mussolini wanted to cajole the British and American conservatives. Since, however, the destiny of Protestantism in Italy is linked indissolubly to the fate of freedom and democracy, the churches at length had to endure the hard times of abolition of civil liberties, muzzling of the press, and limitations imposed upon meetings and free association. A specific ruling forbade free discussion of matters of religion — a fascist bow to the Vatican. An even more welcomed favor was the suppression of Masonry, through destruction of lodges and violent persecution (even to the point of killing) of leading Masons. In practice, Protestant activity beyond worship services within the churches was subject to heavy control and restriction.

Limitations imposed upon the freedom to preach the gospel would have resulted in lively protests in America and England, but the "red scare" (socialism) had now replaced "papism" as the concern of respectable people. Catholicism seemed more and more to be a useful bulwark of social order against subversive doctrines. Mussolini was praised abroad as a champion in the fight against "Bolshevism." It is to their great credit that neither British nor

The Methodist Church in Bologna, early 1900s; drawing by P. Paschetto.

American Methodists joined the chorus of praises for the Italian dictator. They gave voice to their opposition to Fascism in their publications and at their conferences. But the tiny Italian Protestant churches realized that they could no longer enjoy the international support they once had. Italian Methodists had entered a time of trial so dark that there were grave doubts about their ever emerging from it.

5. Through Fascism's dark tunnel

In 1929 Mussolini signed the Concordat between Italy and the Holy See. It became absolutely clear that he would not allow the Italians' spiritual unity in Catholicism to be cracked. The year of the Concordat was also the year of the Wall Street crisis, often noted as the dawn of the Great Depression. In 1931 the world economic crisis reached Italy, sowing disaster. The Methodist Episcopal Church in the United States had to submit to a painful reduction of its missionary commitments throughout the world; in 1932 it cut all financial aid to the Italian Conference and withdrew all American missionaries from Italy. The post of superintendent and the disagreeable job of cutting and saving what was possible fell to Carlo Maria Ferreri, who confronted the storm with a truly indomitable spirit. He had to act fast to liquidate properties lest the fascist government find cause to intervene. Among the specialized ministries which had to be closed were the Monte Mario and Crandon junior colleges in Rome, and the industrial institute in Venice. Church facilities were abandoned in towns where there were other Protestant communities, such as Turin, Florence, Pisa, Naples, and Palermo. The conspicuous patrimony of real estate put together by Burt proved to be a godsend because its sale covered the severance pay of staff which had to be laid off. Most of the churches had to manage with ministers who no longer received a salary, or with voluntary lay workers. When the cutting was over, there had been no disbanding of congregations. The Methodist Episcopal churches, despite all, were still alive in Milan, Alessandria, Bassignana, San Marzano Oliveto, Savona, Sestri, Ponente, Udine, Gorizia, Trieste, Terni, Rome, Perano, Palombaro, and Scicli. Even Casa Materna in Naples resisted the storm without sinking, thanks to the truly exceptional sacrifice on the part of Riccardo Santi and his children.

Every human security had crumbled, many ambitious projects had failed. Only the naked gospel stood intact, and its strength prevented the churches from disintegrating under the blows of adversity.

Through the fascist period, the Episcopal Methodists were so absorbed in the desperate effort to keep up their churches that they had little energy to divert to other causes. A son of one of the pastors won a place of honor in Italian history, however. Fausto Nitti was imprisoned for daring to visit the widow of Giacomo Matteotti — a socialist member of Parliament who was killed by Mussolini's thugs —and then confined on the island of Lipari. In 1929, with Carlo Rosselli and Emilio Lussu, he managed to escape from the island and went into exile in Paris, where he took part in the foundation of "Justice and Freedom," a democratic movement which had an important role in the struggle against Fascism. He then went on to fight in the Spanish Civil War as a major in the Republican Army.

The Wesleyan Methodists were also hit by the crisis, although they managed to save their institutions; right up to WWII they kept open the girls' institute founded by Piggott (which had transferred to Intra some time previously) and the Pestalozzi Institute for children in Florence. In the darkest years of Fascism, they showed a particular vitality because of their courageous faithfulness to what had been Piggott's policy: a generous open-mindedness to spiritual struggle in the life of the nation. The Wesleyans called two people (hated by the fascist regime) with considerable intellectual talents to teach in their theological school — the church historian, Ernesto Buonaiuti, excommunicated by the Roman Catholic Church (because he was a modernist Catholic) and hounded from his chair at the University of Rome (because he refused to take an oath of loyalty to the Mussolini government) and a Jew, Ugo della Seta, a republican and former member of Parliament. The two fearlessly welcomed converts who were politically "hot," such as the former socialist member of Parliament, Dante Argentieri, who became a minister, and the former republican party secretary in Carrara, Jacopo Lombardini. The latter, converted after he had been cruelly beaten by Fascists, became a lay preacher and carried out an admirable ministry among impoverished quarry workers in the Apuan Hills. A Wesleyan minister, Ludovico Vergnano, dared to organize a pacifist association, the Knights of Peace, in an Italy deafened by the warlike shrieks of the *Duce*. A layperson, Ferdinando Visco Gilardi, founded a Milan publishing firm which challenged the dictatorship by publishing works by critics such as Buonaiuti and Benedetto Croce, whom the dictator tried to silence.

All of this was a monument to courage and to clarity of ideas. It must be admitted, however, that even among the best-equipped Methodists, there was a certain aversion to "historical" Protestantism (notably in Calvinist and Lutheran attainments) and hesitance to grapple with theology. Such was the heritage from the *Risorgimento* and perhaps, at least indirectly, from Wesley himself. The dialectical theology of Karl Barth had a pronounced and positive influence on many Italian Protestants during the fascist period: the German *Bekennende Kirche* (Confessing Church) offered a model of a Christian way of resisting totalitarianism. But few Methodists were open to these new ideas and those few were usually laypeople, a good example of whom was Ferdinando Geremia, an intellectual from Padua. A courageous militant in the "Justice and Freedom" underground movement, Geremia was jailed for his politics and later converted to Methodism. The scarce attention given to theological renewal was undoubtedly the cause of a cultural gap that would not be overcome for many years.

To compensate, the Wesleyan Methodists dared to evangelize even during the years of the dictatorship, so that groups were formed in small centers like Vintebbio in Piedmont and Villa San Sebastiano in Abruzzo. In the post-Concordat years of close alliance between Fascism and Catholicism, these movements took on, however involuntarily, the character of revolt against the regime. The Vatican turned to the Fascists for help and the latter intervened with repressive measures. At Villa San Sebastiano the crackdown was particularly harsh: the Methodists were forbidden to hold worship services in their church and their minister, Francesco Cacciapuoti, was jailed. The humble people of Vintebbio and Villa San Sebastiano nonetheless held fast to their Protestant convictions.

In 1935 the Italian campaign against Abyssinia caused tension between fascist Italy and Great Britain, tension that grew in the following years. The Wesleyan branch of Italian Methodism became the target of much state hostility. In 1939, when Mussolini dragged Italy into WWII, the Wesleyans' association with British Methodism became a virtual political crime. All that the Wesleyan Church owned in Italy was declared to be "enemy property" and as such was confiscated. Ministers went hungry, despite the generous help from their people. In 1941, when war was declared with the United States, the Methodist Episcopal Church began to suffer the same fate. The next year, the moderator of the Waldensian National Board, Virgilio Sommani, with a courage that equalled the generosity of his heart, proposed to the Methodists a union with the

Waldensians, so as to alleviate Methodist suffering. Waldensians, whatever their problems during the fascist era, at least were not seen as an alien force as were the Methodists. The preliminary discussions had to be broken off after the allied landings in Italy, the Nazi occupation of a large part of the peninsula in 1943, and the gradual passage of the front from south to north, with its train of death and destruction. There was, for example, the horror of the Nazi massacre at Vinca, a village in the Apuan hills, where all the members of a Methodist group, which Lombardi and Vergnano had created, were slaughtered with the rest of the villagers. For the Methodists, the darkness at the time was penetrated by flashes of brilliant light. Jacopo Lombardini, though getting on in years, joined the Resistance movement as chaplain to the partisans in the Waldensian Valleys. He was captured, tortured and sent to the Mauthausen extermination camp, where he gave witness to his faith in Christ right up to the day of his martyrdom in a gas chamber. Aging ministers found youthful energy in delivering persecuted Jews from death, often hiding them in their own homes. Ludovico Vergnano, in a Florence blood-stained from weeks of street fighting, turned the Methodist church into a sanctuary for homeless families.

From a human point of view, there was faint hope that this little flock could suffer so many trials without losing heart. Yet, when WWII ended, not one Methodist congregation had been disbanded. They were all there, bleeding, mutilated, ready to take up responsibility in a new era. Even Casa Materna had managed to survive, and Teofilo Santi (son of the founder, Riccardo Santi), a physician who had borne the heaviest burden, began to look beyond Casa Materna's charitable and educational work which had now endured for half a century. From the desolation of wartime Naples he nourished the dream of founding a Protestant hospital — a daring dream he was able to realize some years later. Surely the war, for all its violence visited upon human beings, had galvanized the point that Christian faith can stand up to death and not yield its ground.

6. Rebuilding: toward a new Methodism in Italy?

In the wake of liberation, the process of reconstruction, which was to engage Italian Methodists for the next 30 years, was begun. It would be by no means a mere restoration of what existed before the war. Methodist work in Italy was reorganized in view of new opportunities and of a reappraisal of its function in the light of the radical changes that Italy was undergoing after the fall of Fascism and the monarchy, and the advent of a democratic republic.

The first step came in 1946, when the Episcopal Methodists and the Wesleyans united in one body. A new Methodist Church of Italy was formed, administratively related to Methodism in Britain. The urgent next step was in the field of leadership renewal. Without doubt, the body of ministers, symbolized by the strong personality of superintendent Emanuele Sbaffi, under Fascism had withstood 20 years of severe adversity with an heroic tenacity. At war's end, though, there had been no ordination of new ministers for many years. There was a real urgency to renew the ranks of pastors. Likewise, laypeople who had played a key role in the survival of the Methodist churches sought new input. Above all, ministers and laypeople alike needed to catch up with developments in Protestant theology.

A fresh contingent of pastors was trained at the Waldensian Theological Seminary in Rome and the training they received there was invaluable. Equally important was the step which Mario Sbaffi — son of Emanuele — took soon after the war, to build a youth center, Ecumene, for conferences and study sessions in the hills just outside of Rome. At Ecumene a new generation of able leaders was formed.

It became increasingly clear that the postwar situation had made a further step imperative: Italian Methodists needed to become independent of British Methodism. All agreed. Thanks to the intellectual talents and tactful advice of Reginald Kissack, the British Methodist representative, autonomy was reached in 1962, to the satisfaction of both parties.

With other Protestants, Italian Methodists took part in international ecumenical work and national joint initiatives to secure separation-between-church-and-state provisions in the new Italian Constitution, drafted in the late 1940s; to defend religious freedom, following the Christian Democrats' electoral victory in 1948; to organize the national Federation of Protestant Churches in Italy and to win national radio and TV time for Protestant broadcasts.

In no field did Italian Methodists work so effectively as in the search for unity among Protestant churches in Italy. A kind of *koiné diálektos* had developed within Italian Protestantism, especially among its younger members. It came about through a mixture of Barthian theology, commitment to social justice for the sake of those the gospel calls "the least," a rebellion against the nuclear threat and a yearning for peace that took dramatic shape during the war in Vietnam. The language this new generation shared was internationalist in spirit and intent. The indignation of the young people was also aroused against the exploitation of the Catholic religion in Italy by the Christian Democratic Party in furtherance of its conservative policies.

The employment of a common rhetoric was not enough: some new cooperative instrument for mission was needed. In the ensuing search for unity, almost unwittingly, the Methodists found themselves taking on an evermore important role as a bridge between Waldensians and Baptists. The Baptist, Methodist and Waldensian youth led the way and created the Federation of Protestant Youth in Italy (FGEI). Thanks to the vision of young people an Italian Protestant Congress was held in Rome in 1965, leading in 1967 to the constituting of the Federation of Protestant Churches in Italy (FCEI). It seemed obvious to everyone that the Federation's first president should be the Methodist pastor and ecumenical leader, Mario Sbaffi.

The younger generation had actually put to work, perhaps inadvertently, some of the gifts of the Methodist tradition — building Protestant unity and transforming the society. Only united could Italian Protestants hope to make any impact whatsoever upon Italian society. When youth saw radical religious reformation as the foundation for political and social renewal in the nation, it was Piggott's and Vernon's sense of call in the days of the *Risorgimento* all over again. To be sure, Italy after WWII had little in common with former times — the era of "masonic evangelism" was dead and buried forever and nobody dreamed of repeating William Burt's ambitious experiments. Nevertheless, it was not infrequent that the battle cries of old found sympathetic echoes among youthful ranks.

A quantum leap was taken in 1979 when the Waldensian and Methodist churches were federated within one synod and constitution. Each family of churches maintains its own international connections and certain administrative agencies. With their covenant of federation, Waldensians and Methodists have shown that it is possible to concert gifts of ministry received from God, strengthening them and putting them to work for God's purposes, without in any way suffocating the specific identity and tradition of either family of churches. The Methodist-Waldensian federation was truly a courageous step. It has paid off. If, thanks to federation, Methodists have received much, they have surely also brought to the new reality something of their own specific heritage. The Methodist institutions of circuits and lay preachers, for example, have been adopted by the federated church.

231

The job of the historian, as everybody knows, is quite different from that of the seer. But if it be true that reorganization climaxed with the federation of Waldensians and Methodists, it is equally true that in the years to come Italian Methodism will have to face new problems and will have to follow new paths, probably quite different from those trod in recent years. Many are convinced that federation is meaningless, unless it is an instrument for bringing the gospel to Italians with greater intensity, in terms which address the great changes that are taking place in Italy. The forces available to achieve this, at least on a human scale, seem ridiculously small, but the old Wesleyan motto, "The best thing in life is this — God is with us," can surely apply to the small Italian Methodist family, which for over a century of hard testing, miraculously, has made it through to point today's federated church to the grace it has known and sought to live, Christ's very own passion "for others."

Part Six

A CHARGE TO KEEP:
THE WALDENSIAN EXPERIENCE IN LATIN
AMERICA

(1857 ONWARD)

Sisters and brothers, for freedom Christ has set us free; do not use your freedom for self-centered pursuits, but through love look to the interests of others.

— Galatians 5

Va Dios Mismo en Nuestro Mismo Caminar

When the poor have nothing, and still share,
when people endure thirst, and still give to drink,
when the weak offer strength to their brothers and sisters,
it is God who goes the stretch with us.

When people suffer, yet find joy,
when they hope and tire not in hoping,
when they love, though hate abounds,
it is God who goes the stretch with us.

—hymn dear to Waldensian youth, in *Cancionero Abierto* (ISEDET, Buenos Aires, 1982)

We aim—
Within our churches: to intensify Bible study in relationship to social realities; to prepare members for discharging responsibilities in the churches.
Towards society: to seek to discern mission through analysis of social, economic, political, and cultural realities; to strengthen specialized ministries which address contemporary need; to participate actively in public life as biblical people.
To these ends, our churches in the next years must give particular attention to marginal sectors of both church and society, agricultural and industrial workers, and students in high school and beyond.

—from mission statement, synod assembly, Argentina–Uruguay, 1988

I.

TRANSPLANTING: FROM THE OLD TO THE NEW WORLD (1857-1877)

1. Emigration — a matter of survival

Within the enclosure of their narrow and barely fertile Valleys, the Waldensian population experienced a period of relative tranquility throughout the nineteenth century, and grew in numbers. But population expansion, with companion need for broader grazing and agricultural lands, put a severe strain upon land use limitations imposed by mountainous terrain. Farmers by tradition, and restricted by their outcast status until their emancipation in 1848, the Waldensians had no base in industry which might have absorbed the growing labor pool. Moreover, as frequently happens in rural populations, they had developed a ghetto mentality which screened out much of the outside world, with its innovation, change and opportunity. This mentality clearly was related to the fact that for centuries the Waldensians had been persecuted by most of the continent beyond their own small circle.

Still and all, beginning in the 1840s, the growing population had found an outlet in emigration on a non-organized scale, in many cases connected with seasonal jobs in southern France. By the middle of the century, some 450 persons per year were abandoning the Valleys and heading for France, Switzerland and even the Near East.

Devastating crop failures struck in the 1850s. A pastor wrote:

> . . . [I]t is dreadful; if we do not receive substantial subsidies our people will starve by the hundreds . . . [M]ost of our families are ruined. Some have six, eight or ten children — all of them dependent, with no prospect of food for the next day. So great is the poverty that most of our people are on the brink of an abyss . . .

[Crops] have failed for four consecutive years . . . Our villages are destitute.

The phantom of hunger hovered over the Valleys. According to an 1854 report of the Waldensian Board to the synod, no less than 3,000 families that year had to receive aid from the church.

Population increase, agricultural crises, debts and extreme poverty: all pointed to emigration in the interest of survival. In 1855 the Waldensian Christian Union, meeting at Luserna San Giovanni, recommended organized emigration, well studied and with sound guidelines, as the number one remedy. Curiously, that same year the synod dealt with the subject only as a subordinate matter, pointing to the difficulty of choosing a country for emigration and to the problem of obtaining the necessary resources for the undertaking.

In a large sector of the church there was clear opposition to emigration on a major scale, owing to the prevailing ghetto mentality and to the deep fear that the emigrants, in new surroundings, would gradually lose their cultural identity and their faith. In 1856, during a public meeting held to deal further with the subject, there was a confrontation between those (including the moderator, J. P. Revel) who opposed any mass emigration to distant countries, and those (led by Pastor M. Morel) who favored organizing mass emigration to South America, specifically to Argentina. Although no action was taken, a judgement became clear: organized emigration was the way to go.

Subsequent assemblies further examined the subject, but the church consistently declined to sponsor a settlers' venture, notwithstanding the situation of grave poverty and hunger in the Valleys. Individuals continued to leave of their own initiative, their sentiment well illustrated by the words of one who sailed for Argentina:

Neither the love of adventure nor the prospect of wealth drives us to take our families to remote countries we do not know and from which none of us will probably ever return. No, poverty, suffering, and hunger are the forces that expel us.

One settler, J. P. Planchon, crossed the Atlantic and ended up in Montevideo, Uruguay. His correspondence encouraged friends back home to risk the voyage with reasonable hope of finding a beneficial place to settle and induced the first group of Waldensian families to emigrate to the small country called the Oriental Republic of Uruguay.

To present the history of the Waldensians in the *Rio de la Plata*

(Plate River) region of Argentina and Uruguay it is useful to subdivide the narrative into three periods.

The first period (Transplanting) is that of arrival and first settlements. Running from 1857 to 1877, the period includes the launch settlement in the District of Florida, hardships endured there, the move to the area of Rosario Oriental, and establishment of religious and educational structures. Internal tensions and problems of organization pervade the time.

The second period (Expansion and Consolidation) begins with the arrival in 1877 of Daniel Armand Ugón — the patriarch of Waldensian settlements —and extends until the middle of the twentieth century. This is the period of resolution of conflicts in the early settlements and of the formation of new settlements in both Uruguay and Argentina.

The new diaspora presented many problems. The shortage of pastors and the wide dissemination of groups and families created serious difficulties for the church which considered dispersion as a threat to its very existence. Over this period the church became the center of religious and social life in the community. The direction given by the church leaders and religious convictions shared by the majority of the settlers gave the Waldensian settlement process its distinctive character.

The third period (Assimilation and Reorganization) extends from the 1950s to the present. During this period the Waldensian community has had to confront new problems which have served to advance Waldensian integration into the larger society:

— growing urbanization, a particularly traumatic experience for a community with centuries of tradition in a rural setting;

— the secularization of social life, accompanied by the emergence of non-religious volunteer organizations which have deprived the church of its position as the preeminent center of the community;

— the active political commitment of some members of the community, especially of the new generation of pastors, and the attendant polarization of the community during profound political crises experienced by Argentina and Uruguay.

Throughout this period the church has suffered a remarkable loss of influence within its own community, to the effect that it has become increasingly necessary to distinguish the Waldensian community and the Waldensian Church from one another.

2. The promised land

Uruguay came into existence as an independent country in 1830, the result of an agreement inspired by the British and signed by Argentineans and Brazilians. The gently rolling landscape was practically devoid of human inhabitants, although densely populated by roaming herds of cattle. The native population, the Charrùa Indians, had been driven out or exterminated during the first decades of the nineteenth century. Most of the inhabitants of the country were of European extraction (mainly Spanish, Basque, French, and Italian). There were considerable numbers of blacks who had been brought as slaves from Africa — Montevideo had been an important slave market, especially for southern Brazil.

Inhabitants of the east side (Banda Oriental) of the Uruguay River were called *orientales*, but they did not yet possess a clearly defined national consciousness.

Uruguay embarked upon an armed conflict (*La Guerra Grande*, 1838-52) which arose out of a dispute between newly formed political parties of the *blancos* and *colorados*. Argentina, and later Brazil, became involved and at length the conflict acquired international character through the intervention of the English and the French, so that the struggle became an expression of a larger conflict between industrialized powers in Europe and the non-capitalist periphery.

All good intentions notwithstanding, the period after the Great War was characterized by political instability. Between 1852 and 1856 there were seven different governments. From 1856 to 1863, the government was able to stand, despite several attempts at a *coup d'état*.

The political instability did not prevent economic recovery, in particular with respect to ranching and agriculture. New forms of industrialization and new markets integrated Uruguay into the capitalist world market, a process known in Uruguayan history as "modernization."

Such was the country into which the first Waldensian settlers arrived in the late 1850s: a country without a clear national consciousness, of wide open spaces and fertile soil, open to immigrants. The Waldensians' first impression is illustrated by a letter from J. P. Baridon:

> This is a land which can be compared to the Promised Land scripture tells us about. There is abundant natural wealth. There are innumerable herds of sheep, horses and cattle . . . Instead of having

to carry everything on your shoulders, you transport all on horse-back ... I would not exchange what we have here for the properties of the richest man in Villar ... This is a healthy country. No other sickness is known than death.

Another of the pioneers, J. Planchon, encouraged his friends to come by writing: "Do not think that you have to cultivate the ground with a hoe and to uproot trees. It is just a matter of putting the hand to the plow."

And the first pastor to come, M. Morel, in 1860, described his first impressions of the settlement in these terms:

> I have found most of the families living in relative abundance; they all have horses, oxen, cows, pigs and chickens. All their plantations seem to prosper . . . Even the European opportunists are more dangerous than their counterparts in this country. We are living in greater safety here than back in Piedmont. Houses are never locked, not even at night.

3. The first settlement in Uruguay

The first group of emigrants to leave the Valleys for Uruguay, drawn by the encouraging word sent by J. P. Planchon, consisted of just 11 persons, all from Villar Pellice. It was November 1856. Among them was J. P. Baridon, who would become a leader of the settling process in both Uruguay and Argentina. After a first stay at Montevideo, the group moved to the District of Florida, about 60 miles to the north, where they had been offered land at a good price.

In September 1857 a second group arrived, 72 persons, more heterogeneous in its composition, as its members came from different places in the Valleys: Villar Pellice, Torre Pellice, Rorà, Prarostino, San Germano, Pramollo, Inverso Pinasca and Pomaretto. The Montevideo they encountered was totally different from the one the first immigrants had seen: an epidemic of yellow fever was raging in the capital. Baridon's phrase written a few months earlier, "No other sickness is known than death," had turned ironic.

The chaplain of the British Legation in Montevideo, Rev. Frederick S. Pendleton, who was to play an important part in the Waldensians' settlement in Latin America, made contact with the newcomers and directed them to Florida.

A third group, 136 persons, arrived in January 1858, followed by a few more families in the spring of the same year. All considered, 45 families formed the first settlement close by the town of Florida, of which 15 had been moderately prosperous in Italy, while 30 had come over in sheer poverty.

Apart from the difficulties inherent in getting started in a new setting, the first year of the settlement was marked by a long drought. Although most of the settlers were concentrated in the area of Santa Lucía Chico, their farms were distant from one another; thus it became increasingly difficult for them to join forces for their several tasks and to organize their educational and religious activities together. The main difficulty they had to face was the stern opposition of the Catholic priest in Florida, a Jesuit named Majesté. This priest had come from Buenos Aires, where he had worked as a secretary in the diocesan office before being sent to the parish of Florida, where he became the "fashionable sacred orator" of the period. To a Jesuit of his training, the settlement of a number of Protestant families — and Waldensians, at that — was a direct affront to the Catholic Church. In fiery speeches, and through pressure exerted on the local political leadership, he carried on an incessant anti-Waldensian campaign which on several occasions led to violence.

The Waldensians, alarmed at what was happening, turned to Rev. Pendleton for support. Pendleton obtained an interview with the Minister of the Interior, and appealed to him for action. The Minister wrote to the political chief of Florida, urging him to look after the Waldensians' safety in these terms:

> . . . I have [received] favorable information about these people. They are industrious, simple, and peaceful; as our constitution supports economic growth and progress, I believe that they must be granted full liberty and receive full guarantees against the kind of fanaticism which might prevent them from advancing our constitutional aims.
>
> Convinced as I am of the importance of such tolerance, and of the political as well as economic advantage in offering such guarantees, I hope that you will take the necessary steps to avoid their being alarmed, and will see to it that peace among them is not disturbed by strangers . . .

This line of thought prevailed among most of the political leaders of the period. They were influenced by European liberal thinking and most of them were members of masonic or international fraternal organizations. Though the Catholic Church was the official church, leading political figures had marginalized its influence in national life. The Uruguayan Catholic Church was weak: it lacked resources and territorial wealth, and the clergy, in general, had little scholastic training. Intolerance such as Majesté's, however, was not common.

Though the Waldensians were not hounded by the authorities, certain external pressures were indeed evident, so much so that Pendleton thought that the Waldensians should move to another part of the country where they could enjoy greater safety, to the area east of the Rosario River, called Rosario Oriental. In a letter to moderator Malan in Italy he wrote:

They will be far better off in Rosario Oriental than in Florida . . . In Rosario they will be surrounded by the British. That is tremendous protection; I even venture to say it is the only security in this country.

In late 1858 and early 1859 the Waldensians moved to the area of Rosario Oriental. The move was sponsored by the *Sociedad Agrícola del Rosario Oriental*, one of the many projects that had emerged in Uruguay in view of the massive mid-century influx of immigrants. It was of particular interest to the ruling classes to direct the immigrant tide to the countryside to cultivate the land; agricultural settlements had therefore multiplied.

Through the mediation of Pendleton the *Sociedad* had established contact with the Waldensians in Florida; the July 1858 contract stipulated that in exchange for land that had been cultivated and upgraded near Florida, the Waldensians would receive tracts similar in size, but in the rough. Those who did not possess land near Florida would receive land in exchange for a third of their harvests over the next four years. The territory assigned to the Waldensians by the contract consisted of an area of approximately 10 square miles, bounded by the Plate River, 90 miles west of Montevideo.

Doroteo García, the president of the *Sociedad,* went out personally to supervise the measuring of the land. He indicated the place for the future village center and proposed to name it La Paz:

I believe that the name given to this village should point to the very aim of this country. Peace, deeply desired in this nation, is so necessary and indispensable for the success of this enterprise that we should invoke and proclaim it . . . at the moment of founding this village.

For the Waldensians, however, the move was not accomplished without difficulties. Chronicled a settler:

When we arrived at our destination in the District of Colonia, we found ourselves in a vast desert of more than 40 square miles, an immense area inhabited by only two persons, Alexander Malcomb, an Englishman, and Tomás Vila . . . A great quantity of cattle and wild horses was grazing on the land. We were surrounded by

241

vegetation called *chilcas*, taller than our horses. There was no shelter and we were unable to communicate with the town of Rosario because the streams were swollen. It rained every day. We were unable to work. There was no firewood to cook our meals with, if they can be called meals — some flour boiled in water with neither salt nor fat most of the time! ... At night we would huddle under the wagons to protect ourselves from the *pampero* winds; we were always in danger of being drenched by the rain. The children, wet and trembling in the cold, wept and complained all the time...

These adversities, however, were at length overcome. By 1861, the colony had been established and provided with its first pastor, M. Morel, and its first school teacher, J. Costabel. An 1860 census, taken by the pastor, counted 185 persons. The Waldensian Board reported to the synod in 1861 that there were some 800 cattle in the colony, at least four horses per family and that among a total of 240 persons, there had been one death, 19 baptisms and four weddings over the previous nine months. The area showed no hostility, as foreseen. The people in nearby Rosario even raised funds to help the Waldensians, because they knew of the modest means among them. To add to a promising situation, in the early 1860s Swiss settlers started a colony just to the north of the Waldensians' territory, and a close relationship arose between the two groups.

In spite of growing material prosperity, the settlement experienced internal conflict during the first 20 years. There was contention over where the new church facility should be located. One group, led by Morel and supported by the *Sociedad*, argued that the building should be erected in La Paz. The opposition, supported by Pendleton, favored a site nearer the center of the colony. This was part and parcel of a larger struggle between two strong personalities, each striving for dominance among the settlers. Pendleton, the English chaplain who had solved the Waldensians' problem in Florida, who had been instrumental in their move to Rosario Oriental, and who was constantly defending Waldensian interests, was an intricate spirit, and certain questions may well arise with respect to his motivation. For example, at the 1860 synod he urged that for the sake of the tranquility and safety of the settlers, the land should be bought by and put under the protection of the British government. Pendleton found a strong ally for this position in J. P. Baridon, a man of great influence among the settlers.

Morel, the other vital force, opposed such hegemonic attempts on the part of the British chaplain, and observed with growing concern that the settlers needed a strong religious organization, lest they "adopt the customs of the inhabitants of this country, who live like animals, devoid of a sense of God and of hope." Morel developed the idea of a veritable theocracy and attempted to create a colony of rule and discipline "based upon and obedient to the word of God."

In time Morel's heavy hand aroused the opposition of both the settlers and the *Sociedad*. The situation became so tense that the Waldensian Board sent its moderator, P. Lantaret, to mediate the conflict. His mission was successful, although only temporarily so.

The arrival of a new pastor from Italy, J. P. Michelin Salomon, served to polarize the positions instead of solving the conflict. Thus in 1875, accompanied by 10 families from the Latin American colony, Salomon left for the United States, where the group eventually settled down in Monett, Missouri.

Internal conflicts notwithstanding, the Uruguayan colony continued to prosper in material aspects as well as in numbers. New immigrants arrived. The birth rate among the settlers was high. In spite of their divisions, they pulled together in their agricultural tasks as these letters attest:

> When I arrived in 1863, there were 400 souls in our colony. Now, in 1868, we are 700. God is blessing us abundantly. The situation in the colony could not be better: ships from Montevideo and Buenos Aires anchor at the very edge of our lands. Our mud huts have been replaced by brick houses.

> We can live in peace, although sometimes there are clashes between the *blanco* and the *colorado* parties. As settlers we are not disturbed . . . [W]e obtain good results, and the work is not as exhausting as in the Valleys.

There were difficult moments, of course, apart from the internal tension and the confrontations with the *Sociedad*. There were trade and economic ups and downs, as well as an epidemic of cholera.

The steady growth in the colony population brought on a new problem, the need to obtain new land beyond the limits of the 1858 contract. The settlers themselves negotiated the purchase and lease of adjacent lands so that by the mid-1870s the area under cultivation by Waldensians had multiplied six-fold over the area of the 1858 tract.

II.

CONSOLIDATION AND EXPANSION (1877-1955)

1. Daniel Armand Ugón

Arriving from Italy as the third Waldensian pastor, Daniel Armand Ugón found a country in transformation.

During the last 30 years of the nineteenth century, Uruguay was to undergo a process of "modernization," a reworking of social and economic structures in response to the demands of growing world capitalism, making Uruguay a dependent country. Across the whole of Latin America, in fact, large sectors of the national oligarchies got into the act, the result not of national intentions, but of the imperialist policies of the dominant capitalist countries.

In Uruguay, modernization required the establishment of "law and order" — secured by a military dictatorship under General Lorenzo Latorre, who converted the army into a professional corps and introduced the telegraph and railways. The government's power, which had been very limited up to that time, succeeded — perhaps for the first time in the nation's history — in unifying the political space of the nation and in pacifying the country. The methods used were by no means non-violent; the peace achieved was essentially the "peace of cemeteries," but such ethical considerations worried neither the upper class of big landowners nor international capitalism.

Armand Ugón was born in 1851 in Torre Pellice; ordained and married to Alice Rivoir in 1877, he arrived in Uruguay late in the same year to take up the difficult task of organizing the religious life of the Waldensian settlers of Rosario Oriental.

As a man of great intelligence and of incredible working capacity, he was the towering central figure of the Waldensian colonies in the Plate River region for more than 50 years. He was a natural strategist and organizer. Like his predecessors for many centuries before him, Armand Ugón did not devote himself just to pastoral tasks; he was also the political leader of his flock.

Before leaving his native land, in a letter written to the moderator, Armand Ugón set out the strategy he planned to apply in his new ministry:

> ...[T]he church must not abandon the settlers, nor can it permit a foreign society or church to look after the needs of its own members ... Since the young are the hope of the future ... we must train promising young people for our junior college and theologi-cal seminary, so that within a relatively short period of time the settlers will be self-reliant and have their own ministers.

Armand Ugón's objective during his first years in Uruguay was to consolidate the colony of Rosario Oriental and to prepare for expansion. To achieve this, Armand Ugón foresaw that it would be necessary to conciliate opposing groups, set up primary and secondary schools, establish relationships with other Protestant denominations for common approaches to evangelization, and, fundamentally, transform the church into the center not only of the religious but also of the social life of the settlers, so that the religious and civil communities would be practically identical.

In pursuing these objectives Armand Ugón appealed, perhaps unconsciously, to the "ethnic" spirit of the Waldensians, which served in fact to delay their integration into the larger Uruguayan society. New settlements were virtual satellites of the mother colony. The idea throughout was to discourage random dispersion. As A. Griot, one of the founders of Colonia Iris put it:

> There is an urgent need to consolidate the existing groups and to prevent, as far as possible, families from straying away from the centers that have been started, for they will be lost among people of other nationalities and creeds. Let us keep to the principle that strength is in union.

A letter written by Armand Ugón to the President of Uruguay, late in 1879, well describes the situation and shows at the same time the manner in which the pastor represented the settlers in dealings with the Uruguayan government:

> All available land is occupied. We do not know where to send [new] families and those that are coming from Italy. Thirty families have arrived recently, and there is no land for them to cultivate. Experience has shown that when settlers disperse all over the country, they lose their working habits and sober lifestyle. Moreover, when they are widely dispersed, they are unable

The first Waldensian Church built in Uruguay, at La Paz, dedicated in 1893.

to have their own schools and worship centers. We all believe that it is possible to overcome these difficulties, but the lack of capital prevents us from acting accordingly. . . . The only solution is the foundation of a new colony of major proportions, capable of receiving 30 families immediately and another 300 within the next three years. The settlers will not require advances, as those who are established here will be pleased to provide them with what should be necessary . . . If the government were to provide them with a large and well situated area, a new colony would arise in a few years as if by magic.

This letter paved the way for the establishment of the second Waldensian settlement in Uruguay, Colonia Cosmopolita. In 1883 word came that the government had purchased land in Cosmopolita, and that the pastor would be in charge of the distribution and sale of that property. Ten years after its launching in 1883, Cosmopolita was a consolidated settlement, with a church and school in the center of the vast region.

A new pastor left Italy in 1882 to join Armand Ugón in serving the growing Waldensian community in Latin America. The new pastor, P. Bounous, took up residence in Cosmopolita.

By the turn of the century, there were Waldensian settlements all over the District of Colonia and in part of the District of Soriano. Their numbers had grown from 1,450 in 1878 to 3,800 in 1899. Two large churches, at Valdense and La Paz, had been built, along with a number of smaller chapels in the newer settlements. More than 10 primary schools were administrated by local church boards (*consistorios*) and a secondary school at Valdense — an outstanding achievement in the history of the Uruguayan nation — bore witness to the progress that had been made in the field of education and to the value the Waldensian settlers placed upon learning.

2. The launch in Argentina

The immigration of Europeans to Argentina, as to Uruguay, brought people from the Latin countries in the main, Italy and Spain in particular. When the flow of immigrants was trickling to an end in Uruguay in the early 1890s, Argentina was experiencing its highest influx yet; its frontiers had not yet been developed.

The immigration of Waldensians to Argentina during the last decades of the nineteenth century differed from the Uruguayan experience. Most of the early settlements were joint ventures of non-Waldensians with Waldensians. There was no comprehensive plan for colonization, owing to the absence of a permanent pastor.

So there was a dispersion of settlers in Argentina to a degree that far exceeded the experience in Uruguay. Consolidation took far longer than in Uruguay, and several of the dispersed groups ended up being served by other Protestant denominations.

Settlements arose in San Carlos (1860), Las Garzas Norte or "El Sombrerito" (1870), Alejandra (1872), Belgrano (1882), López (1886), and San Gustavo (1891). San Carlos, the first of the settlements, was the result of a contract signed by the government of the Province of Santa Fe and a colonizing society of Basel, Switzerland. The first settlers arriving in 1857 were Swiss. The first group of Waldensians who left Italy for San Carlos passed through Montevideo and, with the exception of one family, decided to stay in Uruguay. A second group of five families and two single persons did arrive in 1860, and more groups followed in later years from Italy, from the colony of Alejandra that started to disintegrate in 1874, and from other Uruguayan colonies. When vice-moderator E. Tron visited the area in 1899, he found some 25 Waldensian families (176 persons) living there.

The settlements of Belgrano, López, and San Martín, to the south of San Carlos, were formed by elements from San Carlos. Belgrano was the first Waldensian settlement in Argentina to be served by a resident minister: briefly, by A. Monnet, followed by E. Beux, the first Uruguayan-born Waldensian pastor trained in Italy. The Waldensian stronghold in Belgrano, at the turn of the century, numbered 335 persons.

Colonia Alejandra was the most dramatic of Waldensian colony failures in the Plate River region. In spite of the pronounced opposition of the leadership in Italy, a group of 226 persons embarked upon this venture in 1872. The hostility of the local Indians, the poor quality of the soil and exploitation on the part of the colonizing firm led to the early abandonment of the project. By 1899 only 25 persons remained, and within a few years they were incorporated into the Methodist Church.

J. P. Baridon and several families founded Rosario Tala, which grew rapidly and by 1899 numbered some 50 families (300 persons). An important center of wheat production, this settlement also passed to the Methodist Church.

Another small settlement was started in 1891 at San Gustavo, in the northern part of the Province of Entre Ríos, on land that had been bought by an Antwerp colonizing agency. There were no more than eight families by 1899, but in the following years it received much encouragement from Waldensian leadership in Europe, which created a commission for promotion of settlement in the area.

3. The early 1900s

During his visit in 1899, vice-moderator E. Tron had established the figure of the Waldensian population in the Plate River region as approximately 5,400. The real headache was the wide dispersion of the Waldensian people in relation to the small number of pastors, six, in the whole area (D. Armand Ugón, P. Bounous, E. Beux, B. A. Pons, P. Davyt and E. Pons), necessitating pastoral charges with reaches of hundreds of miles. The roads in the countryside could be better described as trails, and in rainy times flooding was common.

Until the 1930s, all the pastors who worked in the Plate River region were sent by the Waldensian Church in Italy, except for E. Beux, born in Uruguay and trained in Europe. It is important to note that the immigrant pastors were not considered as missionaries, since the Plate River region (*le nostre colonie laggiù*) was considered a dispersed congregation, and later, a district of the Italian church.

From 1896 onward, annual open conferences were held in which delegates and ministers from the far-flung congregations met to examine church affairs. In 1905 the annual conference was recognized as an official mechanism in the church order, and its actions became binding for the churches of the Plate River region.

A deeply felt need was that of printed communication between the several colonies, and a good link was created in the *Unión Valdense*, first a monthly, then a bi-monthly publication which carried biblical reflections, comment on Christian discipleship and news about the life of the congregations. With some interruption it continued to appear until 1919, when it was succeeded by the *Mensajero Valdense* (Waldensian Messenger).

In the field of publications Spanish was adopted from the outset, as it had very soon become the official language of worship and instruction. In the church-sponsored schools, French was taught in extra-curricular classes. Among themselves, the pastors communicated and corresponded in French, creating in fact, it must be admitted, a certain distance between "leadership" and "the people."

In the light of their training, the ministers exercised great influence upon both the spiritual and the social life of their communities. Ugón was of the theological stream which emphasized biblical scholarship and interpretation of scripture in cultural and social contexts. The next generation, however, more influenced by the pietist movement, was moralistic in posture.

The church clearly was at the center of the communities' life during the first decades of the 20th century, perhaps more than at any other time.

Pastors were teachers at the schools and settlers' representatives in affairs of state. Their wives served as teachers, nurses, midwives, and parish counselors, frequently under conditions they had not imagined when they had embarked for Latin America.

Of fundamental importance for the life of the church was the fact that the first generation of Waldensians born in Latin America had to develop strong lay ministries and equally strong parish councils, since the pastors were far too few.

At the turn of the century, organizations for young men emerged in the larger settlements as contexts in which the youth could hone leadership skills. In time, the local *Uniónes Juveniles* included young men and women. The Youth Federation, founded in 1921, concerted a wide range of activity among the local youth unions, including annual assemblies, sports tournaments and a monthly publication, *Renacimiento* (Rebirth).

The youth unions flourished until the 1960s, contributing to the formation of many lay leaders and playing a vital part in calls to pastors of Uruguayan and Argentinean origin, beginning with Carlos Negrin, ordained in 1932.

During the late 1920s, women started forming local groups, greatly encouraged by Ana M. Armand Ugón de Tron. Within a short time every congregation had its own women's group, an important factor in the life of each community. Apart from organizing meals and visits to the sick, and giving attention to emergency situations, the organizations engaged in Bible study and debates on issues of common interest. The Federation of Waldensian Women's Groups in Argentina and Uruguay was formed in 1935. Both the local groups and the Federation provided continuing opportunities for the training of women for active participation in the congregations' decision-making bodies.

In the field of agriculture, the Waldensians' progress was remarkable within the context of Latin America. In 1902 there were 12 threshing machines in Valdense alone, as well as an uncommon quantity of other heavy farming machinery. Remarkably, Waldensian farmers redesigned and adapted machinery to the requirements of their land and even invented sophisticated machines like an ant-

250

killing device and a combine-harvester.

One Italian observer wrote in 1906:

. . . [A]lthough in the old country [Waldensians] tend to be
excessively linked to tradition, virtually opposed to any change,
over here, they are always looking to perfect their machinery and
methods of cultivation.

The staple products continued to be wheat, corn, barley, and flax.
From 1900 onward plantations of fruit trees and vegetables for the
Montevideo market were started. La Valdesia was a first attempt at
producing jams and preserves on a commercial scale which, though
it did not prosper, pointed to a real future in commerce. Vineyards
had been planted from the very beginning of colonization, and the
production of wine was considerable around Valdense.

4. The education priority

Since the very beginning, particular attention had been given to
education, and there is an undeniable relationship between this fact
and the prospering of the settlements. Within two years of their
arrival at Rosario Oriental, the Waldensians had started a coed
school, and 10 years later, five new schools had been opened in
response to the demand by the growing population. In 1879 the six
petites écoles under the administration of the Valdense parish
council were attended by 292 boys and girls. In 1909, these schools
were recognized and incorporated into the national system upon the
request of the Valdense parish council, although the church continued to underwrite daily French lessons for the pupils.

The most remarkable achievement in the field of education,
however, was the founding in 1888 of the *liceo* (junior college) in
Valdense, the first of its kind in a rural area, the second in the whole
of Uruguay outside the capital and the first in the nation to admit
girls as well as boys. The school was the dream of Daniel Armand
Ugón and Thomas B. Wood, the latter a superintendent in the
Methodist Church in the United States, who, in his work in Latin
America, took particular interest in the Waldensian colonies and in
the educational effort inspired and led by Armand Ugón.

At the time the founders said of the *liceo* that it was "not to
multiply shining lights of culture for the big cities and high places,
but to nurture the lamps for the dark countryside and the common
roads in the life of the nation."

On these lines of material and spiritual growth, the Waldensian
settlements developed as a firmly united community in many

aspects drawn apart from the mainstream of society. Their considerable progress gave the Waldensians a feeling of superiority with respect to their neighbors, save the Swiss, who had performed much as had the Waldensians.

The sense of superiority, while not manifesting itself in depreciation of others, did, nonetheless, keep the Waldensians isolated from the surrounding society by means of subtle mechanisms such as wide-spread in-group marriage, the use of French on occasion in worship services, the teaching of French in the schools, the use of the Historic Valleys' dialect in the homes, the perpetuation of certain traditional Valleys customs, and, ultimately, the exaltation of whatever was considered "Waldensian."

A noteworthy exception to this mentality was to be found in the active participation of several Waldensians in national politics, especially in support of the Batllista reform policy of the *colorado* governments in the first decades of this century.

5. Emigration to Argentina

As the new century opened up, Uruguayan emigration to Argentina caught everyone by surprise.

Contacts by Juan Pedro Rochon with an Argentinean colonization enterprise led to the establishment of a settlement in the southeastern edge of the Province of Buenos Aires. In March 1901, a first contingent of 18 families from Uruguay arrived at what would later be called Colonia Iris; 10 more families followed in the course of the same year. In the next several years the movement increased considerably, and when Pastor P. Bounous made his first visit to the new settlement, there were 122 families, spread over an area of some 800 square miles.

Migration of such magnitude caused concern among Uruguayan authorities. In a 1901 letter to Armand Ugón, the Secretary of Agriculture inquired about causes of the "alarming migratory movement," and for advice about ways to stop it. In his reply, the pastor cited as reasons the growing number of families and the shortage of lands for agriculture at reasonable prices. Armand Ugón offered this advice to the government:

> . . . [B]uy a vast expanse of land where it would not be too expensive, with easy access to a railway line or a navigable river, subdivide it and sell it on installments to families who commit themselves to settle there, in a size proportionate to the number of members of each family, so as to avoid any kind of speculation . . .

No practical solution was advanced by the authorities, however, so the migration movement continued, intensified by civil war. Meanwhile, Colonia Iris — the cluster of Villa Iris, Jacinto Arauz, El Triángulo, Villa Alba (later: General San Martín) and Colonia Bidou — prospered in Argentina, in spite of initial difficulties and some internal tensions. The success of Colonia Iris can be looked upon as confirmation of the Waldensians' great capacity to adapt to new environmental and agricultural challenges. In the Historic Valleys in Italy they had been accustomed to cultivating tiny tracts of land. In Uruguay they had adapted quickly to the new requirements of soil management. In Colonia Iris the challenges were completely different: the *pampa* climate with its dry winds and sandstorms, long and destructive droughts and sudden — and no less devastating — floods.

The settlers started out by sowing only wheat and on several occasions droughts ruined entire harvests. The farmers learned their lesson and diversified their crops, adding corn, barley, and flax.

The Argentinean farms were normally three or four times the size of those in Uruguay. This permitted mechanization of agricultural work on a far larger scale than possible in Uruguay. Since farm machinery was costly, cooperatives emerged early to disperse the burden of debt.

The Colonia Iris experience is a good example of the gradual growth of the church's structures. Six months after their arrival, the settlers were visited for the first time by Pastor P. Bounous. The settlers asked to be considered temporarily as an extension of the congregation of Cosmopolita, some 600 miles away. Wrote Bounous:

> Since the foundation of the settlement, our brothers and sisters have felt the need of assembling for worship, having Sunday school for their children and religious instruction for the young. For a short time, Oscar Griot, an alumnus of the *liceo* at Valdense, took care of these tasks. When he left for Buenos Aires to continue his studies, Benjamin Long [one of the settlers] took over from him. As there was no [church] building, . . . [the community] came together in the homes of those who volunteered to do as much as they could for the well-being of all. A commission of five members was appointed to look after the material and spiritual needs of the community. . .[At an] assembly, heads of families have discussed the need of obtaining, as soon as possible, a building site . . . and of having a minister, or at least a schoolmaster-evangelist.

In such assemblies, and during the yearly pastoral visits by various ministers from Uruguay and elsewhere in Argentina, the elements necessary for a normal congregational structure were taking shape. The building site was donated; the construction of a simple building to serve for school and worship was completed; funds were raised by the settlers, not only for the construction, but also for travel expenses of visiting ministers. Everything was prepared with a view to attaining the status of a constituted congregation. This was conferred in 1905, on the occasion of Armand Ugón's first visit to Colonia Iris.

Lay persons remained in charge of the church school and worship services. By the time Pastor David Forneron arrived in 1908 to take up duties as the first resident minister in Colonia Iris, the congregation had established its basic structures and had even built the pastor's home.

True to its beginnings, Colonia Iris remained a congregation with strong lay leadership. It was the first charge for many pastors, and a common saying in the congregation used to be: "We train them — break them like horses — and then they leave for Uruguay!" In large measure, the training came through serving the five worship centers across the Colonia Iris countryside and the new settlements, 17 de Agosto, Artalejos, and Bahía Blanca.

A word about concurrent national events in Uruguay and Argentina is necessary here. Between 1930 and 1955, the expansion of the Waldensian community through agricultural settlements came to an end in Uruguay (the last group settlement was Colonia Alfèrez, District of Rocha, 1947) and slowed down in Argentina. The disintegration of many of the communities and the complete absorption of others into their respective area populations took place within the framework of severe disruption in the national economies. The 1929 capitalist market crash had a strong impact in Uruguay. The Batllista reforms which worked well in a flourishing economic situation, faltered. In 1933, the Batllista government was overthrown and a conservative and economically powerful government tried to put the house in order with emergency measures and a strong executive. Full democracy was restored in 1946 and another member of the Batlle family, Luis Batlle Berres, governed the country until 1958. The neo-Batllista policy, in a period of economic expansion, sought to give a new impulse to industrialization and development so as to diminish dependence on imports — a line that was shared by other Latin American countries. The economic expansion ended with the Korean War; the country's economy thereafter declined again and entered one of its most severe crises.

What was happening in Argentina was far more interesting. After years of Uriburu's dictatorship and a period of transition, one of the country's most spectacular and contradictory figures, Juan Domingo Perón, arose in the mid-'40s. Aiming his markedly nationalistic economic policy towards the masses — a policy which contained both progressive and fascist dimensions — Peron gave Argentina's economy a strong shot in the arm. Although favored by world-wide economic expansion, he was trapped by his own contradictions, and was unable to bring about structural reform with respect to ownership of land and exploitation. Under pressure from national oligarchies and North American nations, he was overthrown in 1955 by the very instrument that had brought him into power: the military.

III.

ASSIMILATION AND REORGANIZATION
(1955 ONWARD)

1. From an immigrant church to a naturalized church

Scholars make the point that immigrant churches can easily become religious clubs, grounded first of all in the conservation of linguistic and cultural traditions and only in a derivative manner based upon a confession of faith. In such cases, the church becomes an institution which helps the immigrants to overcome the traumatic experience of being thrust into a new society, and to conserve the way of the original culture, effectively delaying immigrants' integration into the new reality. In this perspective, the religious and secular communities are virtually one and the same. What of the Waldensians in Latin America? Through the first decades of this century, almost all who belonged to the circle of Waldensian "people" (those bearing Waldensian surnames) were considered as belonging to the church. But by mid-century, the concept of the church was questioned increasingly. The proliferation of agricultural colonies was over. Links with the Valleys in Italy had been reduced. The languages of the "old country" disappeared from common parlance, and a generation of Latin American pastors who had been trained at Union Seminary in Buenos Aires was taking over from their Italian colleagues.

The rural-based Waldensian community was confronted with profound urbanization and secularization on all sides. A crisis was at hand: although consolidation of the community had been accomplished, its survival would depend on new aims and purposes and upon the community's engagement with new realities — the coming to an end of the colonization period, the scattering of individual farmers and their families to more and more distant places, the exodus of Waldensians to the cities, and the urbanization of agricultural settlements.

Clear-sighted pastors had observed as early as the '20s that the exodus of Waldensians towards towns and cities was complicating matters for the church. No steps were taken, however, throughout the '30s and '40s to come to grips with the changed times. At length, in 1952, in large measure due to the untiring personal efforts of Pastor E. Tron, the Waldensian Church of Montevideo was organized and constituted. Overcoming the opposition of some and the indifference of most, Tron had insisted upon the importance of having a congregation in the capital:

> Eighty percent of the members of our church who move to Montevideo are living on the margin of all church activity. Many of them have lost their links completely, . . . [a] serious and deplorable fact [that] is particularly frequent among intellectuals and professionals. It is an alarming development which must be addressed immediately . . .

E. Tron's premature death prevented his seeing the church facility in Montevideo built during the 1958-1970 pastorate of J. Tron.

The secularization of social life jolted the church, since it had been not only the religious, but also the social, political, and cultural center of the community. The emergence of new and specialized institutions challenged the church's traditional roles and began to restrict its action to "religious" tasks alone. The confrontation between the church and the secularized world became inevitable in the second half of this century. In the '20s E. Tron had written:

> [A]s Waldensians, we have principles of life which characterize us and constitute the reason for our existence... [Although] the Waldensians in South America now cannot escape contact with secular culture, [they] face the imminent danger of losing the principles which have guided our lives and made us a special people... What can we do? Keep ourselves separated from that society? No, Jesus does not want us to withdraw from society. We are called upon to live in our present-day society, but we must struggle to maintain those principles which distinguish us and which are grounded in our faith.

During the '60s, ecclesiastical developments of fundamental importance took place. In 1965 the Plate River region was authorized to conduct its own synod assemblies and to have its own Regional Board, the *Mesa Valdense*, the counterpart, on a full parity basis, to *Tavola Valdese* in Italy. Further, a commission of both Italians and Latin Americans hammered out the text of the Waldensian Discipline, to receive final approval in 1973-74. The Discipline's implications go deep. In the Plate River region, polemics on social and political issues threatened to provoke divisions, but the text of the Discipline calls upon all local congregations to recognize one another as member churches of "one body whose life comes alone from the grace of the Lord." Beyond national and geographical separations, the churches thus affirmed their unity as one body. Institutional forms, adapted to realities on two different continents, stream into the life of *one* synod which unfolds in two annual sessions — the Latin American in February and the European in August.

This put an end to the "adolescent crisis" of the Latin American churches with respect to the mother church in Europe. The Waldensian churches in the Plate River region had achieved their autonomy within the internal unity of the Waldensian Church. The mutual recognition of all local churches on an equal basis was of particular importance in the Plate River region, because it ended the hegemony of Uruguayan churches — earlier in origin and constitution — over the Argentinean churches.

2. The training of the pastors

The need for solid academic training for future ministers in the Latin American congregations had been felt as early as the 1880s, when Armand Ugón and Thomas Wood founded the *Liceo Evangélico* with a view to preparing young people for ministries in the new Protestant churches of the area. However, the sense of urgency among those who felt called to engage in the task of evangelization was so great that it often did not allow sufficient years for solid theological preparation.

In 1926 the dream of an adequate training center for pastors became a reality, when B. Foster Stockwell — sent by the Methodist Church in the United States — was appointed director of the *Seminario Evangélico de Teologia* in Buenos Aires. Dr. Stockwell, a disciplined organizer, transformed a Methodist-Disciples of Christ school into an authentic center of theological inquiry. Courses and admission standards were upgraded. A library was created and the most important works of theologians in Europe and the United States were published by a Protestant publishing house (La Aurora). So many young men and women from all over Latin

America came to receive their training in Buenos Aires, that it became a truly ecumenical and international training center.

After WWII, a decisive change took place in the seminary — change inspired in part by the exchange of leading professors, books and journals, no small thanks to global ecumenism, and in part by the introduction, in the late '40s, of the work of Karl Barth. Contact with the theology of the Confessing Church (the minority experience within the churches in Germany in the '30s and '40s) made a profound difference in the Buenos Aires seminary. The experience of a church that became a minority in its own country by reason of its political challenge impacted in a decisive way the understanding of mission among minority Protestant churches on a continent that had been enslaved, stifled and suffocated by diverse powers of oppression. The example of the Confessing Church gave clarity to the conflict between demonic power and the word of God, and turned the churches to serious commitment to the transformation of societies in Latin America.

Contact with the thinking of Karl Barth, Dietrich Bonhoeffer, and others led the young Latin American theologians to a heightened awareness of issues confronting the church: the church-world dialog, the struggle of faith over ideology, and the Christian's commitment to active discipleship in public life.

In time, the Latin American Protestant churches started to attract the attention of many people in the worldwide ecumenical movement. The Plate River region was well represented in global ecumenism by vitalities who had been trained in the Buenos Aires Union Seminary — most of them members of the Methodist Church (José Miguez Bonino, Emilio Castro, Julio de Santa Ana) which as a "city church" was more versatile, more open to change than the rural and small-town congregations of the Waldensian Church.

3. Tension and conflict

The new generation of ministers who had received their training in Buenos Aires attempted to break through the "splendid isolation" of the Waldensian Church. Writing in the Waldensian weekly in Italy in 1957, an Italian pastor who had served in the Plate River region for seven years offered this incisive analysis:

> All groups of Europeans who have emigrated to Latin America to organize agricultural colonies have gone through three successive stages of development: first, the closing-in of the enclave, sepa-

rated from those who surround it; second, the establishment of contacts with the inhabitants of the new country, the use of the latter's language and some of their customs; finally, the mingling of the whole group with the larger population... At present, our settlements in Uruguay and Argentina are going through a very critical time, that of the transition from the second to the third stage. Increasingly, there is an intermingling with the larger population. The church will have to choose between two alternatives. One is to remain exclusively the church of the Gonnet -Baridon - Geymonat, etc. families, that is, the church of those who are Waldensian by blood ties, even though in many cases the faith is no longer professed. Going down this road the church will become more and more conservative, a museum, a repository of folklore. The second alternative is to become the church of those who are Waldensians in spirit, that is, of those who profess the faith of the Waldensian Church, though they come from, say, Pérez, Quintana, or Montes de Oca stock. Taking this road will make the church more and more different from our church in the Valleys in Italy, but it will be a living church.

Well anchored across the community, the conservative mentality was an entrenched obstacle to efforts for change proposed by the younger generation of pastors and lay people. The conservatives called "communist" or "divisive" all who proposed new ways; similarly branded were all proposals that were meant to insert the church into Latin American and even global struggles.

The advocates of change, fortified with sound intellectual training and theological arguments, made every attempt to convince the community as to the integrity of their posture. The *Mensajero Valdense* and *Renacimiento* papers became platforms of debate and strongholds for exposition of the ideas for renewal.

During the celebration of the first centennial, in 1958, of the foundation of Valdense a member of the new generation put his analysis this way:

The church of Jesus Christ cannot lock itself up in an ivory tower or in an isolated spiritual paradise. It must never do so. That is why we believe it is wholesome that so many "outside elements" converge with this "evangelical" (Protestant) anniversary and join hands with us. If the church sinks more and more into sterile isolation from economic, social and political reality, it will just recite a monologue to itself without making any difference whatsoever in the political, economic and social fields. Those "worlds" and the church, too, will receive no light at all.

All during the '60s and early '70s, the *Mensajero* zeroed in on the process of change and resistance to it. For example, on the Cuban Revolution, the *Mensajero* editorialized as follows:

> Several of our readers have expressed their alarm . . . that our publication should invade the political arena. There are two reasons that have moved us [in this direction]. In the first place, ... as Christians, we cannot remain indifferent to situations which arise in the world and to the problems which move the life of nations. If the church's primary mission is to proclaim Christ — his message of love, justice and truth, and his Lordship over all nations — it is necessary to examine the world and to know about its problems, needs and cries ... A church which is sent into the world and which follows the inspiration of its Lord, must stand up and act in the world... It must have concern for social injustice, ignorance, poverty and privations of all kinds which are suffered by the world's people. Although it must not enter the realm of partisan politics, it must act upon its responsibility to contribute to the relief of suffering.
>
> Secondly, as Christians, we are called to be well informed about the forces which are at work in the world. For this reason we must reach for facts with an analytical spirit and strive for the widest possible base of information.

The *Mensajero Valdense* went on to resource the Waldensian Church with many social, economic and political discussions, such as the stagnation of the rural economy and the need for far-reaching reforms, the United States' invasion of Santo Domingo, the '68 student uprisings, Czechoslovakia, racism, violence, etc.

As the '60s went by, the school favoring renewal became more outspoken, but resistance to it grew stronger. Positions polarized and the terms of the debate hardened, aided and abetted by the general deterioration of the political and economic climate in the region.

In 1968, the editor of the *Mensajero* observed that the Waldensian Church was committing the "sin of turning its back upon reality":

> It appears that we fail to understand that this is a moment of rupture in history — one age is coming to an end and a new age is beginning. If that be true, the mere conservation of religious norms and standards of "the good old times" will never permit the church to offer something to the world ... It will not even permit the church to hold its position, because the tides of change will sweep away everything that is nostalgic memory of the past and no more. The Waldensian Church seems to be asleep, or, worse still, reluctant to wake up.

261

The 1968 synod assembly affirmed the direction taken by the *Mensajero*.

The opposition, however, very much alive, characterized the *Mensajero* as "not representative of the church and its people" as "socialist," as "a cover for the infiltration of communism in our church." There was even a call that the paper should be closed down.

The progressives were accused of belonging to a minority which disturbed the life of the church and its established order. The leadership in the church were labeled a "group of comrades" involved in the leftist campaigns. Criticism came not only from within the community, but also from the right-wing press, which held that in the Waldensian Church in Montevideo, for example, "people are instructed very little about religion and mostly about politics and becoming communists."

While the '60s were characterized by polemics and harsh confrontation within the church, the '70s were marked by a development from without that was new to the Uruguayans and, unfortunately, well-known to the Argentineans: the advent of military dictatorship. The Uruguayan President, Juan Maria Bordaberry, elected in 1973, capitulated to pressure from the military, dissolved the Parliament and decreed a "state of internal warfare" in order to give the armed forces a free hand in subduing the revolutionary movement of the *Tupamaros*. There were arrests without judicial process, imprisonment, torture, the disappearance of persons, threats, and the secret emigration of many in search of exile. The dark days extended to Argentina when Maria Estela Martínez de Perón was ousted by the military who worked in close collaboration with the Uruguayan police and military forces.

We cite several events of particular significance to the Waldensian Church during the dictatorship years. The first was the 1974 shutting down of the Mensajero by the government, on the pretext that the paper reported on "politically persecuted persons" in Chile and Uruguay. In closing down the Mensajero, proclaimed in the government press, along with wild attacks against the World Council of Churches, the government served notice of its intent to exercise close control over what was happening in the Protestant churches and in the Methodist and Waldensian Churches in particular.

All activities in the local congregations, except for regular services of worship (the government did not want to be accused of suppressing the freedom of worship) were subject to prior authorization by the police. Church assemblies, camps, seminars, study groups, cultural activities, special meetings — all required official sanction and submission of names of participants to police authorities.

In Argentina, the town of Jacinto Aráuz, center of the Waldensians' Colonia Iris congregation, was the object of a military search because of alleged "subversive teaching" in the secondary school, a school co-sponsored by the Waldensian Church.

The Waldensian communities had to learn how to endure in a climate in which the pervasive police-military presence was engraved on everyone's mind. They were actually strengthened by the fact that a great number of their educators, expelled from public teaching posts and constrained to find themselves new jobs, were taken on by the church. Awareness went underground and grew in silence.

A most critical moment came during the synod session of 1977. Police authorities let it be known that several progressive pastors who were candidates for service on the Waldensian Regional Board were to be scratched from the ballot! Citing Article 5 in the church's constitution ("The Waldensian Church seeks no privilege from the state, nor does it consent to interference by the state in the church's internal life...") the synod voted unanimously to disregard outright the state's brazen attempt to control the church. Notwithstanding the sharp divisions of the '60s, at the crucial moment when the state sought to shape the church's center of decision, the synod stood tall and rallied to manifest unity.

4. Specialized ministries

The '60s and '70s saw intense activity in the launching of specialized ministries. Earlier, in 1933, the church had organized a home for the aging in Valdense, and earlier still, as we have seen, schools and youth associations were clear priorities.

In 1963 a home for children in distress, Hogar Nimmo, near the town of Colonia in Uruguay, was founded in ecumenical common cause with the Methodist Church. In 1971 El Sarandi, a home for mentally disabled persons, the first of its kind in Uruguay, opened its doors at Valdense. During the '60s, community work had started in a poor area of the town of Rosario; in 1971 a community center, El Pastoreo, was inaugurated there. A second home for the aging was opened in Jacinto Aráuz in Argentina in 1978.

WALDENSIAN CHURCHES IN ARGENTINA, 1989

province	church cluster	
Buenos Aires	Artalejos	Buenos Aires
	Bahía Blanca	San Nicolás
Entre Ríos	San Gustavo	
La Pampa	Iris	
Santa Fe	Belgrano	San Carlos
	El Sombrerito- Reconquista	

WALDENSIAN CHURCHES IN URUGUAY, 1989

district	church cluster	
Colonia	Colonia-Riachuelo- San Pedro Juan Lacaze- Cosmopolita Miguelete	Nueva Palmira- Carmelo Ombúes de Lavalle Rosario Tarariras Valdense
Montevideo	Montevideo	
Paysandú	Arroyo Negro	Paysandú
Río Negro	Fray Bentos	Nueva Valdense- Young
Rocha	Alférez	
Soriano	Dolores-San Salvador	

These ministries, open to persons within the church and well beyond, reveal the church's commitment to the weak and to the "little people." To carry the work forward, Waldensians across the board as well as friends raised the necessary funds and collaborated in many practical ways.

Without ascribing final verity to the saying that "theory divides and practice unites," it must be said for the record that within the realm of traditional social service, conservatives worked together with advocates of change and renewal. Within the framework of the synod's Commission on Social Action and Institutions, space for dialogue was kept open when other points of meeting had disappeared.

The organization which helped mightily to anchor the church during the "heavy" years of passage was the Federation of Waldensian Women. For decades the women had trained themselves for leadership roles; they had served in the local *consistorios* and on synod commissions and as members of the Waldensian Regional Board.

During the turbulent '60s and '70s, the Federation maintained its inner cohesion and matured through collaboration in international women's efforts (World Day of Prayer, Fellowship of the Least Coin, international decades, etc.).

Another decisive factor in deeply troubled times was international ecumenical support. Without encouragement from the churches in Europe and the United States, from the ecumenical movement and the World Council of Churches, it would certainly have been most difficult, if not impossible, to forge a line of thinking and action that strives to practice the mind of the Christ "for others." Ministry exchanges with other countries, and visits and publications from abroad were indispensable nourishment for the Waldensian constituency in Latin America. Moderatorial visits from Italy and the presence of pastors and professors of theology from abroad never failed to bring in fresh air: the visitors said what the local people sometimes could not easily say. They were agents of solidarity in the concrete.

5. For one another: freedom and responsibility

Free elections were held in Argentina and Uruguay in 1983 and 1984, respectively. The restoration of civilian rule brought the liberation of political prisoners, the homecoming of exiles, the end of censorship in the media.

In the midst of rejoicing over the retreat of the military, the image of the two nations as reflected in the world press was one of lands that had been savaged and left with huge debts — debts of dollars to the International Monetary Fund, and debts of restoration to those upon whom the dictators' cruel systems had been visited.

All in all, the Waldensian Church in the Plate River region emerged from the dictatorship years with comparatively few marks of suffering — it had not been "amputated" like the Methodist Church in Uruguay, many of whose leaders had been compelled to flee the country.

The larger society looks upon the Waldensian Church in Argentina-Uruguay as an intentional, serious church, persevering in its work with a message which vindicates human dignity. With other Christian communities the Waldensian churches have a major challenge before them of standing beside political prisoners and exiles of the dictatorship years, and helping them reintegrate themselves into national life. The two countries face staggering international debts, poverty, and grave deficiencies in public education and health. Editorializes the *Mensajero*, "We know that we dare not trust our strength alone, but place our trust in the Lord who rules our vocation, discipleship and obedience. In vain does the witness of our church insist upon the safeguarding of human dignity unless the latter derives from the love of Christ."

Today there is no unanimity within the church as to evaluation of the recent past, nor a clear and concrete vision for the near future. Although it is just too early to analyze the trends abroad in the church in the late '80s, this much can be said: Argentina and Uruguay have been ravaged by the tyranny of military power and "national security" interests. Though democracy in the two nations is a tender experience, they must learn to drink from that well. And in the mystery of God's grace the churches now have Latin American theological inspiration to plumb, and notably, the theology of liberation.

In the first issue of the *Mensajero* to appear just after the 1984 restoration of civilian rule in Uruguay, the moderator at the time, Pastor Ricardo Ribeiro, sounded this note for the reflection of the church as she faced the future:

> The church must open up space for freedom's way. But freedom is meaningless if there is no inner freedom grounded in obedience to God whose will must be discovered each new day and under ever-changing circumstances. We cannot know freedom if we fail to free ourselves from our preconceptions, if we are incapable of

267

examining and judging even the most sacred of institutions, and if there is no respect for the conscience of our sisters and brothers, which will frequently differ from our own.

Obedience to Christ will face us toward the formation of human community more in accordance with God's plan and less dependent upon security and individual interests. As scripture teaches (Matthew 5-7), real freedom consists, first of all, in seeking God's rule and its justice, and trusting to God's hands our personal security and welfare.

25. NEW OCCASIONS, NEW DUTIES: WORDS TO THE CHURCHES (1985)

1) Freedom and responsibility

...We must not view democracy as sheer majority rule: in a deeper sense democracy is space for the freedom and participation heralded by the good news of Christ...

The good news of Christ brings that freedom in which no majorities dominate minorities. We call Jesus "the Redeemer," that is, simply, "the Liberator" who delivers people from the constraints of legalism, the instrument of religious and civil oppression. Paul teaches that Christ has set us free from the power of sin and death — from all powers which suffocate life itself: we live in "the glorious freedom of the children of God" (Romans 8)...

We must be vigilant in keeping freedom alive, working to assure that, as the sun, it illumines all life, for "freedom" for some, but not for all, amounts to the sway of death for all. We must press on unremittingly for the return of freedom that it is fulfilled in reaching to everyone.

Now freedom carries its risks and unsettles many; as in Israel of old, many who have been delivered from domination through the intervention of God's "mighty hand and outstretched arm" lament the loss of servitude's "security" (Exodus 16). We have to recognize that the same faintheartedness which arose in the desert can also prosper among us today.

There are real risks, because freedom, the supreme gift in fully human life, is vulnerable to the snares of sin (which reach well beyond the iniquity of state terrorism and authoritarianism). On this point Paul again teaches: "To freedom we have been called, but not, however, as an open season for indulging in the flesh" (Galatians 5). "Flesh" here means satisfaction of the impulses to greed, self-centeredness, individualism, to the reducing of people to self-serving objects — all ranged against the values of God's rule.

For many, evidently, democracy is "license for the flesh," that is, unbounded opportunity for seeking one's own happiness, one's own fulfillment, one's own fortune at the cost of the others' good. For such

Christ has not set us free! Christ's freedom releases us to work for God's purposes, to struggle above all for God's rule and its justice, for solidarity in place of exclusion, for justice in place of discrimination, with particular regard for the raising up of the weak.

For this Christ transforms us, rescues us from the sin of individualism, of the spirit of "accommodation," of living by the law of the most powerful.

We must receive Christ's freedom with thankfulness, with a spirit of repentance, of readiness to consecrate it to the cause of God's rule for which we must live, militantly, even, in secular and political arenas. Because in a democracy all share power: God will hold us to account for what we do with the measure which falls to us. And because failure to distribute power across the full human community will mutilate life within the community of faith itself.

2) Political action and struggle for justice

At the outset of a new political era in Argentina and Uruguay, we desire to offer the following reflections:

1) We express our joy and satisfaction, giving thanks to God for setting our feet again on the way toward democracy.

2) We confess our churches' passivity and failure oftentimes to give a good witness in the face of a form of government which we have now left behind.

3) We view as illusory the belief that formal resumption of civilian government is the end of the road. On the contrary, we have to be ever-vigilant that injustice and marginalization not undermine God's justice and peace, the service of which is our biblical calling.

4) Though called to the permanent militancy of exercising public responsibility, our final loyalty is to Jesus Christ alone, whose rule we have to announce to all sectors of life in our society.

5) Part of our struggle — our conversion — will be committed to the distribution of resources across our underdeveloped, and to a real extent, retrogressing lands.

We cite, for example, the enormous budgets committed to so-called "national security" (defense, armaments) — to the detriment of vital life sectors, such as health, education, housing, to name just a few.

For this reason, the Waldensian Church commits itself afresh, with sister churches, human rights organizations, and people and political parties of good will:

a) to struggle for total elimination of military outlays and related activities (military service, arms acquisition), thus avoiding major international indebtedness;

b) to oppose the installation of industry intended for arms manufacture;

c) to oppose foreign military bases and satellite monitoring stations for military purposes.

6) The foregoing concerns are not based upon our own discoveries or political formulations. They are based, instead, in the good news of Jesus

269

Christ, who has shown us the true value of life for all human beings, and who has made known to us the "politics" of God, grounded in love, as scripture teaches us in John 13.

—*Acts of the Waldensian Synod,* Argentina–Uruguay, 1985, nos. 1, 77.

Part Seven

WALDENSIAN-METHODIST DISCIPLESHIP IN THE LATE TWENTIETH CENTURY

(1945 ONWARD)

Seek first God's rule and God's justice...

— Matthew 6

To be bearers of Waldensian identity, Protestant progressive-democratic culture, and the tradition of freedom is not enough. Christ is our identity! We aim to live out biblical culture! With our freedom we must stand up for the irrevocable demands of "hungering and thirsting after justice!"

— Pastor Giorgio Bouchard, Italy, 1986

WALDENSIAN-METHODIST DISCIPLESHIP IN THE LATE TWENTIETH CENTURY

1. Bittersweet times

In 1945 the Waldensians wanted to put behind them the terrible period of Fascism and of the war. There was little bread and there were few shoes, but there was rejoicing and imaginative hope for the future. American volunteers, notably from the Mennonite Central Committee, showed up to help rebuild Waldensian facilities and to help provide U. S. scholarships for former partisans. When they left, they were to be remembered for their solidarity and their industrious simplicity.

The Waldensians in the Historic Valleys placed their hope in the reborn Italian democracy and so they did not listen to those who wished to see the Valleys annexed to France, even though the great Republic on the other side of the Alps was considerably more efficient, offered more freedom and was far better organized than its Italian counterpart. A sense of mission to the nation and ties with a huge diaspora were strongly felt across the church. The partisan from Orsara di Puglia who fell at the gates of Turin in the final days of the war was a reminder to Waldensians in the north that on the other side of the Apennines and to the south, there were brothers and sisters who were awaiting them.

It is not surprising that in the immediate postwar years the attention of the Waldensian Church all across the land was centered on *evangelization*. The moment was ripe; many remembered that it was the Catholic Church that had signed the iniquitous pacts of 1929 with the fascist regime, had blessed the Italian aggression in Ethiopia, and had opposed progress and freedom. The postwar

273

aspirations — for justice, freedom, democracy, peace, equality, and education for all — were fueled by the quests for spiritual freedom, for a new relationship with God and for a church which yearned for freedom. In great numbers people turned to the Waldensian churches and tuned in to the weekly radio worship services, authorized by the American military government in 1944. (By 1989 those listening to Protestant radio had reached 1,260,000.) Waldensian speakers attracted people to meetings in squares, theaters, and trade union halls.

There was a certain anti-Catholic bias in Waldensian preaching, true, but also a profound biblical message and a real desire to find an answer to the deep spiritual needs of the nation. In a short time there were some thousands of converts, largely working-class people. New congregations were formed, especially in the south. The church's choice of moderators in this early postwar period reflected the concern for evangelization. Up until 1948 the moderator was Virgilio Sommani, who had been a popular preacher in a Florence suburb; he was followed from 1948 to 1951 by Guglielmo Del Pesco, a convert from the Abruzzo region, and from 1951 to 1958 by Achille Deodato, a Sicilian who grew up in Genoa and received his education at Torre Pellice. In the meantime, a large number of students, those of the war generation, filled the Waldensian Theological Seminary to capacity.

Despite these favorable developments, the Waldensian Church did not find itself altogether at home in postwar Italy. The church had grown during the liberal period, and like the great Neapolitan philosopher, Benedetto Croce, believed that with the fall of Fascism, a liberal-democratic regime would be reinstated in Italy. In 1946, instead, the liberals who had "made Italy" found themselves reduced to a second class party, crushed between two giants: the Christian Democratic Party and the Communist Party, the former supported by the Catholic Church, the latter by the trade unions and the intellectuals. The Waldensians shared the bitter disillusionment of the socialists, social democrats and liberals. Still and all, it was mostly communist workers — excommunicated from the Catholic Church for their party affiliation — who formed the Waldensian churches' new ranks; they had heard of "hungering and thirsting for justice" (Matthew 5) and sought fulfillment in the Waldensian family.

What did the Waldensians think of the Christian Democrats, who right from the first elections in 1946 obtained 35 percent of the Italian votes and who rapidly filled all the key posts in national life?

They had no doubts: the "civilization of the Counter-Reformation" had returned and with it an attempt to bury the liberal *Risorgimento*. Never would a "good Waldensian" give his or her vote to the Christian Democrats, for historical and theological reasons alike. Essentially social democrats, the Waldensians readied themselves for a protracted resistance against the Christian Democrats' regime.

Shortly the boom fell: the Christian Democrats implacably persecuted Seventh-Day Adventists, Pentecostals, and the Brethren and now and then lashed out at the Waldensians, Methodists, and Baptists. Worse still, the Christian Democrats refused to implement the postwar Constitution's Article 8, designed to protect religious minorities. It states:

All religious confessions are equally free before the law.

Non-Catholic religious confessions have the right to organize themselves according to their own constitutions, insofar as they do not contradict Italian law.

Their relationships with the state are established by law on the basis of state agreements with their respective representatives.

The struggle for religious freedom was on. The Waldensian Church put at the disposal of the Protestants, nationally, one of its most able people, a lawyer and university professor, Giorgio Peyrot, who, decades later — in 1978! — would succeed in negotiating the draft of the Agreement sanctioned by the Constitution. (Waldensians, fortunately, having been trained by 800 years of resistance, have no fear of the passing of time!) All the struggle was worth it: "fighting the good fight" for religious freedom really meant fighting for *everyone's freedom*, and for an Italy which would be more open and more democratic.

2. Going through changes

The Waldensian Church in the postwar years found that it had to address significant changes. The churches in the south did not hesitate to inform the synod that a powerful new Pentecostal movement had established itself there. During the '30s the Pentecostals had suffered imprisonment at the hands of the Fascists, while in the '50s they were harassed by the Christian Democrats. During the '60s they reached the northern industrial cities and overtook the Waldensians in numbers of constituents. Other less numerous, but not less active, churches surfaced: Seventh-Day Adventists, Nazarenes, and Churches of Christ. The Plymouth Brethren founded churches throughout the south. This much is clear: the Waldensian Church is stable, but is just a fraction of the Italian Protestant reality, itself increasingly challenged by the Jehovah's Witnesses (thought to be 150,000 in the late '80s) and Mormons.

Within the Waldensian Church itself changes were taking place, the most important of which was within the youth-young adult movement. The young adults had been deeply troubled by the war and were looking for something new — reconciliation, hope, communion with others. Their national secretary and leader was Tullio Vinay, a powerful preacher who during the war sheltered Jews in his home in Florence. A banal turn of events triggered off a movement that in the succeeding decades would impact the church in a dramatic way. Young Waldensians wanted to buy up some abandoned barracks at Prali in the Historic Valleys, where for two years running they had held summer camps; the government, however, was unwilling to sell the properties to them (ten years later they were sold to a Catholic organization). So Tullio Vinay decided to build a new center outright. A brilliant architect from Florence, Leonardo Ricci, drew up designs which were daring and full of meaning to the young people. All the good old Waldensian traditionalists predicted that the venture would be a failure, but the young people, ex-partisans and ex-Fascists alike, Italians and non-Italians, buckled down to work and within four years of international workcamping the central facilities were completed. Right from the beginning, in 1947, Agape, which in Greek means "the love of Christ," had a well-defined sense of mission. Europe was still littered with war ruins and the cold war was coming on, but Agape was preaching *reconciliation*. While in Italy there was a counter-reformationist regime, Agape was living out *ecumenism*. Above all, Agape stood for a challenge to Protestant individualism and offered *community* instead.

During these same years, the Iona community in Scotland was founded; certainly this was a splendid experience, but a bit elitist and anyway, rather "religious." The neo-Catholic monastery of Taizé in France, too, captured the attention of many Protestants. Agape, on the other hand, had nothing monastic going for it. Though led by deeply-committed Christians, it was no "religious" center. There was not even a chapel in the whole complex — all was left to the power of the Spirit through preaching. Sufficient was the Bible on the table in the huge conference-dining hall, open for all to see, believers and non-believers alike. After 40 years, Agape is still a lively center, a "school of contradictions," to be sure, yet the lungs through which the churches breathe the air, albeit a little sharp, of the contemporary world.

The Agape ministry in its early decades could stir up "hot" debates at synod meetings. Its coming on the scene ended definitively the church's conservative tilt — running back to the onset of WWI — and most certainly created the critical mass which led the church into far more liberal, and even radical, years.

3. The challenge of secularization

In 1958, when the young Republic entered the European Common Market, it was difficult to recognize the backward agricultural country which Mussolini had led to war. The secular era had arrived. The Christian Democrats were in power, but the number of people attending mass was diminishing, while the number of young men going into the priesthood was falling rapidly.

Secularization affected the Waldensian Church in two ways. First of all, many young intellectuals left the church, professing a Marxist faith. Next, depopulation of the countryside, which filled the industrial cities (and emigrant ships), struck at the rural roots of the Waldensian Church, whether in the Historic Valleys or in the south. Typical Waldensian villages like Massello, Angrogna, and Bobbio Pellice lost two-thirds of their population; in the south many rural congregations were snuffed out when their members moved to Turin or even to Toronto. The uprooted people found it difficult to adjust themselves to new situations, and sometimes were lost to the church or remained on the periphery of church life. By the early '60s the danger became blatantly obvious: there was a real risk that the nation's industrial transformation would overwhelm the Waldensian Church, or at least deprive it of its hinterland base, leaving it alone with urban middle-class churches. The Waldensians stood up to this great challenge by taking a good number of initiatives.

We begin with the south and will anticipate events in our story by considering the Waldensian and Methodist experiences together. In Naples-Portici the faith of a Methodist pastor, Riccardo Santi, and his family had established in 1905 an orphanage, Casa Materna, which today is a major educational center, serving 400 children. Again, in 1944 (supported by the chaplains of the 5th Army, especially by those who were members of the then Congregational Church, now the United Church of Christ), in the suburb of Ponticelli in Naples, the Santis had established a small, and to this day, active community center called Casa Mia. During the war the idea came to Dr. Teofilo Santi (son of Riccardo Santi) and a Waldensian pastor, Achille Deodato, to build a Protestant hospital in Naples. It would be 24 years before their dream could be realized, but at length, in 1968, the hospital, Villa Betania, was inaugurated at Ponticelli. (Here, too, the help of the former American chaplains, who by then had become ministers of large congregations in the United States, was crucial.) The hospital is owned by the Waldensian National Board, but representatives of all the Protestant denominations in the city sit on its administrative council. Various Protestant communities have sprung from the Sunday evening worship services in the hospital: truly the word of God cannot be chained down.

Following the 1980 earthquake, the Federation of Protestant Churches in Italy built a village with a splendid community center at Ponticelli for 60 displaced families. It is obvious, then, that in Naples, in Italy's most "religious" city, Protestants did not make their presence felt with speeches alone, but also with tangible forms of solidarity to confront the distress of the times.

In Palermo in the early '60s, an Italo-American Protestant woman offered a Waldensian pastor, Pietro Valdo Panascia, an old building in a suburb, La Noce, dominated by the mafia and oppressed by poverty. After 12 years of hard work and with the support of Swiss and German churches, an important *centro diaconale* was set up. It now has a school, attended by 400 children, a health center, and a center for assistance to immigrants and refugees. La Noce has become a pulpit from which the local minister (currently a Methodist) courageously challenges the mafia and equips the Noce people to be protagonists in life and to claim Christ's freedom which shatters the mentalities of dependency, so pervasive in the south and exploited by the mafia.

At about the same time, in the early '60s, Servizio Cristiano of Riesi was founded. In the heart of Sicily, it was another arresting Vinay initiative. If Agape is essentially a place for dialog and for hammering out fresh visions for ministry, Riesi is a center intended to transform or at least to offer hope to a poverty-stricken, dispirited town in the Sicilian wilderness. It started with a nursery school; then came an elementary school, a library, a medical center and two agricultural cooperatives. Servizio Cristiano also organized a trade school for mechanics, and with the cooperation of a Swiss industrialist, launched a small factory called Meccanica Riesi (which provides 30 non-mafia controlled jobs!). The latter is an attempt to challenge the extreme concentration of industry in the north of Italy. It remains a small, but significant, sign. At the core of Servizio Cristiano, as at Agape, is a community of international volunteers, at times as many as 20. The group tries to incarnate the love of Christ in the midst of a culture of hopelessness. Once again Vinay entrusted to the architect Ricci the task of designing a splendid complex which attracts visitors from all continents.

Certainly, the "big three" centers in the south — Casa Materna, La Noce, and Servizio Cristiano — are perhaps more than a church as small as ours can handle, but the picture is even larger. Other specialized ministries in the south were set up in the postwar years — schools, cultural and social centers, and cooperatives. Why? There can be no doubt that Waldensians and Methodists felt that behind the Italian "economic miracle" something was amiss: there was still too much poverty, too much emigration, too much injustice, and they decided they had to do something about it, that they had to become socially committed, to live and to practice the good news of Christ (Matthew 25) and not just talk about it. Naples, Palermo, Riesi, and other social ministries add up to *schools for witness*, space for freedom's way, in tormented landscapes so vulnerable to corruption and exploitation.

In the Historic Valleys, in the north, for over a hundred years there had been Waldensian hospitals, homes for the aging, and schools, but they had become out-of-date. They had been run on the good will of dedicated workers, but faced with the challenges of modern society, good will was not enough. So a lively debate on the question of the hospitals in particular engaged the Waldensians in the '60s. The conservative elements wanted our hospitals to become modern private clinics. The "left" wanted to hand over the hospitals to the state (which, in other words, meant closing them down), claiming that the church's primary concern should be preaching and the training of Christian doctors and nurses, who, in the secular climate of public hospitals, could witness like the "salt" and "light" in the New Testament sense. But Waldensians who really knew the public hospitals knew only too well that they are by no means strictly secular; rather, they are run by, and for the benefit of, various interests within the sphere of the Christian Democrats.

In the end a compromise was struck: the hospitals remained in Waldensian hands, but they became part of the public health service. The church, with the support of its friends from abroad, spent major sums to bring the buildings and equipment into state-of-the-art shape. Specific agreements were signed with the various

Italian regional authorities to protect the autonomy of these Waldensian institutions. First-class doctors, nurses and administrators gave up promising and lucrative careers to serve in these small, but caring hospitals where love is plainly on the map, up every corridor, in every room. The church's homes for the aging, likewise, were found to be in grave need of rehabilitation, and they, too, in recent years, have been largely renovated. In both hospitals and homes for the aging, we can see how the church has adapted itself in a creative way to the problems of the "welfare state" which inexorably has replaced the old society grounded in the care of the nuclear family.

In contrast to the service-oriented ministries just outlined, we return to the Agape story and the ensuing issue-oriented impact of youth and young adults upon the church. The fruit of four years of international workcamps, Agape was inaugurated in '51, the same year a federation of Waldensian, Methodist and Baptist youth movements came into being and the journal, *Gioventù Evangelica* (Protestant Youth), which for four years had been the mouthpiece of the Waldensian youth-young adult movement, was put at the disposal of the youth and young adults from all three denominations. In the '60s Agape, the youth federation and *Gioventù Evangelica,* working together, became an explosive catalyst. Agape was the hub of radical thought both within and without the Protestant world. Thanks to successful conferences with Africans, dialogue with the Prague Christian Peace Conference and innovative ecumenical conferences, Agape became an extraordinary center for dialog, certainly the liveliest and most controversial within all of Italian Protestantism. The dialog with Marxism had begun. For many years there would follow an attempt to reconcile socialism and freedom. In this search the most progressive vitalities in Italy would make their way repeatedly to Agape.

This activity was in full swing when in 1968 the student uprisings burst upon the scene. Protestant students interrupted worship services and distributed manifestos, declaring that western society was rotten, and that revolution was necessary. Vietnamese resistance became the symbol of the world's struggle for emancipation from the "bondage of capitalism." Christian vocation was seen in terms of anticapitalist struggle. Even the Waldensian synod was disrupted, scandalizing the conservative forces. Unfortunately, that public action took place just three days after the Soviet occupation of Czechoslovakia; the students simply were not able at the moment to understand the import of that tragedy. Under the impulse of the student movement the Federation of Protestant

Youth-Young Adults in Italy (FGEI) was founded in 1969, formally gathering Waldensian, Methodist and Baptist youth and young adults in one organization. FGEI set out to address both reform of the church and transformation of society. At the outset its interest was primarily revolution; it would widen its scope to include the issues of peace, the environment, and feminism. FGEI's stance towards the churches was harsh. It considered the churches to be too closely tied to bourgeois society and values. Over its first 20 years FGEI schooled at least half of the church's future pastors, leaders and directors of specialized ministries. Although some members became completely secularized, others discovered Protestantism and became believers through FGEI. In the context of the FGEI experience Marxists and ex-Marxists discovered Jesus Christ, professed their faith and joined the churches. Later on pacifists and others were to make the same discovery. Always a thorn in the flesh for the churches, FGEI would remain a necessary forum — small but hard-hitting — for critical examination of the churches' thought and practice.

Halfway between the large "service institutions" of the south and the Historic Valleys and the FGEI movement "on the issues" was the attempt by the Waldensian and Methodist churches to establish a new urban strategy in the north. Too many of the church members were being swallowed up in the dismal suburbs of the "economic miracle." In Turin there was an effort to decentralize the church and open new meeting places in the working-class peripheral areas. The idea was not to limit the Waldensian presence to one downtown "cathedral" where great preachers might hold forth, but fail to reach people at the grass roots.

In Milan, capital of the "Italian miracle," there was a more complex strategy. The Methodists, by now oriented towards federation with the Waldensians, moved out of their old buildings, in order to become the "Protestant parish" of northern Milan. In 1968 the Waldensian publishing house, Claudiana, opened a successful bookstore in Milan. Later a flourishing "cultural center" for conferences was to become part of the bookstore. Also in 1968, in Milan's working-class industrial suburb of Cinisello Balsamo, the Jacopo Lombardini center was founded. Named after a Methodist lay preacher and partisan who died at the hands of the Nazis in Mauthausen, the center launched evening classes for young migrant workers from the south, a conference center, a Bible study group and a community of some 20 people who shared a rather austere, committed life-style. It was the same experience as Riesi in Sicily, but in an industrial context, with a special emphasis upon political activity. The Lombardini center was perhaps the most Marxist in all Italian Protestantism. In theology it was pronouncedly Barthian.

Although these particular experiences were very lively, the Waldensians and Methodists generally were unable to find a viable strategy for ministry in the cities. The typical pastor was still, in a sense, cut from the cloth of the Historic Valleys preacher who read Melville and Tolstoy and could quote them ably on the right occasion, but who, at the same time, was somewhat lost in the emerging computer world — on the elite side, not really in step with mass culture.

To overcome this difficulty, the church in the '60s embarked upon an intense *cultural campaign*. Over the next several decades the Waldensian Theological Seminary increased the number of its full-time professors from three to five; its library has become a splendid resource for students and scholars. The seminary's quarterly journal, *Protestantesimo,* first published in 1946, has become an indispensable tool for anyone who seriously wishes to study theology in Italy today. Since the '60s the Seminary has been an ecumenical reference point both nationally and internationally.

The Claudiana Publishing House underwent a thorough transformation. It published in translation works of German theologians, like Gollwitzer and Kaesemann, along with the works of Luther, Calvin and Barth. It also published the rather militant works of Catholic dissenters, the history of Italian Protestantism, Bible commentaries, and the important *History of Anabaptism* by the independent evangelical scholar, Ugo Gastaldi.

On the occasion of the 1974 celebration of the Waldensians' first 800 years, Claudiana published the first in a monumental three-volume series on the Waldensian experience. Writing from his native Prague on the Waldensians' medieval movement, Amedeo Molnár surveys the situation of Christians in a society which has been secularized from "above." The medieval Waldensians protested against a Christianity concerned with wielding power; the question posed by Molnár is: Can Waldensians today still teach how to witness when confronted by non-Christian power? The perspective of the second volume, written by the liberal democrat Augusto Armand Hugon, teacher at the Waldensian Junior College and former prestigious mayor of Torre Pellice, is quite different. His scientifically faultless book deals with the history of the Waldensians in post-Reformation times and once again puts forward the theory of the "people-church" led from on high. Quite different again is the concluding volume by the former dean of the Waldensian Seminary, Valdo Vinay, published in 1980, which tells the Waldensian story across the last two centuries. It is Vinay's judgment that the time for traditional evangelization, to which he personally made a great contribution, is over and that it is now necessary that Waldensians be a *critical leaven* within Italian Christianity and culture.

A synthesis of these three interpretations of Waldensian history and vocation is Giorgio Tourn's volume, *I Valdesi*, the first edition of which appeared in 1977. The most important of Claudiana's publications in the '70s and certainly the most widely read in Italy (and abroad in translations), it is the history of "a family of believers" and their sense of vocation tempered by the trials encountered by each new generation. It is a Calvinist interpretation, filtered through Dostoyevsky — an interpretation, I dare say, which is destined to last.

4. The Vatican Council and Catholic dissenters

It is often impossible to foresee moments of testing. In the '60ʳ Italian Protestantism had to deal with one of the most delicate moments in its history, Vatican Council II (1962-65). Protestants were taken by surprise. They had been fighting against an intolerant Christian Democrats' regime which persecuted minority denominations, and now, all of a sudden, the Catholic Church projected itself as a leader among the progressive and ecumenical forces which it had snubbed in 1948, when it had refused to take part in the Amsterdam Assembly which constituted the World Council of Churches.

The Waldensian Church was divided over two interpretations of Vatican II, each led by an eminent Barthian theologian at the Waldensian Theological Seminary. Valdo Vinay gave the Council an historical interpretation: he saw it as a break with Vatican I. Vatican II was Christianity on the move; the various confessions could, in the long run, become "of a family" within a universal church, that would be "catholic" without being "Roman." Vittorio Subilia offered a systemic interpretation, concluding that the unchanging features of Catholicism were all to be found in the Council. Vatican II completed rather than contradicted Vatican I. This interpretation was to be confirmed by the militant pontificate of John Paul II and for the moment it is the interpretation which is most widely accepted by Italian Protestants. Even though the systemic interpretation stiffened Italian Protestantism's backbone, it did not sufficiently tone up the muscles.

Two phenomena demonstrate the Waldensian stance towards the Catholic Church: a "Bible-based" ecumenism and interaction with dissenting Catholic movements. An exponent of the first trend is the tireless Waldensian minister, Renzo Bertalot, who, as director of the Italian Bible Society, was a major force behind the 1985 interconfessional translation of the Bible (the Italian equivalent of *Good News for Modern Man*). Although Protestants hesitated for some time before embarking upon this ecumenical translation, and though they represent only 0.5 percent of the national population, they actually did 30 percent of the work.

The second trend, shared by most Waldensians, is that of dialog with dissenting Catholics and with Catholic "base" communities. This was affirmed by the 1970 synod and put into practice also by the Federation of Protestant Churches in Italy. Before long the churches had a journal for furthering this relationship: a Protestant weekly merged in 1974 with a mainly Catholic publication and became *COM-Nuovi Tempi* (now *Confronti*, a monthly). Its articles cover a wide range of issues from Christians for Socialism to feminism and peacemaking. At an international level, the journal supports Third World struggles, with a keen interest in Nicaragua.

Catholic "dissent" as a whole was not really much interested in Protestantism. Max Weber's much-quoted but little-read books led it to oversimplify and to identify Protestantism with capitalism, and to describe the problems of American society in a rather grotesque way. Waldensians were seen as too few to be of consequence, born losers, and so were of little interest to these rebellious children of the Counter-Reformation. When they discovered the Waldensians' real strength, it was rather late, because marginalization of their dissent itself had begun to take place. Paradoxically, however, from this movement some significant people joined the Waldensian Church — Catholics who saw in Protestant theology backbone for real protagonists, not crutches for the lame.

5. On the Protestant front

In the meantime, within the Waldensian and later within the Methodist churches a profound internal reorganization was being carried out. The Waldensian centralized organization, which had functioned since about 1915, was modified. The key to the system was again the synod, but a synod now realigned toward a type of responsible congregationalism, open to mission and social commitment. Gradually the various agencies of the church (Agape, Palermo, Riesi, Casa Materna, Ecumene, the hospitals, and the seminary) became largely autonomous, but at the same time they had to submit to an increasingly thorough review by the synod, as did the Waldensian National Board itself. A review commission became the most important and powerful feature of the synod. Each year it works for a month prior to the synod, examining minutely what has been done in the previous year, raising questions and offering proposals for action.

The Waldensian Discipline (1974), in Italian and Spanish, codifies the new relationship which had been established in the '60s between the Waldensians in Italy and those in Argentina-Uruguay. Now there is a relationship of full interdependence among sister churches in one denominational family. The "blood ties" have loosened, but the two communities on both sides of the Atlantic share common views on theology, and have a mutual passion for democracy which, warmed by "latin" temperament, has found fulfillment in resistance to military regimes. For many church leaders in Italy the journey to the churches on the other side of the Atlantic has been a climactic moment of intense joy.

Reorganization within the church has certainly meant innovation. In 1962, with a majority of five votes, the synod voted to ordain women; by the late '80s half of the church's theological students were women. In 1980 the role of the full-time deacon, provisionally introduced in 1967, was sanctioned; by 1988 there were 30 deacons. The deacons are brothers and sisters who have been entrusted by the church to run the many specialized ministries that have been launched or reshaped since the '60s.

On this basis of responsible congregationalism, the Waldensian Church has encouraged major initiatives in the interest of the unification of Italian Protestantism: the founding of the Federation of Protestant Churches in Italy, the Waldensian-Methodist federation and the continuing dialog among all Protestant churches.

In 1946 the synod decided to encourage the founding of the Council of Protestant Churches in Italy. At the outset the Council included only Waldensians, Methodists and Baptists. Later, when the problems of religious freedom worsened, the Council represented in a united front practically all the denominations at work in Italy. In various quarters, however, the desire for something different was growing. There were the models of the Federation Protestante de France, an efficient and important body, able to influence public life in France; the National Council of Churches (U.S.), with its specialized agencies famed throughout the world (such as Church World Service) and ability to place the church on the new frontiers of American life. Above all, there was the growing importance of the World Council of Churches and its embracing of churches from the Third World.

The first Congress of the Italian Protestant Youth (GEI), held in Milan in 1951, triggered a movement which would grow in different, but complementary, directions. One led to the creation of the Federation of Protestant Youth-Young Adults in Italy (FGEI) in 1969, and the other advanced mightily a desire for unity within the "historical" denominations of Italian Protestantism — the Waldensians, Methodists and Baptists.

The Protestant churches, absorbed in their difficult postwar reconstruction, had strengthened their international ties, but had paid little attention to the concerns of the youth and young adults. So, in 1962 the GEI Congress in Rome made a solemn appeal to the churches and to the Council of Protestant Churches to convene a second Protestant Congress (the first having been held in 1920), with the clear aim of unifying Italian Protestantism. After some hesitation, the appeal was accepted. All the churches active in Italy from the Lutherans to the Pentecostals agreed to take part; the Plymouth Brethren alone expressed reservations. GEI, the leading light of the Congress, untiringly stimulated the churches to put into practice hopes and promises for Christian unity.

The Congress took place in Rome in the spring of 1965 in an absolutely unforgettable atmosphere. The feeling of unity between "old Protestants" and "new evangelicals" was palpable. The ancient Waldensian Church, the churches founded during the *Risorgimento* and those born during the harsh fascist era met and gave each other the "right hand of fellowship." At the close of the Congress, however, some of the new denominations (the Pentecostals) announced that they would not become part of the proposed new federation, which was thus limited to the "historic" churches: the Waldensians, Lutherans, Baptists, Methodists and later on, the Salvation Army. The Federation of Protestant Churches in Italy (FCEI) was constituted two years later, in 1967, in Milan.

The Federation inherited certain joint activities which were already successful, like the Sunday School committee and the Protestant Radio worship service with its wealth of evangelistic potential. New initiatives were also taken. In 1973 the Federation launched the television program *Protestantesimo* upon which the public image of our churches largely depends. Today, the biweekly program has 500,000 regular viewers.

The 1980 earthquake in the Irpina-Naples area highlighted the persistent "southern issue" on both civil and religious levels. In the wake of the catastrophe the Federation was foremost in galvanizing national and international Protestant advocacy on the south through national conferences, the publishing of several books and a five million dollar program. Today two villages for those who lost all they had in the earthquakes have been built at Naples-Ponticelli and at Monteforte (Avellino); with several community centers and farming cooperatives they are fit examples of the effectiveness of the Federation's ministry in Italy's deep south.

Through the earthquake emergency service and community development work the Federation was considerably strengthened, enabling it to forge a united Italian Protestant voice on the question of church relationships with the state. In the '80s it has intervened authoritatively in the serious controversy with the state over the question of the teaching of the Catholic faith in state schools.

Over the past decade the dramatic increase in the number of Third World immigrants to Italy has transformed the Federation's immigrant-refugee unit, which works vigorously, in the face of pervasive racism in the nation, to help local churches embrace the newcomers. The Federation has also generated continuing legislative advocacy so that national immigrant-refugee policy can be made as just and humane as possible.

The Waldensians sometimes unconsciously seek to model the Federation on the experience of the Waldensian Church, so that the triennial assembly should, as much as possible, resemble the synod, and the Federation's governing council, the Waldensian National Board. The Federation, however, has managed to resist this; its assembly is more a congress than a synod, while its council is more a forum than a powerful executive organ like the Waldensian National Board.

The Methodists, for their part, have served as presidents in crucial moments and have taken an active part in the Federation's initiatives and assembly debates. It can be said that Methodists find the Federation a suitable place to express their specific gifts and their enthusiasms. This fact, noticeable in the assemblies of the '80s, is worth mentioning, because it belies a common fear that the Methodist-Waldensian federation is no more than fresh paintwork to cover up the assimilation of the Methodists into a Waldensian

Church, able and willing to stretch itself, but not really prepared to be transformed.

6. An autonomous region

Working side by side the 94 Waldensian communities with some 80 ministers and 50 or so specialized ministries, there are 37 Methodist communities with nearly 20 ministers and 10 specialized ministries. The common cause runs to the '30s, the heyday of Fascism, which proved to be extremely difficult years for the two small Methodist groups in Italy. The Methodist Episcopal Church (U.S.) attempted to reorganize itself and became self-supporting, while the Wesleyan Church (Britain), in 1942, started talks to unite with the Waldensian Church. Quite correctly, the Waldensian National Board and the synod accepted the Methodist proposal in principle, but expressed the judgment that before being put into effect, it should receive the approval of the British Methodist Church, upon whom the Italian Methodist mission still depended. In the meantime, without any fuss, the Waldensians extended indispensable financial support. It was indeed the poor sharing with the poor.

Shortly after the end of the war, in 1946, the Wesleyan and Episcopal streams unified and the Methodist Church in Italy was born, with considerable British backing. The church reached full independence in 1962.

The Methodists' theological seminary, however, was not re-opened and a whole generation of future pastors was sent to the Waldensian Seminary, creating a network of informal relationships which would break down many barriers. Talks for union with the Waldensians were resumed in the early '50s. It was believed that from the merger of the two churches a new church would emerge (Chiesa Evangelica Italiana — Italian Protestant Church) and the name "Waldensian" would be linked to a purely geographical area in the Historic Valleys and to earlier historical periods. After a remarkable debate, the synod of 1955 rejected this proposal for historical, theological and ecumenical reasons, and proposed instead a "solemn covenant" between the two churches and federation instead of merger. Received with skepticism at first, the idea proved to be effective, because it enabled the two churches to begin a prudent trial period, during which they could better get to know each other and learn to cooperate. In 1957 ministers were recognized reciprocally, from 1958 there were pastoral exchanges, in

1969 and then from 1972 joint sessions of the Waldensian and Methodist annual assemblies were held — probably the decisive factor. After 20 years of increasing cooperation, the process could quickly become the Covenant of Federation, approved in 1974-75, and then gradually be put into effect until the first unified synod was held in 1979.

The covenant contains some significant innovations:

It is based theologically on the principles of the Reformation rather than on that generic "Protestantism" which has been the foundation of many unsuccessful attempts of union in the past. The so-called Waldensian Confession of Faith of 1655 was accepted as a common base (the confession is nothing more than a summary of a sixteenth century French Reformed Confession of Faith: a Calvinist text, therefore). At the opening of each synod assembly, the new ministers, Waldensian and Methodist, promise to preach and to teach in line with the Confession's affirmations. The covenant is between local churches, not between denominational bodies, so those seeds of congregationalism which were already within the traditional Waldensian system and were further developed in the '60s and '70s became the norm in this ecumenical encounter.

The integrity of the Methodist churches, clearly a minority, is guaranteed in the covenant. Their name and organization cannot be changed; their ecumenical and financial interests are dealt with by a special synod commission, *Opera per le Chiese Evangeliche Metodiste in Italia (OPCEMI)*; the Methodist traditions of lay preachers and circuits have been welcomed and adopted throughout the federated churches.

At the center of the system is a typically Waldensian body, the synod, with its executive National Board. Two of the seven members of the National Board have to be Methodists, a pastor and a layperson.

In this light it can be easily seen how the "question of the name" was solved. In previous negotiations this had been one of the main sticking points. Under the covenant, when the Waldensian and Methodist churches need to present themselves as one family to the world beyond, the name *Chiesa Evangelica Valdese* (Waldensian Church) is used, but it is understood that this name means "the federation of Methodist and Waldensian congregations." The name, "Waldensian," which cannot be relinquished, was thus confirmed in the ecumenical context of the covenant.

Federation has brought profound changes into both the Waldensian and Methodist worlds. To give a pictorial image, let us imagine that most of the American states from Maine to California had been

Waldensian, but some, say Georgia, Florida, Alabama, Louisiana, Mississippi, Texas, New Mexico, and Arizona had been Methodist; that to this day each group has both close ties within its own ranks and an identity within the national federal scheme. For Italian Methodists the key to this identity is the beautiful center of Ecumene, a few miles south of Rome, where each year a consultation of Methodist churches is held. On this occasion the problems common to the Methodist communities are discussed.

Significantly, the 37 Methodist churches brought into the synod that part of the Protestant world which had emerged during the Italian *Risorgimento*. In the past, Waldensians considered the Middle Ages and the Reformation the "classical" moments of their history; now the Waldensian Church can acknowledge its debt to the Italian *Risorgimento*. It means giving up a certain piemontese bias, which has conditioned it for centuries.

Federation has thus changed the Waldensian Church, just as it has put the Methodist churches into a new framework. After ten years it can be considered a successful venture of unity in freedom.

7. The twelve tribes of Israel

Italian Protestantism is, in fact, far more complex and diverse than the Waldensians like to believe. The churches which make up the mosaic of Italian Protestantism can be likened to the twelve tribes of Israel, each with its own history and identity, each with its own specific vocation. Certainly, they could be gathered together in a "sacred league," but they could never be unified under the same administration. Torre Pellice might become the Gilgal in this "sacred league," but it could never become the Jerusalem and certainly never the Samaria!

This has been shown in the last 20 years through a series of bilateral talks held by the Waldensian National Board with the encouragement of the synod. The first is the relationship between Baptists, Methodists and Waldensians. Thirty-five years of joint youth-young adult work; 20 years of cooperation in the Youth Federation; similar points of view on the issues of peace and the relationship between state and church; cooperation in certain specialized ministries; plans to hold a joint session of the synod and the Baptist assembly in 1990 — all suggest that there is major cooperation between these churches. It may or may not result in full federation, but certainly something extremely lively and meaningful is likely to emerge.[9]

Next in time came the accords with the "free churches," a group of active communities from the Naples area. Joint social and evangelistic projects have cemented this relationship.

In 1973 the Waldensians signed the Leuenberg Agreement which abolished the old barriers between Reformed and Lutheran churches in Europe. A few years after the Agreement there was an echo in Italy, and the relationships between the two denominations have become closer. The Lutheran Church in Italy has a glorious history which goes back to the times of the Reformation (Venice), the Enlightenment (Trieste and Milan), and nineteenth century liberalism (Naples, Rome, Genoa and Florence). Most of its members are of German, Austrian, Hungarian and Swiss extraction. The opportunity for dialog is considerable because most Waldensian pastors have been influenced by German culture, at least as far as theology, music, psychology, philosophy, sociology and politics are concerned.

In the '70s the dialogue with the Plymouth Brethren, which had been interrupted halfway through the last century, was resumed. They have 230 congregations and are slowly but surely expanding. The number of active members is now roughly the same as that of the Waldensians. The Brethren have agreed to share in the running of three institutions of the Waldensian Church in the Florence area.

The relationship with the Brethren opens up the problem of relationships between Waldensians and evangelicals, among whom there has too often been reciprocal misunderstanding and even occasional diffidence. Here are two schools of spirituality which can and must give each other the "right hand of fellowship" with a view to a common witness despite the differences in culture.

The Waldensian Church is well aware that it is not itself Italian Protestantism (some 300,000 persons of which Waldensians and Methodists, Lutherans and Baptists, Pentecostals and non-Pentecostal evangelicals are 10-5-77-8 percent, respectively), but all the same it is equally aware that without the Waldensians, there would be only a generic Italian "Protestantism," subordinate and forever paying homage to others. Whether it would be subordinate to national Catholicism, foreign Protestantism or one of the secular cultures is irrelevant, because any type of subordination threatens a most precious gift that a family of believers can have: *spiritual autonomy*.

Since the relationship with God is lived in history and not in "private," the Waldensian Church presents itself as a community which has never lost its taste for good theology; which loves to distinguish the classics from books that are merely in vogue; and which presents itself as the custodian of the historical memory of Italian Protestantism. It is a church that has deep historical roots. It expresses and "guarantees" the participation and grounding of Protestantism in all phases of Italian life, from the very dawn of national culture in the twelfth century to the present day.

8. Waldensian is beautiful . . .

The mid-'80s were times when the Waldensian Church enjoyed high visibility, a season which would be difficult to repeat.

The first opportunity, and spiritually the most important, was the Lutheran Year (1983). Up until a few years before, Luther had been in Italy what the Germans call a *Feindbild*, a negative image, something to exorcise. For Catholics, Luther was the one who had broken the unity of the Church.

By 1983, though, the reevaluation was complete. Dozens of Catholic seminaries invited professors from the Waldensian Seminary to lecture on justification by faith and the teachings of the great reformer. A Catholic theologian wrote a beautiful book on Protestant spirituality, largely dedicated to Luther; the communist publishing house commissioned a Waldensian, Professor Mario Miegge, to write a splendid book on the life and work of the reformer. On every side taboos fell; if Italy wouldn't get in step with the Reformation, it certainly did need the reformers.

Italy also felt the need for the Reformed. When on February 21, 1984, the moderator signed the *Intesa* (Agreement) with the state, there was a resounding echo throughout the country. Was it merely because of the timing with the state's signing of a very questionsable "new" Concordat with the Roman Catholic Church just days before? It seems unlikely. The Agreement was rapidly approved by Parliament. The then President of the Senate, the liberal Catholic, Francesco Cossiga, officially greeted the Waldensian delegation and offered a speech which was memorable in its high cultural and ecumenical tone. In 1985 Cossiga visited Torre Pellice, as a guest of the Society for Waldensian Studies. Elected President of the Republic, he paid an official visit to the Waldensian Church at the Theological Seminary in Rome on February 17 (the Waldensian Freedom Day), 1986.

What is the reason for this public attention? Representing 30 years of hard work, the Agreement certainly is a remarkable document. In it the Italian Republic takes note of the "autonomy and independence of the Waldensian order;" it removes the effects of the old fascist laws, and affirms that Waldensian ministers have the right to visit prisons, barracks, hospitals, homes for the aging, etc. with no limitations imposed (and with no compensation, at Waldensian insistence). The freedom of Waldensians to elect not to attend Catholic instruction in state schools is guaranteed. Ministers continue to have the right to perform weddings, and the autonomy of the Waldensian institutions, like their hospitals or the Theological Seminary, is recognized. Separate agreements are foreseen for the protection of the cultural heritage reposed in the Waldensian and Methodist properties. This is an Agreement for freedom, clearly distinguishing the sphere of a free-standing church from that of the state. In American terms, it is "a line of separation," even though it is not the "wall" which Jefferson would have liked.

All this was encouraging. It aroused the jurists' and politicians' interest in Protestants, but it does not explain the popular appeal of the Waldensians — due, in our opinion, to the process of modernization which transformed the Waldensians, in the public eye, from a minority to a *social component*. In fact, today, sociologically there no longer exists a northern "industrial block" and an "agrarian block" in the south; there is, instead, a classical western *complex society*, a society that is founded on the middle class. It marginalizes the south and watches the duel between the "great families" of private industry (like the Agnelli family) and the Christian Democrats, who inefficiently run the state industry. This society no longer has many children; hires immigrants from more impoverished lands to do its dirty work; legalizes abortion and divorce; is full of Catholics, but is no longer the Catholic society that Italy was until the early 1960s.

Culturally, Italy is a *pluralistic society*, in which all confessions can live peaceably side by side, believers and non-believers, Christians and Muslims, Jews and Catholics, Orthodox and Protestants, Mormons and Jehovah's Witnesses. Who better than the ancient Waldensian Church, now rooted across the peninsula and Sicily, can symbolize this opening to pluralism, to legitimize it and give it an historical perspective as old as the nation?

In fact, from the ethical-political perspective, this is a *democracy in search of legitimization*. For 40 years the "Italian case" had benefitted, paradoxically, from a dual legitimization: on the one hand, the Catholic tradition, lightly forgetting its excommunication of the *Risorgimento* and its dealings with Benito Mussolini, saw itself as the way of leading the masses into the life of the young

Italian Republic; and on the other hand, the communist tradition, which had given Italy one of its most intelligent citizens (Antonio Gramsci) and had thousands of its members condemned during the Resistance to Fascism, and for 40 years had taken part in the democratic life of the new Italy. Today, Catholic authority over conscience is declining and many communist myths have collapsed.

Today, Italy seeks the *legitimization of an open society*, which, with the healing of its ancient wounds, guarantees the practice of justice and freedom for all. An open society presses on towards inclusion, with all of its components, however large or small, drawing breath in freedom.

It was not just by chance that the highest authorities of the state asked the Waldensian National Board to be present at the religious consecration of this "legitimization" and to offer a prayer at the monument which is called the "altar of the nation" during the 40th anniversary (1986) of the founding of the Republic. And it was not by chance that the churches were unanimous in backing the Waldensian National Board's polite but firm refusal to participate on these grounds: the state in its invitations had failed to respect the multicultural situation in Italy today, where there are millions of Italians who do not profess to be Christians; moreover, offering prayer on that occasion would have meant giving to "Caesar" that which belongs to God.

There have been other occasions when overtures from the state have drawn sharp debate in the churches. In the '80s the Waldensian Church in an heroic effort completely renewed the Torre Pellice Hospital, a project which cost two million dollars. The hospital has made an enormous contribution to the quality of life in the whole area and can be considered a great success. The regional authorities have now asked that its services be further extended and have offered nearly a million dollars to cover the cost. The 1987 synod debated the issue and agreed to accept the offer. There are, however, people who feel that the wall of separation has been lowered.

The issue of pass-through of certain income tax revenues from the state to the churches (along the lines of the state-Catholic model) generated hot debate in Waldensian-Methodist churches in the late '80s (moreso than sex or Marxism had ever done!). The 1988 synod, on a close vote, declined the option for the Waldensian-Methodist churches (until total review of the 1984 Agreement in 1994), seeing in the measure a privileged and too-cozy relationship with the state — the real issue!

Once marginalized, the Protestants in Italy now claim respectful public attention. New roads in church-state relationships are being opened up. "Waldensian is beautiful." Ah, but there are temptations . . . Will the salt lose its flavor?

9. Three currents

Since the military and moral catastrophe of the fascist regime, there have been three basic streams in the worldviews of Waldensians and Methodists. They are not always clear-cut and luckily they shift somewhat from year to year.

First, there is an old *liberal-democratic* current that judges the historic mission of the "open societies" still valid. Conservative in politics, the pietistic liberal democrats believe that it is essential to preserve the spiritual identity of free societies, as they are fragile and surrounded by merciless enemies (as in the '30s). The job of the church basically is to educate — to train men and women, correct the young, console the aging, and mold converts to be like the ancient nucleus in the Historic Valleys' traditional Calvinist way, which they consider to be the sole successful experiment of that ethic in Italy. They believe that the Puritan-Victorian ethic is the definitive ethic. They hold, therefore, that the present sexual permissiveness means really bad news. They are especially against homosexuality, because they believe it jeopardizes the traditional family, one of the basic values of Protestant society.

At the center of the Waldensian-Methodist churches we find a *social-democratic* current, which recognizes the fundamental importance of social justice. Industrial development has caused and cost too much suffering and injustice, and the peoples of the Third World have the right to free themselves from our domination. Money, social democrats feel, is not everything. In theology they tend to be followers of Barth. Social democrats are cautious about the great revolutions of our century: there have been too many concentration camps, too many tanks and too many lies. Antifascist to the core, the social democrats find their spiritual fathers and mothers in the generation of the Resistance. Most of the Waldensian-Methodist people (north to south) adhere to this stream, and accordingly, normally vote in roughly equal measure along the lines of Italy's two major parties of the left.

The creed of the social democrats could be summed up in two ideas: personal fortitude and social justice. Giuseppe Gangale said

that the Waldensian Church "mistrusts both mystical and rational-
istic apocalypses;" the "apocalyptic" (revelatory) claim, a feature
of the revolutions of our time, leaves Waldensians cold. The
Waldensians prefer to look under the revolutionary surface to the
substance of ethical commitment, the attractive secular counterpart
to Christian discipleship.

Fascism, as the social democrats see it, revealed blemishes in the
national consciousness; the rule of the Christian Democrats is an
attempt to reinstate a new Counter-Reformation, which has, with
difficulty, adapted itself to a prosperous industrial democracy. The
social democrats believe it is necessary to rebuild a free and just
country with the cooperation of those elements which strive for
justice and the modernization of the country.

The Waldensian-Methodist social democrats are theologically
allergic to any political metaphysics and believe that ethical passion is the sole and inexhaustable driving power behind political
involvement. Although scrupulously honest (the Waldensian and
Socialist member of Parliament, Valdo Spini, is a good example),
they are rarely engaged at an ideological level.

This leads to the third current, which we will call the *radical-
democratic* stream. Under this one term can be placed groups which
are seemingly quite different from one another, such as the extra-
parliamentary Marxist groups of the '60s and '70s and the pacifist
"greens" of the '80s. "Reds" and "greens" share a common middle-
class intellectual background. This current, which came into being
with the 1968 student movement, basically believes that the West
must be critiqued and radically transformed and that transformation began with the great revolutions of this century. They hold that
the massacres and infamy that characterized these revolutions
cannot be valid reason for discrediting them, just as the slave trade
did not discredit liberal England. Daniel Ortega's and Ernesto
Cardenal's Nicaragua and the African National Congress are proof
that the revolutionary process can offer hope and justice. In recent
years the movement has put more emphasis on disarmament, the
environment and feminism. Certainly the step from a revolutionary
stance to a non-violent one is arduous, and perhaps it was taken with
insufficient self-criticism. Nevertheless, the desire for radical change
and collective repentence remains firm, as does the insistence on
the importance of grassroots participation. Without a doubt, young
people, especially students, identify with this current. Within
Protestant constituencies, the Agape and Adelphia centers, the
Protestant Youth-Young Adult Federation, the journals *Gioventù*

Evangelica and *Confronti* and the political commentary pages of the Waldensian-Methodist weekly, the *Luce*, are the radical-democrat strongholds.

There have been times when these groups have agreed and other times when they have clashed. An occasion when they shared a common point of view was in 1974, when the referendum on divorce split the country in two. If we consider how much conservatives value the role of the traditional family, there was a real risk that the Waldensian Church would be split, too. Instead, something quite different happened. In the months leading up to the referendum all the churches, without specific direction or counsel from the synod, started to discuss the problem in house groups and Bible studies. The results were spectacular; at Bobbio Pellice, which is 95 percent Waldensian, votes in favor of the legalization of divorce reached 96 percent (the highest in Italy); in fact, throughout the Waldensian Valleys, the vote was massively in favor, not of divorce per se, but of *freedom of choice*. Liberal democrats, social democrats, and radical democrats found themselves on one and the same side, *libertà*.

It is suprising that the same unity was found once more, in 1981. This time the referendum was on abortion, which, even more than the divorce issue, unsettled Protestant moral sensibilities. Despite the fact that abortion was not common practice among Protestants, the church was united on this issue. Was it a form of anti-Catholicism? It seems unlikely in a church where at this point 70 - 80 percent of marriages are mixed. The only credible explanation is the age-old Waldensian tradition of freedom and, above all, the practice of distinguishing between the law of the state and the law of conscience.

In the time between the two referenda, there was a sharp clash in the Waldensian-Methodist churches. In the mid-'70s the power of the Christian Democrats began to decline. The Italian Communist Party began to loosen its ties with the Soviet Union, accepted NATO and seemed able to lead the country in a sound reformist direction. In this climate, the Communist Party offered numerous Catholics the chance to run as "independents" on communist lines. To give an ecumenical veneer to this arrangement, the Communists decided to include a Waldensian pastor and their choice naturally fell to Tullio Vinay, who had founded Agape and Riesi. In 1974 Vinay had gone to Washington to back the National Council of Churches in its demand that American troops be withdrawn from Vietnam. The Communist Party's initiative and Vinay's acceptance caused a storm. The pietistic liberal democrats felt that Vinay had betrayed his mission, that the church was now prisoner of the "powers of this world" and of the Soviet world, at that. The "people of the church" voted for Vinay, believing that in him they would have a good voice in Parliament. They were right: in the Senate Vinay spoke up on many national and global peace and justice concerns; unfailingly the preacher, he brought to Parliament some extremely good sermons (attracting the attention of Francesco Cossiga, who has since been elected President of the Republic, and who, through the witness of Vinay, as President tells his nation that the Waldensian passion for freedom promotes everyone's freedom). The controversy exploded. The 1976 synod had to deal with a petition signed by 15 percent of the Waldensian-Methodist constituency, solemnly asking that the church review the entire matter. The Synod chose not to repudiate Vinay, with the result that the minority, believing that it was misunderstood, founded the *Testimonianza Evangelica Valdese* (TEV). Although TEV knew exactly what it was against (perceived political excesses), it was not so clear about what it was for, and in the end managed to get the support of only a fraction of the church. It was to lead continuing protests against Marxist tendencies in the church, and, later, against the liberalization of sexual mores. But TEV is unlikely to offer a viable alternative to the church's centerline.

In the late '70s the issue of women came again came to the fore. Throughout the century the Waldensian Church has increasingly opened its doors to the participation of women. In 1905 women received the right to vote in church affairs. In 1962 the first Waldensian woman became a pastor (today 14 percent of the Waldensian-Methodist pastors in active service are women and the percentage will surely rise rapidly, since roughly half of today's Waldensian Seminary students are women). In 1970 a woman was elected to the Waldensian National Board (in 1989 two of seven members are women). In the mid-'70s this "wise gradualism" was overturned by stirrings of the international women's movement. In 1976 the Federation of Protestant Women in Italy (FDEI) came into being, alongside the collective of women in the Federation of Protestant Youth-Young Adults in Italy. The church faced a real challenge. Harsh articles appeared in the church press and, as usual, Agape played a crucial role with its feminist camps.

It was not enough to introduce women gradually into an ecclesiastical structure planned and run by men. The feminist movement questioned the way work was distributed, along with the subordi-

Waldensian-Methodist Ministries in Italy, 1989

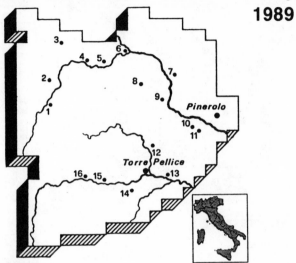

1st District

- TORRE PELLICE ⌐ H ◇ ⚕ ⚕ ⌂ ⋒ ⌥ ⌦ ⌐ ⚙ ⚲ ⊛ᵏ
- PINEROLO ⌐
1 Prali ⌐ ⚖ ⋒
2 Rodoretto ⌐ ⋒
3 Massello ⌐ ⋒
4 Perrero ⌐
5 Villasecca ⌐
6 Pomaretto ⌐ H
7 Villar Perosa ⌐ ◇
8 Pramollo ⌐ ⋒
9 San Germano ⌐ ⚕ ⋒
10 Prarostino ⌐   11 San Secondo ⌐
12 Angrogna ⌐ ◇ ◇ ◇ ⋒ ⋒
13 Luserna S. Giovanni ⌐ ⚕ ⚕ ⚕ ⚕
14 Rorà ⌐ ◇ ⋒
15 Villar Pellice ⌐ ⚕
16 Bobbio Pellice ⌐ ◇

⌐	Constituted Congregation
H	Hospital
⚖	Conference Center
◇	Hostel-Guest House
⚕	Home for the Aging
⚕	Children's Home
⊛ˢ	Community Development Center
⟐	Theological Seminary
⌂	Pre-School
⌂	Elementary School
⌂	Middle School
⌂	Junior College
⌂	Trade School
⋒	Museum
⌥	Press
⌦	Bookstore
⊡	Publisher
⚙	Library
⚲	Radio Station
⊛ᵏ	Cultural Center

Symbols in negative (apart from congregations) indicate ecumenical ministries.

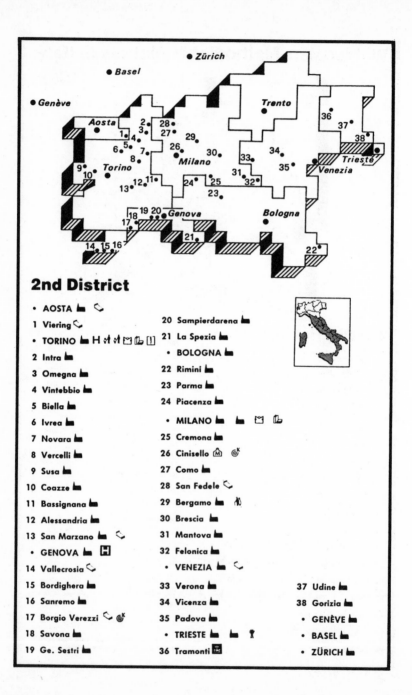

2nd District

- **AOSTA** 🛏 ⌣
1 **Viering** ⌣
- **TORINO** 🛏 H ⚲ ⚲ ✉ 🏛 ⊡
2 **Intra** 🛏
3 **Omegna** 🛏
4 **Vintebbio** 🛏
5 **Biella** 🛏
6 **Ivrea** 🛏
7 **Novara** 🛏
8 **Vercelli** 🛏
9 **Susa** 🛏
10 **Coazze** 🛏
11 **Bassignana** 🛏
12 **Alessandria** 🛏
13 **San Marzano** 🛏 ⌣
- **GENOVA** 🛏 H
14 **Vallecrosia** ⌣
15 **Bordighera** 🛏
16 **Sanremo** 🛏
17 **Borgio Verezzi** ⌣ ⦿
18 **Savona** 🛏
19 **Ge. Sestri** 🛏

20 **Sampierdarena** 🛏
21 **La Spezia** 🛏
- **BOLOGNA** 🛏
22 **Rimini** 🛏
23 **Parma** 🛏
24 **Piacenza** 🛏
- **MILANO** 🛏 🛏 ✉ 🏛
25 **Cremona** 🛏
26 **Cinisello** 🏛 ⦿
27 **Como** 🛏
28 **San Fedele** ⌣
29 **Bergamo** 🛏 👤
30 **Brescia** 🛏
31 **Mantova** 🛏
32 **Felonica** 🛏
- **VENEZIA** 🛏 ⌣
33 **Verona** 🛏
34 **Vicenza** 🛏
35 **Padova** 🛏
- **TRIESTE** 🛏 🛏 ⚱
36 **Tramonti** ⊞

37 **Udine** 🛏
38 **Gorizia** 🛏
- **GENÈVE** 🛏
- **BASEL** 🛏
- **ZÜRICH** 🛏

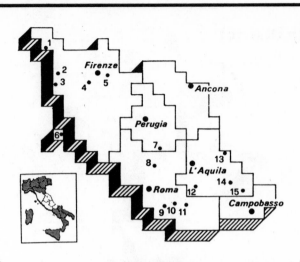

3rd District

- FIRENZE 🏭 🏭 🐂 🧑 🧑 📷 👞
1 Carrara 🏭
2 Pisa 🏭
3 Livorno 🏭
4 Tresanti 🌾
5 Reggello 🌾
6 Rio Marina 👞
7 Terni 🏭
- ROMA 🏭 🏭 🏭 🏭 👞 🏛 📖 📚
  🗿
8 Forano 🏭
9 Velletri ⚜
10 Colleferro 🏭
11 Ferentino 🏭
12 Villa S. Sebastiano 🏭 ⊚ˢ
13 Pescara 🏭
14 Palombaro 🏭
15 S. Giovanni Lipioni 🏭
- CAMPOBASSO 🏭

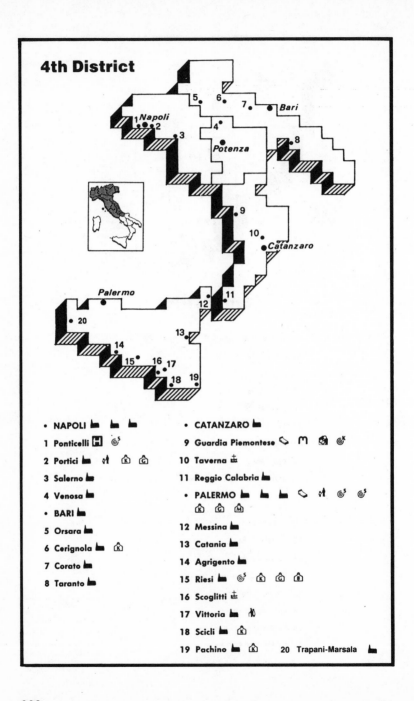

4th District

- **NAPOLI** ⌐ ⌐ ⌐
1 Ponticelli 🅗 ⊙ˢ
2 Portici ⌐ ⚒ 🏠 🏠
3 Salerno ⌐
4 Venosa ⌐
- **BARI** ⌐
5 Orsara ⌐
6 Cerignola ⌐ 🏠
7 Corato ⌐
8 Taranto ⌐

- **CATANZARO** ⌐
9 Guardia Piemontese ◇ ⋒ 🔲 ⊙ᵏ
10 Taverna ⚓
11 Reggio Calabria ⌐
- **PALERMO** ⌐ ⌐ ⌐ ◇ ⚒ ⊙ˢ ⊙ˢ
  🏠 🏠 Ⓜ
12 Messina ⌐
13 Catania ⌐
14 Agrigento ⌐
15 Riesi ⌐ ⊙ˢ 🏠 🏠 🏠
16 Scoglitti ⚓
17 Vittoria ⌐ 🚶
18 Scicli ⌐ 🏠
19 Pachino ⌐ 🏠   20 Trapani-Marsala ⌐

302

nation of "feminine" roles. It also questioned the service ethic that had sustained the avant-garde Waldensians from Agape to Riesi and Cinisello.

In the meantime, something unheard of has taken place: self-acclaimed homosexuals are knocking at the door of Protestant churches, asking to be accepted as partners in dialog and to be received at the Lord's table. Again the Agape center is at the fore: since the early '80s Agape has been hosting ecumenical conferences for homosexuals. The Agape initiative towards homosexuals was, in fact, the first institutionally-sanctioned initiative of its kind in Italy.

10. Set free for discipleship

In this past decade youth and young adults, disappointed by party politics, threw themselves into issues like ecology and, above all, disarmament. Two events set the stage: the installation of nuclear missiles at Comiso in Sicily and the Chernobyl incident. The synod expressed its support for the "peacemakers," backed demonstrations and even started a disarmament dialogue with the then Prime Minister, Bettino Craxi. A peace research and action center (CEDIP) was founded at Catania and was hailed in German, Dutch and American churches, and in the Valleys a peace hostel (cà d'la pais) was dedicated at the Bagnóou, site of a WWII partisan command post.

In this context, the passion for politics which characterized the '60s and '70s has been succeeded by a new form of ethical passion: the search for a different quality of life. Authentic *solidarity* has become the main spiritual question. Some grumble that the interest in theology has diminished. Maybe so. The neo-Calvinist orthodoxy which was the backbone of three generations of Waldensian-Methodist ministers and laypeople seems to have turned down "Sunset Boulevard." In its more serious moments, however, the church still seems to hark to the '30s theology, otherwise why should there have been so much rapt emotion at the opening service of the 1984 synod, when three young pacifists read the Barmen Confession, that manifesto of Protestant freedom and of Christ-centered faith, written by Barth 50 years earlier against Nazism? Why, otherwise, should that same synod have accepted the plea of Rosanna Ciappa, a convert, that the burning issue of terrorism should be debated in terms of theological, not socio-political language? The neo-Calvinist turn of the '30s, in my judgement, will stand secure. It is necessary, though, that it move forward in a completely different context.

The Waldensian Church which was persecuted until 1848, and marginalized until the 1960s, is now a part of the life of the nation, and, moreover, it is well-accepted, even courted, a recognized *component* of national life. In present-day pluralistic Italy, the Waldensian Church is like a little *republic of faith and culture*. With neither regional nor ethnic boundaries, it does have certain well-defined contours, as anyone who steps within Servizio Cristiano at Riesi or in the museum at Torre Pellice cannot fail to note.

The Waldensian experience is a culture, ready to shoulder responsibility. The small republic is decentralized, very pronounced in its ways, fine-tuned in its order and administration. This becomes apparent in the willingness of its people to take on the administrative and executive posts of the church. Brilliant men and women agree to serve for years on even obscure committees. Waldensians and Methodists know that democracy has a price, and they are willing to pay for it.

When all is said and done, it will not be the "democratic," "committed" or "progressive" elements that will open to our churches the pathway to the future: no, that will depend on the way we interpret our vocation. For some time now I have personally been convinced that Waldensian and Methodist believers interpret their *vocation* in Italy in terms of *Christian discipleship*. This has not always been the case. Nineteenth century Waldensians understood penetration of Italy in terms of *mission*, in the fascist era they interpreted their call in terms of *resistance*, but from the end of WWII to the present day, the most important issue has been *discipleship*. It is this theme which is apparent in the efforts of the Barthians to build truly "Reformed" congregations, in the setting up of intentional communities to counter the myths of success and prosperity. The call to discipleship is the engine which drives youth's passion to reform the church and the women's challenge to the obsolete mental structures of the church. From "service" to "militancy" the centerline is the same: discipleship, the substance of the cross. For such Christ has set us free.

This is the reason why people still want to join the Waldensian-Methodist churches, whether they are Marxists or former Marxists who decide to live with us their rediscovery of God, monks and priests tired of crusades, left-wing Catholics dissatisfied with a "socialist Christ," or "evangelicals" wanting a more complete theology and a church open to new ideas. Will these new people be able to fill the gaps in the traditional Waldensian-Methodist ranks caused by dispersion and secularization? Will old and new Waldensians together be able to create a meaningful minority component in the Italy of the future?

Flesh and blood cannot answer these questions right now. We do know that the future of the "evangelical" Waldensian-Methodist churches will depend on two things, the quality of its message and the quality of living it stimulates in its people. This is a gift more than achievement, so what counts is the prayer of Psalm 130:

Our souls long for the Lord,
Yea, more than the night watch longs for the morning!

26. FOR RELIGIOUS FREEDOM (1946)

Italians:

... Since authentic civil and political freedom cannot flourish unless there be the foundation of freedom of religion equal for all, we must eliminate every vestige of the old confessional state. Therefore, we Protestant Christians advance the following principles:

1. The full and complete freedom of conscience and of religion for all, so that anyone — if a believer — can worship God and witness to God's truth as conscience directs;

2. The full independence of all the churches from the state ...

3. Impartiality and neutrality in matters of religion on the part of a non-confessional state — which means citizens' equality before the law, regardless of faith professed, and no confessional teaching in public schools ...

In freedom and in parity of faiths before the law, no one's rights are diminished.

Rome, May 20, 1946.
Protestant Christians in Italy.

—poster affixed across Italy preparatory to elections for the national constituent assembly of June 1946.

27. SENT TO SERVE (1960)

The time has come for an urgent reexamination of our mission as Christian communities.

Mission in this world is the reason for the church's existence, but that mission must be seen in a double perspective: in the world and in the light of the rule of God. The church cannot live for herself. Her criterion is not that of success. The church's calling, rather, is to serve as Christ himself served, and to give her life that the world may live. She is the body by which today the Lord gives himself to the world.

We ask you, therefore, to consider what the world needs today. The world does not need the private piety of those who are concerned above all for their personal salvation. Nor do we need it, for Christ had already secured it. The world has no need for our success. What the world does need is a new sense of meaning for life and a new hope.

Our generation has spent itself in an exhausting search for self-aggrandizement, for possessions, for dominion and power. Even if it has always been more or less thus, it is also true that in a desire to save itself the world in our time risks final destruction.

But if its existence has become precarious, this same world is open to the proclamation of the "new world" which Christ in his own person has brought to us. This is the new world of service, of love which gives freely of itself . . .

Today, brothers and sisters, the world can see in all clarity that the way of Christ, living for others, is the one true way; and it can also understand how dangerous and empty is the recourse to false remedies.

The world will receive this good news only if it is the way of life for us, as we proclaim Christ through serving others and by renouncing our own particular interests. Our words and reasoning alone will have little effect. When our communities demonstrate that they are new men and women in Christ, who know how to practice reconciliation and love, our cities and villages will have understood Christ, and they will embrace and love him.

The gospel in every period of history has reached people when believers have brought it to bear on the real concerns of men and women . . .

Let us not fail to hear in the precise moment in which we are called. We are but few and we are not rich, yet the Living One can take our mere nothingness and from it bring forth new creation, the creation which the world he so loved awaits, consciously or unconsciously.

Christ who lives and is present among his people will cause faith and hope to spring up from the seeds of our life, seeds we shall sow in love in the difficult soil of our society.

—*Acts of the Waldensian Synod,* Italy,1960, n. 21.

28. WITNESS FOR PEACE AND JUSTICE (1980s)

1) Acting for disarmament

The synod, recognizing that the message of Jesus Christ overcomes hate, power, and death, and is the love, service, and life which build a new world where all are brothers and sisters to one another; and confessing that its witness for peace heretofore has not been sufficiently firm on the arms issue —

— *affirms* the promise of life without the homicidal protection of arms;...

— *asserts* that conventional, nuclear, chemical and bacteriological arms alike constitute crime against humanity;

— *holds* that Italy's having agreed to the installation of a missile base at Comiso — beyond the hundreds of already-existing NATO and American nuclear devices around the nation — is intollerable; . . .

— noting that Italy is the fourth largest exporter of arms in the world, *urges* the nation to embark upon a program of conversion of its arms industry to peaceful purposes;

— *recognizes* conscientious objection to military service and arms research and production as a choice worthy of maximum support;

— *calls upon* parents and educators to promote peace education and education on non-violence, truth and love for justice;

— recognizing that disarmament negotiations often yield little fruit and do not preclude the possibility of global catastrophe, *affirms* that unilateral disarmament alone holds promise for concrete results;

— *calls upon* all religious bodies to take note that millions suffer and die because of military arms, the staggering financing of which impedes human development and assaults human dignity;

— *urges* the churches to grapple more and more with the theological dimensions of the arms issue and to promote ecumenical initiatives — among and beyond the churches — for peace and disarmament;

— *calls upon* the Waldensian National Board to name a commission on peace and disarmament to connect with national and international peace units, to pursue work launched by the Comiso conference, to promote peace education, to generate theological materials, and to stimulate and support action in the churches . . .

—*Acts of the Waldensian Synod,* Italy, 1982, nos. 74, 75.

. . . The synod . . . adopts as its own the World Council of Churches' Vancouver Assembly's solemn condemnation (1983) of the production, use and diffusion of nuclear arms; . . . calls for the suspension of the installation of cruise missiles at Comiso, . . . recognizing that nuclear disarmament — even unilateral — is the way most consistent with our faith...

—*Acts of the Waldensian Synod,* Italy, 1983, nos. 22, 26.

2) Loving the stranger within our gates

The synod, concerned about the advance of racism in our nation . . .

1) calls upon the churches

a) to examine — in dialog with theological reflection — the phenomenon of immigration in all its political-economic-social complexity;

b) to promote and back up initiatives to safeguard immigrants and their families, and to encourage intercultural dialog;...

c) to fight racism at home and abroad, where our life-styles have the effect of nourishing it;

2) reminds the churches that the Immigrant-Refugee Ministry of the Federation of Protestant Churches in Italy can resource and assist churches

in the study and condemnation of situations incompatible with the principles of justice and the biblical message;

3) calls upon the Waldensian National Board actively to pressure the government to deal with the immigrant-refugee issue in full regard for human rights accords and the precepts of the Italian Constitution.

—*Acts of the Waldensian Synod*, Italy, 1988, n. 74.

EDITOR'S END NOTES

(1) The name *Valdesius* has come down in French, Italian, and English, respectively, as Valdès, Valdo, and Waldo; the English *Waldensian(s)* is derived from the latter. Archaic forms (as Waldenses) are in use in some circles to this day, but the preferred singular, plural, and adjectival forms in English are *Waldensian, Waldensians, Waldensian* (as Presbyterian, Presbyterians, Presbyterian).

(2) The Waldensians at length were to survive in settlements located on the Italian side of the French-Italian border. The *Valli Valdesi* in the Cottian Alps ("Waldensian Valleys" or "Historic Valleys") today include the Val Germanasca, Val Chisone, Val Angrogna and Val Pellice. The Waldensian population there (15,000) constitutes roughly one-half of the Waldensian-Methodist population across Italy today.

(3) Since Waldensian people were dispersed all across the continent, variant forms of spiritual leadership emerged from region to region. In some areas there were actual hierarchies—not elaborate, but nonetheless highly structured. Elsewhere organization was more fluid and collegial. Early leaders of the Poor were itinerant preachers; when the movement was constrained to go underground the leaders were seen preeminently as teachers. By the fourteenth century a distinct form of spiritual leadership, the *barba* (from *barbanus*, uncle, meaning an elder who commands respect), had developed in the Alpine region; in the German lands the leaders were called variously "apostles" or *Meistern,* masters. After the Reformation the *barba* increasingly served particular communities in Italy in the fields of preaching and spiritual formation, and at length came to be called pastors.

(4) The Waldensian diaspora in the German lands at the time thus streamed into the Lutheran ranks of the Reformation. The Alpine Waldensians, through the "Geneva connection," aligned themselves with the Reformed ranks. Waldensians adhere to the World Alliance of Reformed Churches, their Confession of Faith being a 1655 statement of French Reformed inspiration.

(5) Even at the end of the twentieth century the struggle for equal treatment of all the components of Italian society, including religious and racial minorities, goes on. Stirring indeed is the Waldensian-Methodist and Federation of Protestant Churches' advocacy in the nation for *everyone's* freedom—for authentic practice beyond the national rhetoric of democracy and pluralism.

(6) In Italian: *chiesa evangelica* or *chiesa cristiana evangelica. Evangelica* normally means "Protestant." To this day many Waldensian and Methodist congregations are known first of all as *chiese evangeliche,* even though actually each congregation is either *chiesa evangelica valdese* or *chiesa evangelica metodista.*

(7) "Waldensian" people in the U.S. today (apart from the New York City congregation, the sole congregation in the U.S. organically related to the

309

church in Italy) are effectively Waldensian-*heritage* people. While found all across the ecumenical spectrum, most Waldensian-heritage people in the U.S. are members of Presbyterian and other Reformed denominations, largely because emigrants from the sending church overseas, Reformed since the sixteenth century, have welcomed the promise of streaming into and applying their talents to the wide dimensions of Reformed discipleship lived out in North America. The church overseas has always understood and accepted this development.

(8) The *Tavola Valdese* and *Mesa Valdense* in this volume normally are cited, respectively, as the Waldensian National Board in Italy and the Waldensian Regional Board in Argentina-Uruguay.

(9) The Baptist churches in Italy first arose through British and American initiatives in the 1860s. Today there are some 90 churches (constituency: 8,000) across Italy, particularly in the central and southern regions. Though congregational in polity, the congregations belong to the Baptist Union in Italy—*Unione Cristiana Evangelica Battista d'Italia* (UCEBI)—which meets in an annual assembly and is a member of the Federation of Protestant Churches in Italy, the Baptist World Alliance, and the World Council of Churches. UCEBI (president: Pastor Paolo Spanu; headquarters: Piazza S. Lorenzo in Lucina 35, 00186 Roma, Italy) has close ties to the Southern Baptist Convention (USA), although it is becoming a free-standing body in its own right. Specialized ministries include two homes for the aging, five camp and conference centers, two periodicals, and departments on theology and evangelization. Collaboration between the Baptist churches and the Waldensian-Methodist churches is very close and in fact may well eventuate in a three-way federation.

310

FOR FURTHER READING

1. Periodicals

The semi-annual *Newsletter* of the American Waldensian Society (475 Riverside Drive, Room 1850; New York, NY 10115) reports on the shape and direction of Waldensian-Methodist ministry in both Italy and Argentina-Uruguay. New publications in the Waldensian field are also cited, as well as 'crossings': opportunities for service with Waldensian-Methodist ministries overseas, and mission-to-the-USA visitations by Waldensian-Methodist leadership.

Published in the United Kingdom are the *Waldensian Review* of the English and Irish Waldensian Church Missions Committees and the Scottish Waldensian Missions Aid Society (c/o Ms. R. Farrer, 157 Waldegrave Road, Teddington, Middlesex TW11 8LU) and the *Waldensian Fellowship Newsletter* of the United Reformed Church (c/o Dr. R. Cowhig, 21 Priory Road, Sale, Cheshire M33 2BS).

The *Bollettino della Società di Studi Valdesi* (Journal of the Society for Waldensian Studies), published in Italy on a semi-annual basis, reviews continuing serious research on the Waldensian experience across the centuries. Included are synopses in English of major articles. Facsimile copies of the entire series since 1884 are available. Subscription inquiries via the American Waldensian Society.

Among the seminaries and universities in the U.S. which receive the *Bollettino* are Bethany Theological Seminary (Church of the Brethren), Oak Brook, IL; Mennonite Historical Library, Goshen College, Goshen IN; Princeton Theological Seminary (Presbyterian Church in the USA), Princeton, NJ; United Theological Seminary (United Methodist Church), Dayton OH; and Virginia Theological Seminary (Episcopal Church), Alexandria, VA.

The *Boletin de la Sociedad Sudamericana de Historia Valdense* (Journal of the South American Society on Waldensian History) has been published since 1935 at irregular intervals in Uruguay; currently it is not published. Information via Biblioteca y Archivo Valdense, Casa Valdense, Avda. A. Ugon, 70202 Valdense (Dpto. de Colonia), Uruguay.

Information on the following can be secured from the American Waldensian Society: the Waldensian weekly (*La Luce*, in Italian) and monthly (*Mensajero Valdense*, in Spanish), the quarterly journal of the Waldensian Theological Seminary in Rome (*Protestantesimo*, in Italian), the bi-monthly journal of the Federation of Protestant Youth-Young Adults in Italy (*Gioventù Evangelica*, in Italian) and the press service (Italian and English) of the Federation of Protestant Churches in Italy.

2. Books

The most extensive bibliography (3,500 entries, all relevant languages) in the Waldensian field, *Bibliografia Valdese*, by A. Hugon and G. Gonnet, was published in 1953 by the *Società di Studi Valdesi* as no. 93 in the *Bollettino* series, which periodically includes updates to the 275-page base document. A revised, updated edition is in preparation.

311

In the U.S. exceptional Waldensian collections are found in the libraries of Princeton Theological Seminary, Princeton, NJ, and of the Presbyterian Church in the USA's Department of History (Box 849, Montreat, NC 28757, and 425 Lombard Street, Philadelphia PA 19147).

Recent titles in English are relatively few. Classic nineteenth century works [such as W. Beattie, *The Waldenses* (London, 1838)—notable for its engravings; A. Muston, *A History of the Waldenses: the Israel of the Alps,* 2 vols.(London, 1866); Presbyterian Board of Publication, *The Waldenses* (Philadelphia, 1853)] may be found in some libraries. Facsimile reprints of a number of seventeenth-nineteenth century texts in English are available from Church History Research and Archives (220 Graystone Drive, Gallatin, TN 37066) and AMS Press, Inc. (56 E. 13th Street, NY, NY 10003). Late twentieth century critical scholarship has surpassed certain earlier views concerning the origin and early centuries of the Waldensian experience.

Titles in French, German and, of course, Italian, abound, most of the latter being the work of the Waldensian publishing house (Claudiana Editrice, Via Principe Tommaso 1, 10125 Torino, Italy). Claudiana's catalog currently carries over 500 titles—booklets and volumes alike on .theology, biblical studies, church history and the ministry of the church today in both global and Waldensian attainments.

The most recent comprehensive treatment of Waldensian history developed by Claudiana (apart from G. Tourn's *I Valdesi*) is the monumental three-volume *Storia dei Valdesi*—A. Molnár, *Dalle origini all'adesione alla Riforma, 1174-1532* (origins to the Reformation), 1974, 370 pp.; A. Hugon, *Dal sinodo di Chanforan all'emancipazione, 1532-1848* (Reformation to emancipation), 1974, 330 pp.; V. Vinay, *Dal movimento evangelico italiano al movimento ecumenico, 1848-1978* (Great Revival into the ecumenical movement), 1980, 530 pp—which builds upon E. Comba's *Storia dei Valdesi,* likewise published by Claudiana in 1923 and revised editions.

Of interest to scholars will be G. Gonnet, *Enchiridion Fontium Valdensium, I* (1179-1218 accounts concerning Waldensians), 1958; G. Gonnet, *Le confessioni di fede valdesi prima della Riforma* (Waldensian pre-Reformation confessions of faith), 1967; V. Vinay, *Le confessioni di fede dei Valdesi riformati* (early Reformation-era Waldensian confessions of faith), 1975— all published by Claudiana. The Waldensian publisher has undertaken to offer to the public a series of volumes on the celebrated collections of ancient Waldensian texts found in the university libraries of Cambridge, Dublin and Geneva. The Geneva series is well underway, with three volumes (introduction and the '206' and '209' texts) having been published to date. Texts are presented in the original languages.

On occasion of the 300th anniversary of the 'Return' of exiled Waldensians to Italy, Claudiana in 1988 published two titles by authors associated with the present volume: G. Bouchard, *I Valdesi e l'Italia* (the meaning of the Waldensian presence in Italy over the past three centuries); G. Bouchard, A. De Lange, B. Peyrot, G. Spini, G. Tourn, *Il glorioso rimpatrio dei Valdesi* (history, European context and significance today of the 'Return').

A full statement (378 pp.) of the Waldensian experience in Latin America to the mid-twentieth century is E. Tron and E. Ganz, *Historia de las Colonias Valdenses Sudamericanas, 1858-1958* (Valdense, 1958).

312

3. Waldensian-heritage people in North America

A detailed narrative (309 pp.) of the dispersion of Waldensian immigrants across the continent is G. Watts, *The Waldenses in the New World* (Durham, Duke U., 1941).

Further information on Waldensian settlements in the U.S. may be secured from the Waldensian Museum, c/o Waldensian Presbyterian Church, 104 E. Main Street, Valdese, NC 28690.

The American Waldensian Society has a modest collection of unpublished monographs and graduate theses on Waldensian-heritage people in the U.S. and their overseas forebearers. Owners of such materials are invited to make their existence known to the Society.

ADMINISTRATORS SINCE EMANCIPATION, 1848

Moderators, Italy		Presidents, Committee on Evangelization, Italy	
G.P. Revel	1848-1857		
B. Malan	1857-1859		
G.P. Revel	1859-1860	G.P. Revel	1860-1971
B. Malan	1860-1863		
P. Lantaret	1863-1874	M. Prochet	1871-1906
J.D. Charbonnier	1874-1880		
P. Lantaret	1880-1887		
G.P. Pons	1887-1909	A. Muston	1906-1913
B. Léger	1909-1915	E. Giampiccoli	1913-1915

Moderators, Italy

Ernesto Giampiccoli	1915-1921
B. Léger	1921-1928
V.A. Costabel	1928-1934
Ernesto Comba	1934-1941
Virgilio Sommani	1941-1948
Guglielmo del Pesco	1948-1951
Achille Deodato	1951-1958
Ermanno Rostan	1958-1965
Neri Giampiccoli	1965-1972
Aldo Sbaffi	1972-1979
Giorgio Bouchard	1979-1986
Franco Giampiccoli	1986-

Moderators, Argentina-Uruguay

Wilfrido Artus	1965-1966
Delmo Rostan	1967-1973
Mario Bertinat	1974
Wilfrido Artus	1975-1978
Mario Bertiant	1979-1982
Ricardo Ribeiro	1983-1987
Hugo Malan	1988-

Presidents, Methodist Commission in Italy since federation, 1979

Sergio Aquilante	1979-1986
Paolo Sbaffi	1986-1988
Claudio Martelli	1988-

THE WALDENSIAN CHURCH: ADMINISTRATION

1. Denominational Names

    Argentina-Uruguay: Iglesia Evangélica Valdense del Río de la Plata
    Italy: Chiesa Evangelica Valdese (Unione delle Chiese Valdesi e
    Metodiste)

    The Church is cited in English as The Waldensian Church in the Plate
    River Region (Argentina-Uruguay) and The Waldensian Church - Union
    of Waldensian and Methodist Congregations (Italy), since, in the case
    of the latter, in the federated arrangement, dating from 1979, local
    churches retain their historic identity.

    The Churches on the two continents are organically related to a single
    synod, which meets in two annual sessions: in mid-February, for the
    Latin American session, and in late August, for the European session.

    The Churches are members of the World Council of Churches, and
    the Methodist and Waldensian components belong, respectively, to the
    World Methodist Council and the World Alliance of Reformed Churches.

2. Executive Boards

    Regional Board, Argentina-Uruguay   National Board, Italy

    Mesa Valdense   Tavola Valdese
    Casa Valdense   Casa Valdese
    70202 Valdense (Dpto. Colonia)   Via Beckwith 2
    Uruguay   10066 Torre Pellice (To)
                                         Italy

3. Executives

    Waldensian Moderators (part-time in Argentina-Uruguay;
    full-time in Italy)

    El Moderador   Il Moderatore
    Casa Valdense   Tavola Valdese
    70202 Valdense (Dpto. Colonia)   Via Firenze 38
    Uruguay   00184 Roma
                                         Italy

    President, Methodist Commission (part-time)

    Il Presidente
    OPCEMI
    Via Firenze 38
    00184 Roma
    Italy

4. Regional Organization

The Waldensian and Methodist communities in Europe are organized into 16 circuits, which in turn are related to four districts (regional conferences) as follows:

districts-circuits	regions	number of communities Waldensian	Methodist	constitutents
1/1-3	Waldensian Valleys	19	0	13,000
2/4-9	Switzerland, northern Italy (except Waldensian Valleys) through Emilia-Romagna	28	21 1 united church	9,000
3/10-12	central Italy - Toscana, Marche through Lazio, Molise	20	8	4,000
4/13-16	southern Italy - Campania, Puglia through Sicilia	26	7 1 united church	4,000
		131 communities		30,000

The Waldensian communities in Latin America (Plate River Region in Argentina-Uruguay) are organized into six presbyteries, embracing 24 constituted church clusters, as follows:

	Argentina	Uruguay	Total
presbyteries	2	4	6
larger parishes	9	15	24
constituents	4,000	11,000	15,000

SPECIALIZED MINISTRIES, 1989

In Italy

1. Theological Seminary

   Facoltà Valdese di Teologia
   Via Pietro Cossa 42
   00193 Roma, Italy

2. Publishing-Broadcasting Units

   a. Publishing House
      Claudiana Editrice, Turin

   b. Book Stores
      Milan, Rome (E), Torre Pellice, Turin

   c. Periodicals
      Bollettino, Società di Studi Valdesi (Journal, Society for
         Waldensian Studies
      Confronti (Catholic base community-Protestant
         journal)(E)
      Gioventù Evangelica (journal, Federation of Protestant
         Youth-Young Adults in Italy) (E)
      La Luce (weekly newspaper)
      Protestantesimo (journal, Waldensian Theological Seminary)

   d. Bible Society (E)
      Rome

   e. Radio-TV
      national Protestant radio hour (weekly) (E)
      national Protestant TV hour (bi-weekly) (E)
      Torre Pellice: Radio Beckwith (24/24 hrs.)
      Trieste: Radio Trieste Evangelica (24/24 hrs.)

3. Research-Archival Units

   a. Torre Pellice Historical and Cultural Center
      archives, library of Waldensian National Board
      museum
      office, Society for Waldensian Studies

   b. Society for the Study of Protestantism in Southern Italy
      (Società di Studi Evangelici)

   c. Museums

Historic Valleys		Calabria
Angrogna (4)	Rodoretto	Guardia Piemontese
Balsiglia	Rorà	
Massello	San Germano	
Prali	Torre Pellice	
Pramollo		

317

4. Cultural Centers

Cinisello-Milan
Guardia Piemontese (Calabria)
Milan

Naples (E)
Rome (E)
Torre Pellice

The centers have proliferated as conference points where the Protestant experience and public issues are examined, normally in public-at-large settings for reaching new people. Some of the conference-reading room areas are within worship centers; others are in adjacent facilities. Cited are major centers; several dozen others are found across the churches and specialized ministries.

5. Hostels-Guest Houses

Historic Valleys
Angrogna (3)
Torre Pellice
Villar Pellice

Guardia Piemontese (Calabria)
Palermo

The cited accomodations are for church-related visitors. Many churches and specialized ministries not cited have overnight facilities for small numbers of church-related visitors.

Three units can accept large numbers of church-related and non-church-related visitors:
Florence (*Foresteria Valdese*)
Rome (*Casa Valdese*)
Venice (*Foresteria Valdese*)

6. Conference Centers

Adelfia (Sicily) [3]
Agape (Historic Valleys) [1]
Bethel (Calabria) [3]
Casa Cares (Tuscany) (E) [2]

Ecumene (Rome) [2]
Monteforte (Campania) (E) [3]
Tramonti di Sopra (Friuli) (E) [3]

(1) open year-round; program in the main developed by international resident staff team
(2) open most of the year for program developed by staff and visiting groups
(3) open on seasonal and special event basis for programming developed in the main by visiting groups

7. Vacation Centers

Located in the main in Liguria, Lombardy, Piedmont, Tuscany, and Valle d'Aosta. Programming is self-organized by visitors.

8. Education Centers

    a. Pre-Schools
        Cerignola (Puglia)   Palermo
        Monteforte (Campania) (E)   Riesi (Sicily)
        Naples   Scicli (Sicily)
        Pachino (Sicily)

    b. Elementary Schools
        Naples   Riesi (Sicily)
        Palermo

    c. Middle Schools
        Cinisello-Milan   Palermo
        Naples

    d. Junior College (*liceo linguistico*)
        Torre Pellice

    e. Home-School for physically-mentally disabled children
        and youth
        Luserna San Giovanni (Historic Valleys)

    f. Homes-Schools for children from families in crisis
        Florence (2)   Palermo
        Naples

    g. Community Centers
        Florence (E)   Villa San Sebastiano (Abruzzo)
        Naples (2, one of which is E)

    h. Dormitories for out-of-town students
        Florence   Turin
        Torre Pellice

    i. Trade School
        Riesi

9. Community Development Centers

    a. Centro Diaconale, Palermo
        schools, preventive medicine center, village for
        families uprooted by earthquake

    b. Servizio Cristiano, Riesi (Sicily)
        schools, agriculture center, preventive medicine
        center; international staff resident team

    c. Villages for families uprooted by earthquakes
        Monteforte (Campania) (E)   Vita (Sicily)
        Naples-Ponticelli (E)

319

d. Cooperatives (agriculture, livestock, textiles)
    Vita (Sicily) (2)   Senerchia (Campania) (E)
    Riesi (Sicily) (2)   Villa San Sebastiano (Abruzzo)
    Ruvo del Monte (Campania) (E)

10. Centers for immigrants-refugees (in development) (E)

Florence	Palermo
Genova	Rome
Milan	Turin
Naples	

11. Hospitals

Historic Valleys	Genova (E)
Pomaretto	Naples (E)
Torre Pellice	Turin

12. Homes for the aging

Historic Valleys	Bergamo (Lombardy)
Luserna San Giovanni (3)	
San Germano	Florence
Torre Pellice	Vittoria (Sicily)
Villar Pellice	

13. Ministries of Federation of Protestant Churches in Italy (FCEI), Rome (E)

church school curricula	immigrant-refugee ministry
earthquake resettlement	radio-TV-press service
disaster relief	

14. Commissions and special units (partial listing)

Federation of Protestant Women in Italy (FDEI) (E)
Federation of Protestant Youth-Young Adults in Italy (FGEI) (E)
Federation of Waldensian-Methodist Women (FFEVM)
Union of Lay Preachers (UPL)

synod commissions on
church-state issues	specialized ministries
ecumenical relations	studies for lay preachers
evangelization	women-men in the church
justice, peace and	worship and liturgy
integrity of creation	

synod special committees on
historical sites in	solidarity with conscientious
the Valleys	objectors

In Argentina-Uruguay (Uruguay unless otherwise noted)

1. Theological Seminary

   Union Theological Seminary (ISEDET),
   Buenos Aires (Argentina) (E)

2. Publishing-Broadcasting Units

   a. Book Store
      Valdense

   b. Periodical
      Mensajero Valdense (monthly newspaper)

   c. Radio
      Valdense

3. Research-Archival Units

   a. archives, library of the Waldensian Regional Board, Valdense
   b. museum, Valdense

4. Conference Center

   Parque 17 de Febero, Valdense

5. Education Centers

   a. Home-School for physically-mentally disabled children and youth
      Valdense

   b. Home for children from families in crisis
      Colonia (E)

   c. Community Center
      Rosario

   d. Dormitories for out-of-town students
      Buenos Aires (Argentina)   Montevideo (also medical
      Bahía Blanca (Argentina)   patients)

   e. Church Education - Continuing Theological Education Center
      Valdense (E)

6. Homes for the aging

   Valdense   Jacinto Aráuz (Argentina)

7. Commissions and special units (partial listing)

Women's Federation (FFEV)
Youth Federation (FJV)
synod commissions on
    agrarian development   liturgy-music
    Christian education   social ministries
    dispersed constituents   youth

Notes: 1. E = ecumenical ministry
          2. The majority of the above ministries has been developed
              since WWII.
          3. Particulars (directors, addresses, populations served, etc.) may
              be secured via the American Waldensian Society.

VOICES IN THE 1980s

God's rule and "all things new"

Is the rule of God a garden of the faith which the Christian community cultivates, a ghetto, within the fence, well-protected from the wolves without? No, the rule of God is the reality of life made new, set free: it has the whole world in mind—South Africa, the Middle East, Chile—the same world that is threatened with self-destruction.

The rule of God propels us to seek out our sisters and brothers, to love them, to care for them. So God's rule, never an institution, is love at work in the extremities *(diaspora)*, always new, always liberating . . .

The inquisitors said of the early Waldensians, "Nude, they follow a nude Christ." That's just the point: our faith means commitment to the poor, and free preaching not kept "in line" by church authorities. Discipleship, fundamentality, is not a matter of "certification." Openness to God's will *(disponibilità)* is all that is needed.

In this light *diaspora* takes on a whole new meaning. To say it is far-flung little groups of believers is not enough. *Diaspora* is the vocation of the whole church of Christ. It places the whole church in the stream of God's rule, which never fails to meet life's Jericho Roads head-on.

Pastor Gianna Sciclone, Italy

Key elements in authentic ecumenism:
* recovery of the rule of God as the central motif;
* explicit appeal to the liberating movement of the Spirit;
* resistance to the forces of evil in this present age;
* reformulation of the role of women in the church;
* search for a new catholicity which is bound to the indivisibility of humanity;
* the church's becoming the home of everyone's freedom.

Professor Paolo Ricca
Waldensian Theological Seminary, Italy

Our ministry raises up hundreds of young people who are being shaped to take charge of their own development, to think critically, to take responsibility, to decide and act as free agents. Meanwhile,

323

the church community, instrument at once of theological reflection and of the practice of the good news of love and hope—this community keeps saying to the people of Palermo that God, who raised Jesus from the dead, remakes all things, that freedom from the chains of the past—of sin, of death—is open to us, that therefore we no longer need to continue on life's treadmills, but can become artisans of a whole new way *(costruttore di novità)* which God has imparted to us in the love of Christ . . .

Pastor Sergio Aquilante, Italy

The student generation speaks up

The Federation of Protestant Youth-Young Adults is not a "youth department" annex to the churches; it is a movement which dialogs with the churches. As we live our faith in constant interaction with global realities—nuclear arms and militarism, Italy's deep south, Third World immigrants, Central America, South Africa—we raise these same issues as believers within the household of faith . . .

We are discovering "another America" beyond the America obsessed with flag, "national security," anti-communist crusades, trust in nuclear arms, etc. It is taking time, but in Italy young believers—my generation—are finding that the global network of solidarity for the practice of justice and for the culture of peace does extend well into the U.S. after all. We are connecting with U.S. contemporaries who, with us, choose to lodge their identity in the gospel which risks all for others *(vangelo scommodo)* and for which resistance to evil structures in society is the inescapable path of Christian witness and faith-made-visible . . .

How shall we work for authentic public life? Shall we settle for a false pluralism which advances privileges for those who can finesse the system? Or shall our faith place us in the struggle for the freedom which reaches everyone, far beyond ourselves alone?

Debora Spini
university student, Italy

This year in the U.S. has permitted me to get to know other ways of being Protestant in our world and has stimulated me to reflect upon why, after all, I should serve in the Waldensian Church. I have come up with several reasons: 1) The church has deep roots in its history, throughout which its people found their identity in their faith. 2) We engage in a wide spectrum of activity. I attach

324

particular importance to work at the frontiers of social life: working class people, Third World immigrants, etc. 3) The church is open to participating in the political life of the nation. The challenge of the peace movement is an example. 4) We insist upon theological reflection, which gives breadth and depth to our life, preaching, and action, and which keeps us in dialog with the Italian culture. 5) Our small size reminds us that we have to choose among many urgent concerns: we have to find a way to be significant through the prophetic content of our activity and words, not through trying to take on everything . . . And finally, this: 6) Our world is deeply divided between a north, affluent and powerful, and a south, poor and dependent. Two-thirds of our small church is in Italy, in the rich world; one-third of the church is in Argentina-Uruguay, in the poor world. We are not allowed to forget for one minute that some nations have a high standard of living at the expense of the rest of the world, because we are in both worlds. So we do not understand ourselves as a center, in Italy, and a colony (mission) in South America; instead we see ourselvs as one church in two continents, with a singular opportunity for witness to Jesus Christ who is overcoming the dividing walls of north and south.

Daniele Bouchard
seminarian, Italy

Theology

. . . I say to all the delegates: return to your churches, and when they ask you what you did at the synod meeting, tell them, "We did theology: what stood out was the relevance of theology and reflection upon the word of God for confronting the issues of these times."

Pastor Giorgio Bouchard, Italy

In the face of pervasive social change, our Latin American churches cannot settle for the teaching of personal morality alone, with a few social ministries mixed in. The real question is, do we have an across-the-board serious commitment to the poor? Will we walk with the poor in the search for justice and social transformation? While we will always give close attention to European theologies, we know that we must move beyond them and come to terms with liberation theology, fruit of the Latin American experience of the poor. We cannot look over our shoulders for European answers.

325

That will surely fail us. The emerging Latin American theology is risky all right, but we think it points us to "a future and a hope."

Pastor Hugo Malan, Uruguay

Witness and solidarity

(The church's) first vocation is evangelization—arousing and confirming faith in the Lord Jesus Christ . . . Preaching and service are constituitive dimensions of witness. We call upon the churches and specialized ministries to see the connection between these two aspects of witness, and to recognize that action to strengthen the one must not serve to diminish the other.

synod assembly, Italy, 1988

Our solidarity with suffering people is an expression of our faith; it is our response to a God who did not evade dying for us. In today's world, solidarity adds up to the struggle for justice. It is a way of preaching the love of Christ . . .

In the midst of pervasive secularism, our church fails to animate a new humanity at life's peripheries . . .The commandment to love makes this clear: Truth is opened to us only as we are joined to others. Unless we are in communion with (converted to) emarginated people, we are not the assembly which is the church.

Pastor Carlos Delmonte, Uruguay

Personal commitment and social responsibility are joined in the word solidarity, the secular term for *agape*, Christ's love. Solidarity does take us down the road of engaging political realities—risky, yes, for harmony in the church. But the greater risk for faithfulness on the part of believers and the church is the eventuality that the agape of Christ should be muted and make no difference in the public life of our times.

Pastor Franco Giampiccoli, Italy

Paul teaches that in bearing one another's burdens, we fulfill the law of Christ (Galatians 6). Christ's own incarnation, life and death bore the full weight of our troubled humanity. This is the standard of authentic life for the church of Christ, for God's people in the world. It is the standard of active solidarity, of voluntary and sacrificial giving of self by those who are "rich," whether spiritually

326

or materially, to set free others who are in need . . .

Christ's church in this world is one. It has one solidarity to live out in the search "first of all," as Jesus put it, for God's rule and its justice, for the glory of God's name. May Christ so live his life in each of us that we may surrender our wills to the purposes of God.

Pastor Ricardo Ribeiro, Uruguay

Let's be clear: to opt for life with Christ means going down a difficult road with no security and no hope other than that which God alone renews each day. Living with the cross, the community of believers makes common cause with all who suffer and die for freedom and for conscience. We aim for a culture of resistance to anything that would make victims of human beings anywhere. In Italian we call this action *solidarietà*. We cannot pretend that those who "hunger and thirst for justice" are of no concern to us. Jesus Christ took all human suffering upon himself and set us free for making concrete, in every time and place, the good news of Light to the world!

Pastor Giuseppe Platone, Italy

What does it mean to labor under the call of God in the vineyard (Matthew 20) of the *mezzogiorno*, Italy's deep south? It means to confront the economic dependency of the region. It means to confront the poverty of values in urban areas. It means to confront the "salvation" of militarization of the region. It means to confront the grip of the mafia, so rooted in consent, dependency and the "sacrament of the recommendation." It means to confront the ancient mentality of non-acceptance of responsibility (*mentalità della delega*) which, ingrained in an exasperated and defensive individualism, undermines the formation of a mentality for sharing, for working together, for all taking responsibility for each one and each one for all . . .

God accomplishes works of liberation for his people, because God is good. And because God is good, God calls us to work in the vineyard with him. . . . It is the call of God, and no human station, which confers value and dignity upon believers. Before us, therefore, is the blessed opportunity, in the midst of a troubled humanity, of being an instrument and sign of God's rule which is coming.

Pastor Salvatore Ricciardi, Italy

327

We have been given to one another, across many ideological, religious, political and racial backgrounds. The Lord has bound us to his work and the upshot is that we are not an association to propagandize in favor of a certain society, social policy or philosophy, nor still to cling to traditions of times past. We are called to be witnesses to Christ and his good news. We are not a religious circle which gathers for the sake of rites, nor are we a club of Jesus fans. We are witnesses to the good news of Jesus Christ, crucified and raised up. A community which bears up those who have need, which shares suffering and joy, which takes upon itself the burdens of others . . .

Pastor Valdo Benecchi, Italy

Justice, peace, and integrity of creation

There is no sector of life which is not confronted by the word of God. If this be true, then in faithfulness to this word, the church cannot escape speaking out against unjust forces which reduce people to "objects" to be used or to be trampled over by any form of violence. Christ the Lord has chosen the path for the church, and that is to inspire hope for life and human dignity among the most wretched of this earth . . .

Waldensian Regional Board in its message,
"Jesus Christ is Lord,"
to the synod assembly, Argentina-Uruguay, 1987

The practice of justice is the measure of fidelity to the covenant between God and God's people. We aim to build a just society on the foundation of truth and love, the way of the cross, not the way of political compromise. When political calculation becomes the rule, truth and love are the victims . . .

Pastor Carlos Delmonte, Uruguay

I think that some of the most beautiful pages in our history were written by Christians who, while they may not have had a strong sense of social or political responsibility, did understand that their faith compelled them to risk their lives for a higher value: to save life. In the Catania sanctuary case, we are not really risking anything. We are not risking our lives. We are only trying to affirm that there is a higher value than obedience to unjust laws.

328

Our history, the history of the persecution of the Waldensian Church, the struggle against Fascism and Nazism in Europe, the civil rights movement in the U.S., all of these things show us that there is a point, a crossroads in your life, and you must decide which road you will take: to go along with human conventions, or to obey a higher law which sometimes resists human conventions. The latter is our tradition in the Waldensian Church. Many, many times we have simply had to choose whether to obey the prince, which would have meant abandoning our faith, or to obey God. Our church is alive in our times because we chose—and hope today to choose—to obey God.

Paolo Naso, Italy

(The U.S. churches' campaign against contra aid and for a negotiated peace in Nicaragua) has greatly impressed us as it expresses clearly much of what we Latin Americans feel and think on the subject... It hurts us that such a powerful nation as yours, called to be a sister in solidarity with the smaller nations of this hemisphere, occupies itself with...reducing them to submission if they try to make their own way... It hurts us that one of our smaller sister nations is obliged to spend its resources—which otherwise would be used to improve and dignify the life of its people—on the folly of war, to defend its liberty and dignity against the most powerful country on earth... May the Lord give you the blessing of the peacemakers, and of those who hunger and thirst for justice.

Waldensian Regional Board in Argentina-Uruguay, 1986

The gospel goes beyond "western culture," so a multi-cultural society (Third World people in Italy) opens up opportunities for understanding the reach of God, who is Spirit . . . The gospel does not "belong" to us; where it is preached and lived there is created freedom's way (*spazio di libertà*) both for ourselves and for others. It is in encounter with "the stranger" that Christ's liberation is known and experienced.

from a theological reflection
developed at a Federation of Protestant Churches'
Immigrant-Refugee Ministry conference, Italy, 1987

Surrounded as we are on all sides by resignation, weariness, and confusion, it is reassuring to note that our churches in Sicily—

especially their youth—are among those who refuse to give up. The Pachino Waldensian Church was among the first to call for a nuclear-free declaration in the city. The same is true of the Methodist Church of Scicli. Last year the Adelfia center coordinated the most telling peace actions in the Comiso (missile base) area, culminating with a demonstration on 6 August, the Hiroshima anniversary. At the Servizio Cristiano (Riesi) and Noce (Palermo) schools, peace education goes forward. At Catania, the Waldensian and Baptist Churches have taken up the cause of undesired Senegalese immigrants. These are the forces that have not yielded the ground of the "Christ who is our Peace."

Bruno Gabrielli, Italy

Humanity has come to the point at which it must choose either life or death. As Christians we believe that the distinctive sign of life, love, is the sole instrument that Christians must use to shape the future—a future for people, in which the quality of life is measured not in terms of domination but of brotherhood and sisterhood, peace's way.

In this light the business of peace must not be left to the politicians: it is the business of everyone everywhere. God has committed responsibility for creation to each of us . . . Let us therefore be promoters of a culture for peace . . .

Taranto Waldensian Church, Italy,
"nuclear-free" declaration

Is there not room on this planet for peace, made of love, for respect of nature, for economies and cultures built by human beings for human beings on the foundation of sharing, solidarity, justice? Lord of Peace: grant us the grace to testify in the world, with our words and our lives, that without you and the work of your Spirit there is no peace, no security, no justice, no bond among peoples.

We place no trust in the "security" of arms and the "power" of the nuclear idol. We place no trust in the great powers' "peace" whose way is violence and injustice . . . We place our trust in Jesus Christ alone, who is agape, love for humanity, our supreme law, our determinative political principle, our salvation.

from prayers and confession of faith,
the churches' march for peace,
Comiso, Sicily, Good Friday, 1986

Agape—Christ's love—is nothing theoretical. It is concrete, it is the living Christ. The problem of refugees around the globe can be solved only by that truly revolutionary force, love's way "for others." National "interests" will never do it. When calculation takes over, love is out.

Which way, then, to go? For a start, what strikes me as right is the "sanctuary" ministry of the Americans and its consequent civil disobedience in the eye of the authorities who cling to a line regarding refugees different from that of the churches. Sanctuary ministry is a prophetic act: it directs light right on the question of why so many people should be driven to take flight from their very own land.

Pastor Tullio Vinay, Italy

The crux of sanctuary ministry is not the "stranger," the emarginated person, the one in misery, or, if you will, ethics. The heart of the matter is meeting Jesus. As Luther put it, *Tu ama Deum in creaturis; non vult ut eum ames in majestate* (You love God in God's creatures; God does not wish to be loved in God's majesty).

Pastor Sergio Ribet, Italy

The "Return" and the "living of these days"

Do we want to celebrate ourselves or shall we seek to actualize our heritage in the present and for the sake of God's coming future? Remember, our forebears in 1689 decided this way—to forsake the security of Switzerland for the unknown of Piedmont. That's living to actualize responsibility. In the interest of ecumenism and social engagement I hope we will live up to that mandate in our world city today.

Professor J. Alberto Soggin
Waldensian Theological Seminary, Italy

One danger with celebrations is that, basking in our history, we neglect to keep our aim sufficiently focused on living out today's hard choices. Confirmed by the past, unconsciously we may play down responsibility for "the living of these days." Enthusiastic afresh for the faith of our fathers and mothers, we may fail to ask, What is involved in living with God today?

Professor Sergio Rostagno
Waldensian Theological Seminary, Italy

331

The past is what it is. There is no reason to magnify it. What matters is how we live today. To celebrate the glorious "Return" really amounts to rethinking what our presence and responsibility in this land add up to.

Pastor Giorgio Tourn, Italy

Remembering that the Waldensians 300 years ago suffered, fought, and prayed for return to their native land, and recognizing that the identity of a people is essentially tied to the right to land and to freedom there, the synod expresses the hope that the 300th anniversary of the Waldensians' "Return" will be occasion for all Italian Protestantism to renew its commitment to international solidarity, and in particular, 1) towards the Middle East, where a solution must be found which recognizes the right to land and self-determination for the Palestinians and the guarantee of existence, with secure and recognized borders, for the state of Israel, and 2) towards South Africa, where the black population sees negated in its own land the rights to freedom and self-determination.

synod assembly, Italy, 1988

The synod points to the relevance of the Waldensians' exile and "Return" 300 years ago for our churches' sense of mission today in the context of millions of exiled and persecuted people, beyond and within their lands, across the globe and in Latin America in particular.

synod assembly, Argentina-Uruguay, 1989

INDEX OF PERSONS (SELECTED)

Massimo Olmi
PROTESTANTI E SOCIETÀ IN FRANCIA
Dalla Rivoluzione a Michel Rocard
pp. 192, 14 cartine a colori, L. 21.000 («Nostro tempo» 45)

La presenza discreta ma significativa dei protestanti nei governi francesi dalla Rivoluzione ad oggi e la loro influenza sulla costruzione dello Stato moderno. Il rapporto fede-politica e le scelte etico-sociali dei protestanti francesi. Il libro di un giornalista italiano, profondo conoscitore della Francia e attento alla crescita della nuova Europa.

Allan A. Boesak
SE QUESTO È TRADIMENTO, SONO COLPEVOLE
pp. 178, L. 18.000 («Nostro tempo» 46)

Discorsi, conferenze, sermoni di uno dei **leaders** della lotta anti **apartheid** in Sudafrica, autore di **Camminare sulle spine** (Claudiana, 1986). Teologo e pastore della Chiesa Riformata Missionaria Sudafricana è anche il presidente dell'Alleanza Riformata Mondiale. Acuto teologo della nonviolenza, forse il maggior **leader** politico del momento in Sudafrica.

David Haslam
NICARAGUA:
Chiese evangeliche e rivoluzione sandinista
Fede nella lotta: l'esperienza dei cristiani del Nicaragua
pp. 176, 15 ill.ni f.t. e 18 nel testo, L. 18.000 («Nostro tempo» 47)
Edizione italiana aggiornata a cura di Aldo Comba

In Nicaragua il 15% della popolazione è protestante. Come hanno reagito le chiese evangeliche alla rivoluzione sandinista e qual è stato il loro ruolo nella lotta e nella ricostruzione nazionale di questi dieci anni? Il Nicaragua si rivela un «laboratorio teologico» di estremo interesse per le chiese del «primo mondo». Ampia documentazione originale.

Marga Bührig
DONNE INVISIBILI E DIO PATRIARCALE
Introduzione alla teologia femminista
pp. 120, L. 13.000 («Nostro tempo» 48)

L'insegnamento di Gesù e l'esperienza delle prime chiese erano stati rivoluzionari rispetto alla tradizione d'inferiorità della donna: ma si trattò di una breve stagione. Quanto hanno perduto le chiese per aver messo a tacere le donne? L'Autrice, che ha dedicato la vita a questa battaglia, ci offre una chiarissima introduzione alla teologia femminista che è anche un bilancio delle più importanti acquisizioni della nuova teologia vista dall'altra metà del genere umano.

Hans Ruedi Weber

ESPERIMENTI DI STUDIO BIBLICO
Nuovi metodi e tecniche

pp. 250, L. 24.000 (Collana P.B.T.)

Il responsabile dell'Istituto biblico del Consiglio Ecumenico delle Chiese mette a disposizione degli addetti ai lavori (monitori, catechisti, animatori, pastori ecc.), la sua vasta esperienza internazionale nel campo degli «studi biblici», con esempi pratici di grande utilità.

Ugo Gastaldi

I MOVIMENTI DI RISVEGLIO
NEL MONDO PROTESTANTE
Dal «Great Awakening» (1720) ai «revivals»
del nostro secolo

pp. 208, L. 18.000 (Collana P.B.T.)

Storia di un fenomeno tipico che ha segnato il protestantesimo di ogni paese d'Europa all'insegna dell'**«ecclesia semper reformanda»**. Un avvenimento ricorrente che ha dato la sua impronta ad un settore larghissimo del cristianesimo mondiale, oggi in piena espansione (movimenti carismatici ecc.).

Giorgio Tourn

(con G. Spini, G. Bouchard, R. Geymonat)

«YOU ARE MY WITNESSES»
The Waldensians across 800 years

pp. 320, ill.ni f.t., L. 28.000

Nuova traduzione inglese de **I Valdesi** di Giorgio Tourn, con varie appendici a cura di G. Spini (I metodisti in Italia), G. Bouchard (gli ultimi 10 anni) e R. Geymonat (I Valdesi in Sudamerica). Edizione a cura dell'American Waldensian Aid Society di N. York.

Martin Lutero

L'ANTICRISTO
Replica ad Ambrogio Catarino (1521)
Il Passionale di Cristo e dell'Anticristo (1521)

a cura di Laura Ronchi De Michelis (Opere scelte, 3)
pp. 208, con 4 ill.ni f.t. e 30 nel testo, L. 19.000

Grazie ad un'acuta esegesi del cap. 8 di Daniele e della II Pietro, Lutero giunge alla conclusione che il papato in sé, indipendentemente dalle persone che l'incarnano, è una potenza spirituale negativa che si contrappone all'opera di Cristo nel mondo. Il libro è un'analisi esauriente della dittatura papale e delle sue conseguenze nefaste per il «corpo cristiano». **In appendice:** il famoso **Passional**, ornato da 27 splendide incisioni di Luca Cranach.

Stefania Biagetti
EMILIO COMBA (1839-1904), storico della Riforma italiana e del movimento valdese medievale

pp. 128, con 4 ill.ni f.t., L. 22.000
(Collana della Facoltà Valdese di Teologia, n. 16)

Vita, opere e attività del maggiore storico della Chiesa Valdese nel XIX secolo, l'ideatore della prestigiosa «Rivista Cristiana». Audace demolitore di miti, combatté una nobile battaglia fra molte incomprensioni, acquistandosi una chiara fama di accurato ricercatore nell'Europa protestante del tempo.

Sergio Carile
I METODISTI nell'Inghilterra della Rivoluzione industriale (sec. XVIII - XIX)

pp. 364 + 8 tav. con 14 ill.ni f.t. e 18 nel testo, L. 33.000
(Collana «Riforma Protestante nei secoli», 5 - diretta da Salvatore Caponetto)

Dalle memorie, dai resoconti, dalla voce stessa dei protagonisti, emerge il profondo coinvolgimento metodista nella rivoluzione sociale e ideologica del Settecento e primo Ottocento: una lenta e pacifica rivoluzione che ha forgiato il modo di vivere e l'etica anglosassone. Le grandi battaglie per l'abolizione della schiavitù, della povertà, per l'uguaglianza, la predicazione femminile, la pace ecc. Per la prima volta in italiano i testi essenziali opportunamente inquadrati. Per il 250° anniversario della conversione di J. Wesley.

Giorgio Bouchard
IL PONTE DI SALBERTRAND Il ritorno dei Valdesi in Italia (1689)

f.to 21,5 × 30, pp. 80, 47 disegni e 33 grandi foto in b/n, cop. a colori, L. 18.000

L'Autore fa rivivere vivacemente la più famosa pagina della storia valdese di cui ricorre il III centenario. I magnifici disegni di U. Stagnaro e le incisive foto di A. Merlo immergono visivamente il lettore nei luoghi storici e tra i personaggi dell'epoca. A richiesta con traduzione tedesca e inglese.

Domenico Maselli
VILLA BETANIA Un'avventura della fede

pp. 153, 19 ill.ni f.t., L. 15.000

Nel ventennale della fondazione dell'Ospedale evangelico di Napoli che è la risposta ad una chiamata, una sperimentazione dell'amore di Cristo nel tempo presente. Un'opera che porta l'impronta del dr. Santi e di tutti gli altri evangelici che hanno lottato aspramente per realizzare il loro «sogno».

Finito di stampare il 21 Luglio 1989 - Sagat, Moncalieri (Torino)